200 Years of Grammar

A History of Grammar Teaching in Canada, New Zealand, and Australia, 1800–2000

Dr. Laurence Walker

iUniverse, Inc.
Bloomington

200 Years of Grammar
A History of Grammar Teaching in Canada, New Zealand, and Australia, 1800–2000

iUniverse books may be ordered through booksellers or by contacting:

iUniverse
1663 Liberty Drive
Bloomington, IN 47403
www.iuniverse.com
1-800-Authors (1-800-288-4677)

ISBN: 978-1-4620-5165-6 (sc)
ISBN: 978-1-4620-5167-0 (hc)
ISBN: 978-1-4620-5166-3 (e)

Library of Congress Control Number: 2011916171

Printed in the United States of America

iUniverse rev. date: 11/21/2011

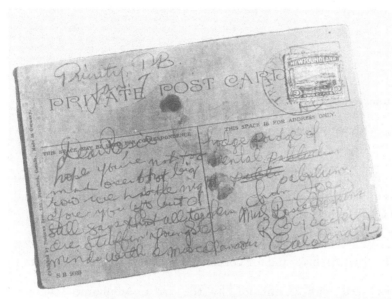

Frank LaPointe, "Mental Pablum", Newfoundland Postcard Series, 1976.
Colour photolithograph on woven paper. (Image courtesy of National Gallery
of Canada, Ottawa, and used with artist's permission.) Seen by the author
in 1985, on display at the Confederate Art Centre in Charlottetown, PEI.

Message reads: "Dear Rosie, hope you're not too mad over that big row we had
the night afore you left but I still says that all teachers are stuffin' youngsters minds
with a miscellaneous hodge podge of mental ~~pablulum publu~~ pablum. From Joe."

Copyright

Acknowledgments

First and foremost, to my wife, Hilda, for her support over the forty years of my career, in which I attempted to finish this book and its research; our daughters, Gillian, Jennifer, and Stephanie, for their love and interest; Stephanie in particular for her prodigious computer skills, artistic talent, and editing insights that helped me finish this book.

To Mr. T. C. Byrne and Helen Fowler, for their gracious donation of time and responses to many questions about their professional history.

Thanks are also due to Mount Saint Vincent University's Committee on Research and Publication for funding during the early years of research, and to funding from the Alberta Advisory Committee for Educational Studies, and the University of Lethbridge, without which this book would not have been possible.

Thanks to Kathleen Burgess for her keen editing eye, and to Sue Ducharme for her excellent comments and suggestions.

Finally, warm thanks to all my colleagues at the University of Lethbridge, for their assistance and fellowship over the years, both during my career there and afterward.

Author's Note

Much controversy has arisen over the teaching of grammar (or lack thereof) in our schools over the past two hundred years. No doubt this issue, with advocates for and against, all in the pursuit of providing teachers and students with crucial skills as speakers and writers of the English language, persists even today. This informal book may help readers to see and understand the issues that teachers have grappled with.

Dr. Laurence Walker, Professor Emeritus
University of Lethbridge
Lethbridge, Alberta
May 2010

Compiler's note

This book is the culmination of nearly four decades of the author's efforts and nearly two years of my own. There are copious amounts of other data and research that didn't make it into this book, equally interesting to the topics that are included. Some of this unpublished research will be provided through the author's website, canadiangrammar.com.

Any errors or omissions in citations or references are entirely mine, and not the responsibility of the author. Comments and suggestions are welcome at the above website.

Stephanie Sedgwick
Windsor, Nova Scotia
August 2011

Contents

Introduction

For years, grammar has not been a strong candidate for attention in the school curriculum. The professional consensus among school people is that grammar is neither palatable nor useful to children. In the words of one nineteenth-century school inspector in Nova Scotia, it was "more a torment than a benefit."

On the other hand, some parents, journalists, politicians, and even some professors mistrust this consensus. They wonder aloud why knowledge of the structure and rules of a language would not help young speakers and writers to use their mother tongue more effectively. Is using a language like riding a bicycle— something you can do well without knowledge of the physics of balance? As Steinmann (1966) stated, "Neither sort of knowledge entails the other." In other words, you can know *how* without prior need to know *that* (Ryle (1949); Scheffler (1965); Polanyi (1958). Or is the analogy defective?

Since 1800, millions and millions of child hours have been spent learning English grammar. In the nineteenth century, it was common for children to spend more time on grammar than on composition. As children and teachers toiled at parsing and analysis, under the occasional and watchful eye of the inspector, dreading the exam at the end of the year, the debate about the real value of learning grammar raged. Nowhere were the arguments as passionate as in the English-speaking colonies of North America, New Zealand, and Australia.

Immigrants from Britain had a special anxiety about their mother tongue, which they feared did not travel well over all the thousands of miles of ocean. New experiences and the absence of good language models put a strain on the Queen's or the King's English. Without vigilant supervision, dreaded colonial "twangs" were springing up. Communities of immigrants looked to their schools to defend the mother tongue, and the defense they wanted was grammar—the rules of good speech.

Conviction in matters of language is a function of a discourse larger than valid and reliable statistics. It emerges from a set of assumptions about the aims of language instruction, about the nature of language, about the use of language in a society, and about the psychology of learning. To the detriment of the debate about grammar, these assumptions are generally not articulated by either side of the issue.

The essays in this book attempt to present the story of grammar teaching in the provinces of Canada, the states of Australia, and the unitary state of New Zealand during the two centuries between 1800 and 2000. As former British colonies, all three countries shared an educational heritage. In the case of non-English-speaking immigrants, it was important to the authorities that they too learned to speak good English in order to maintain the Imperial culture. English grammar was considered to be part of the maintenance kit, an important bulwark against deterioration of the Imperial language, English, as local speech adapted itself to new conditions.

Parents and citizens wanted their children to learn grammar as the route to proper use of the standard language. After 1960, instead of standard English as a unitary institution, the concept of variable standards developed, such as "standard Canadian English," "standard New Zealand English," and "standard Australian English." Thus there is logic to including all three countries in this exploration.

If the basic question of grammar's proper role in the English language arts curriculum is too complex to be turned into anything less than a formidable array of empirical research questions, and if, in any case, convictions on both sides of the debate tend to be too firmly rooted to be swayed by that kind of evidence, a historical perspective on grammar teaching might contribute to a broader inquiry agenda.

This study is an attempt to provide that contribution. It also reveals the residues of older convictions that, although in official disrepute, may linger as ritualistic survivors in current practice or participate unconsciously in the debates and controversies. I spent most of my forty-plus career years in education, and most of those were spent in the education of teachers. From the classrooms at university, to the teachers I mentored, to the development of an education curriculum in Kosovo in the 1990s, the role of grammar in the curriculum has been a constant issue and a source of interest. Geoffrey Nunberg (1983) appealed for an end to the "invective" that has often attended the debate about grammar and a "return to civil discussion of the problems of grammar and their social importance." A history of grammar's role in the curriculum and an assessment of its changing claims to educational significance will be a contribution to this civility. In the sense of grammar's inclusion as one of the *basics* in education, there would be value in attaching some useful meaning to part of that slogan.

CHAPTER 1
The School Grammar Debate

Magrath School House with outbuildings behind the fence and a barbed wire fence surrounding the buildings at the right. Magrath, Alberta, 1903. (Courtesy Galt Museum & Archives, UID 19640357029.)

Enquiry into grammar

Grammar was once the most autonomous of that loose aggregation of subjects that grew into English in the school timetable. Grammar was indispensable to the timetable, appearing as a separate subject or in combination with composition, dictation, rhetoric, or even orthoepy. Its rationale, implicit or explicit, was assured as a commonplace of educational theory. Its demise since roughly 1960 has left a curious void in the subject of English. On the one hand, in the face of apparently unanimous research evidence that the teaching of formal categories and rules, exercised through the analysis of sentences, produces no benefits in expression or comprehension, it is hard to make a serious and well-informed case for a return to traditional grammar teaching.

1

On the other hand, to omit it leaves the English program vulnerable to the question of how the study of language as an important and defining part of human experience can be properly conducted without learning the language used to talk and think about language. In no other school subject, it is claimed, are you not allowed to use a technical vocabulary. It is, as one issue of the *Guardian* newspaper described, like trying to discuss painting without being able to use the names of the colors (*Guardian*, 1988).

The dilemma is to find an appropriate technical vocabulary about language to replace traditional school grammar, now discredited. Attempts to develop an alternative curriculum strand from the "new grammars," structural grammar and transformational grammar, failed in North America in the 1960s and 1970s. The 1984 British report *English from 5 to 16* observed that although there appeared to be a broad consensus that some knowledge about language should be included in school English programs, there was a lack of professional unity that would be required to implement any specific policy. (This report is discussed in detail later in this book.)

There is a temptation to think that grammar as it existed as a school subject at the height of its popularity in, say 1875, or prior to its removal from English, was a homogeneous thing, consisting of defining and identifying the parts of speech and analyzing sentences. This was not so. Apart from problems of definition within English, which have variously included under grammar the mechanics of punctuation and the social etiquette of usage alongside propositional information about language structure, the more parsimonious term, grammar, was constantly being transformed in its content, method, and rationale through the eighteenth, nineteenth, and twentieth centuries.

For example, as many as 297 different enumerations of the parts of speech in English grammars were published before 1801 (Michael, 1987). Parsing as a teaching method was not widely established until about 1800. Sentence analysis did not stabilize until after 1850, when the linguistic concepts of clause and subordination were established, permitting the distinction between compound and complex sentence and the division of the latter type into principal and subordinate clauses. A succession of justifications attended grammar teaching: its value as a mental discipline; its necessity as a foundation for correct usage; its assistance in the discrimination of good from bad usage; its value to the subsequent study of a second language; and its provision of a technical language, or meta-language, with which to think and talk about writing.

Perhaps there is less revolution and more evolution in the changes that have affected English teaching since the 1960s. It may be helpful to consider the vexed question of what information about English may, or even should, be usefully taught to school children in the light of the history of grammar teaching.

THE DEBATE ABOUT GRAMMAR AND THE VALUE OF A HISTORICAL PERSPECTIVE

In 1987 the *New Zealand Listener* reported the claim by an Australian writer in her forties that her generation was the last one schooled in English syntax (McLeod, 1987). The claim implied that her ability to earn a living by writing owed something to her Geelong primary teacher, who had drilled her sixth-grade classes in parsing and analysis. It also implied that the benefits of instruction in syntax had been denied to later generations of school children by the elimination of grammar teaching from the school English curriculum, presumably in the 1960s and 1970s.

Confronted with such a charge, education officials in New Zealand, Canada, or Australia could have made two responses to the claim: first, that children's control over English syntax is an important objective of modern programs for teaching English even though its explicit teaching as a separate part of the subject is not recommended; and second, that there is no evidence that teaching the rules of English syntax separately and directly produces any benefit in either speaking or writing. The same officials might also point out that some teachers do continue to teach grammar in the traditional, formal sense, in spite of official disapproval.

By the 1970s and 1980s, curriculum guides for English or English language arts published by provincial, state, or national departments of education in Canada, Australia, and New Zealand were unanimous in their exclusion of grammar as an explicit, identifiable component in authorized or recommended programs. Nova Scotia's 1983 program for secondary school English includes a categorical denial that teaching formal grammar leads to any benefit in language use. The 1987 Alberta guide for junior high school language arts relegates it to a very minor role in the editing phase of the writing process.

Recent documents on the teaching of English published by the New Zealand Department of Education fail to even mention grammar, an indication that the policy based on an alternative ideology of language learning is so widely established that denials of the value of grammar teaching are no longer necessary in that country. In Australia, curriculum guides for English embrace the ideology of the personal growth model of English teaching, which, from the late 1960s, took over from the cultural heritage and the skills models under which grammar had been maintained. In both Australia and New Zealand, any treatment of language as an object of study in the higher grades leading to propositional understandings about it has been broadened beyond a narrow set of structural categories and rules to focus on characteristics of language as it is actually used in various social situations.

In 1987 the Canadian Council for the Teaching of English held its annual meeting in Winnipeg. The extent to which grammar teaching was out of favor with the English teaching establishment was evident when a motion from the Council's Resolutions Committee was passed. It read as follows:

> Whereas there is no evidence that teaching any grammar at all of any theoretical persuasion has any beneficial effects on students' use of language; and whereas there is considerable evidence from research that the level of abstraction in grammatical study is so high that it remains incomprehensible to most students; and whereas the time wasted on formal study of grammar could be better used to develop fluency in the use of writing and speaking English or studying literature; move that the teaching of grammar be replaced by activities that are known to foster literacy. (1987)

It would be fair to say that the confident consensus against grammar represented by this successful motion still prevails in the authorized discourse in English language arts education, particularly as found in the deliberations of curriculum committees, in most of the pages of contemporary language arts journals, and in the official and unofficial substance and business of English language arts conferences. Grammar teaching is beyond the pale.

However, there is occasional evidence that the wider community does not accept the curriculum demise of grammar. The *Listener* reference above was an expression of anxiety that an important part of literacy learning is being neglected. That anxiety emerged in a 1986 Canadian radio discussion about literacy on CBC's national program "Morningside." In response to a university student's claim that she had not studied grammar in school, host Peter Gzowski asked, in apparent astonishment, "If you didn't study grammar in your English program, what did you study?" (1986)

The assumed neglect of grammar in school programs is implicated in popular concerns about linguistic deterioration and a retreat from language standards on contemporary usage. This is frequently attributed to a failure of schools to thoroughly teach the basics. Business organizations, including Chambers of Commerce, have criticized school English programs on these grounds. Universities have expressed concerns about the literacy abilities of their freshman intakes from the schools, and the media have been quick to publicize such criticisms. Some teachers share this disquiet and, under official curriculum policies that are permissive rather than prescriptive, continue to teach grammar in spite of prevailing professional opinion.

While it is possible for professional consensus to set aside the contrary opinions of some practitioners as unscientific and the reports of "establishment journalists" as sensational, there is also an academic dissent that has been largely ignored rather than countered. This dissent has criticized the claim that research findings show that grammar teaching does not achieve better performance in speaking and writing. That claim was articulated in a 1963 review of the research, one section of which has gained the status of a manifesto against grammar teaching:

> In view of the widespread agreement of research studies based upon many types of students and teachers, the conclusion can be stated in strong and unqualified terms: the teaching of formal grammar has a negligible or, because it usually displaces some instruction and practice in actual composition, even a harmful effect on the improvement of writing. (Braddock, Lloyd-Jones, & Schoer, 1963, pp. 37–38)

This fifty-six-word quotation "has appeared over and over again in books, articles, convention papers, classroom, and casual conversations" (Kolln, 1981). However, as Neuleib (1977) pointed out, it was preceded in the article by a cautionary statement that is usually overlooked: "Uncommon, however, is carefully conducted research which studies the effect of formal grammar on actual composition over an extended period of time." Without taking that statement into consideration, others have claimed that the studies reviewed by Braddock *et al.* were representative of the best kind of thoroughly designed educational research.

As one of the apparently most dependable propositions about the teaching of English, the Braddock *et al.* conclusion about the absence of transfer between traditional grammar teaching and composition was extended to the transformational-generative version of grammar. On the basis of findings from a three-year investigation in New Zealand by Elley *et al.*, the conclusion drawn was that the effects of transformational-generative grammar study are negligible (Elley, Barham, Lamb, & Wyllie, 1976). Several researchers judged the validity of this conclusion to be unquestionable, but others disagreed; Newkirk (1986) argued that the authors went beyond their data in claiming that grammar teaching was ineffective. He turned the authors' conclusion around to say, "The grammar groups read and wrote as proficiently as the group which free read and wrote extensively." After considering the diverse judgments, Hartwell (1985, p. 107) concluded that "it may well be that the grammar question is not open to resolution by experimental research." The issue of whether or not grammar should be taught in school may not, therefore, have been resolved as satisfactorily as official policies on English teaching suggest. The empirical foundation of the visible consensus of the English teaching establishment may be more fragile than its rhetoric admits.

That is not to be more critical of that establishment than of others in education, nor to be more skeptical of that consensus than of others. It is no longer fashionable in educational research (itself prone to fragile consensus) to put faith in a positivistic view of social science's ability to reveal stable and enduring laws of human learning. To state that research shows that teaching formal grammar does not transfer to speaking and writing would indicate a wish for an abiding and dependable truth, which an anthropologically-based view of social science would deny. Knowledge is not a mirror of an absolute reality that exists separately from the knower but is culturally and socially formed. Within this science, the nature of a relationship between propositional knowledge about language and language performance would be necessarily local and transient, depending on where you were looking from and what you were looking with. Or, as James put it many years ago, truth is "what it is better for us to believe," not "the accurate representation of reality" (Rorty, 1979). Convictions, according to this view, emerge not from the findings of research but from some other construction of reality by whatever communities we belong to or seek to join.

From this perspective of the cultural relativism of knowledge and hence of professional conviction, grammar, in its exclusion from the modern English curriculum, has been an ideological victim of shifting conceptions of English as a school subject. Its demise is the result of a particular social formation of subject English; its pre-eminence in that loose aggregation of subjects that constituted English studies one hundred years ago was the result of a different social formation. As Morgan (1987) noted, older social formations or paradigms of school subjects are not wiped cleanly off the syllabus by new visions: they deposit residues in the folklore of schooling. According to Kliebard (1986), the curriculum is a site of struggle among different visions, paradigms, or social formations. A better explanation of the current English curriculum is to attribute its form to the temporary ascendancy of one vision over others than to the march of progress within a liberal, celebratory view of curriculum history.

COMPETING VISIONS OF GRAMMAR TEACHING

With regard to the teaching of English grammar, we have a clear recent example of different ascendancies in current practice. On one hand, there is the **conservative** return to the mandated study of grammar in the late 1990s in the National Curriculum in British schools. On the other hand, in sharp contrast, is the survival of a **progressive** orientation to grammar's role in the English curriculum that had been established in school programs in Canada, New Zealand, and Australia in the 1970s and 1980s (an idea which had actually originated in Britain). Britain had made a 180-degree change. Interestingly, grammar failed to make a comeback in Canada, New Zealand, and Australia when conservative outcome-based models of the English curriculum became the vogue in those countries in the 1990s.

In the early years of the development of colonial education in Canada, New Zealand, and Australia, it was natural that officials and teachers should look to the mother country for guidance. Indeed, as far as teaching the mother tongue was concerned, there was a special anxiety about language standards in the face of the natural development of nonstandard dialects to represent new experiences. Immigrants wanted their children to learn only the Queen's English, and they thought that learning English grammar from English textbooks was the only way to safeguard the British language and culture, as well as their children's prosperity and social standing. British theory and practice about language learning continued to be influential through the 1970s—for example, the 1975 report *A Language for Life*[1] (also referred to as the *Bullock Report*) was enormously popular in Canada, New Zealand, and Australia.

Ironically, curriculum ascendancies have now diverged. Progressive ideas about language learning (with emphasis on child-centered personal growth and integration) have continued to guide curriculum policies in these three

---

1   *The Bullock Report. A language for life.* Report of the Committee of Enquiry appointed by the Secretary of State for Education and Science under the Chairmanship of Sir Alan Bullock FBA, London: HMSO, 1975.

countries. This survival has occurred despite the outcomes movement of the 1990s, a conservative shift that might have brought grammar back into the mainstream curriculum. Not so in Britain: in the 1980s the Thatcher government began a process of bringing grammar back into the public school curriculum.

Although the focus of this book is on grammar teaching in three former colonial countries without the inclusion of the British experience, the story of this restoration in Britain is a useful starting point. The new ascendancy presents a sophisticated model of grammar teaching with a comprehensive rationale, detailed curriculum, thorough mandatory training of teachers to teach grammar, and clear accreditation requirements. In the two hundred years that grammar had been on the defensive, there had never been such a complete and plausible intervention by governing authorities, whether to promote teaching of grammar or to eliminate it.

THE ATTACK ON PROGRESSIVE EDUCATION IN BRITAIN

The British press in March and April of 1988 was unusually exercised about the teaching of English. Scarcely a publication day went by without at least one of the so-called "quality newspapers" carrying a story about declining language standards that were usually attributed to an apparent lack of rigor in school English programs. The language of the ideological right was often strong. A *Daily Telegraph* article on March 5, 1988, described British Broadcasting Corporation (BBC) English as having degenerated to a "grisly patois." In a March 21 article on illiteracy, the *Sunday Telegraph* indicted "rubbishy education theory," saying that current practice in the teaching of basic subjects was the culprit.

Other press references, hostile to the progressive teaching of English, called the education policies of the Labour Government in the 1970s "the Shirley Williams' holocaust." Advocates of the personal growth model of English as a school subject were referred to as "those muddled theorists," or those "tired gurus in their wax museums." Other groups attacked for their support of so-called left wing approaches to English teaching were English specialists in teacher-education institutions and civil servants in the Department of Education and Science, who were accused of having "hijacked" the curriculum. One letter writer to the *Sunday Times* on April 17 related an example of illiteracy in high places: a school head of English had been unable to explain the function of an "intransigent verb." Perhaps the anecdote was more telling than the correspondent intended!

A COMMITTEE TO REMEDY THE NEGLECT OF GRAMMAR

In 1984 Her Majesty's Inspectors of Schools (HMI) published a discussion booklet, *English from 5 to 16,* which set out proposed aims and objectives for English language arts. Four aims were listed: oral language, reading, writing, and knowledge about language. This fourth aim was further elaborated as follows:

To teach pupils about language, so that they achieve a working knowledge of its structure and of the variety of ways in which meaning is made, so that they have a vocabulary for discussing it, and so that they can use it with greater awareness, and because it is interesting. (p. 3)

In 1986 a *Second Edition, Incorporating Responses* was released. The first three aims had been well received, with widespread support. However, the fourth aim was more contentious. "Nothing divided the respondents more than the question of what knowledge about language should be taught to either teachers or pupils," and the report later concluded that, "it will be a long time before the professional unity required to implement a policy can be arrived at." (pp. 39–40)

To attempt to reconcile these divergent views, the Kingman Committee was struck. The anticipation over the April 1988 release of the Committee's report caused the media furor mentioned in the preceding section. The Committee's task was to recommend to the secretary of state for education and science a "model of the English language as a basis for teacher training and professional discussion, and to consider how far and in what ways that model should be made explicit to pupils at various stages of education" (p. 1).

Behind this wording was the issue of grammar and Prime Minister Thatcher's desire to bring it back into the school curriculum. One term of reference of the Committee said simply, "To recommend what, in general terms, pupils need to know about how the English language works and in consequence what they have been taught, and be expected to understand, on this score, at ages 7, 11 and 16." (ibid.)

THE KINGMAN COMMITTEE'S RECOMMENDATIONS

The Committee steered a middle course between those who wanted a return to pre-1960s prescriptive teaching of grammar rules and those who favored a curriculum based on language learning "by osmosis." The report firmly rejected a return to old-fashioned grammar teaching and learning by rote; yet the Committee rejected the claim that knowing how to use the terminology of language is unnecessary. It also rejected the argument that effective language use can be achieved without explicit knowledge of the structure of the language or of the ways it is used in society. "There is no positive advantage in such ignorance," it claimed.

The report recommended that children be taught broadly about language structure, use, and variation. They should know the terminology of language structure, such as *word, sentence, noun*, and *paragraph*. This knowledge should be acquired "through an exploration of the language they themselves use, rather than through exercises out of context. In the hands of sensitive teachers, a move from spontaneous practice to considered reflection upon language could be a natural and interesting process."

The Committee also made strong statements about the training of teachers. "All intending teachers of primary school children should undertake a language course in which the larger part of the course to be spent in direct tuition of knowledge about language. All intending teachers of English should undertake a course which enables them to acquire, understand, and make use of knowledge about language" (pp. 62–3).

THE GOVERNMENT TAKES ACTION?

The release of the Committee's report did not lead to any immediate action by the government. There was a sense of official disappointment that traditional grammar had not been unreservedly endorsed. However, the Kingman Report was influential in the longer term; its recommendations began to show up in the new National Curriculum, under firm state control, and in requirements for teacher education. By the end of the century the study of language as a body of explicit knowledge had been incorporated into the curriculum of English as required study and into programs for the training of teachers, both pre-service and in-service. Universities and colleges authorized to offer teacher-training programs were rigorously inspected to ensure that teachers themselves had sufficient knowledge of grammar and language to enable them to teach the curriculum.

THE GRAMMAR PAPERS (1998)

In 1998, the Qualifications and Curriculum Authority (QCA), responsible to the minister of state for education in England, Wales, and Northern Ireland for the National Curriculum, issued a set of guidelines and discussion papers on the topic of teaching grammar. The *Grammar Papers*, six of them, were a thorough analysis of the historical role of grammar teaching in schools, of the role of grammar in the new English curriculum, of issues in the training of teachers for instruction in grammar, and the assessment of students' work in grammar.

These papers presented an uncompromising position on grammar in United Kingdom schools. The question was not *whether* to teach grammar but *how* to teach it. The *Grammar Papers* noted that with the demise of grammar in school English after the 1950s, there was much confusion and an absence of consensus about the role of English grammar in schools. The aim of the *Grammar Papers* was to dispel that confusion and create a consensus. Two key questions were posed:

1. How can grammar teaching be systematic if it is taught only as and when it arises in the context of pupils' work?

2. How can systematic approaches to the teaching of grammar that are responsive to the living language be developed? (p. 5)

A number of key points were presented related to the curriculum requirements for grammar in schools:

- Schools were to ensure that pupils were familiar with grammatical terminology and able to make independent use of their grammatical knowledge in relation to their own and others' work.

- The grammar requirements should be met within an overall program of English work, which integrates speaking, listening, reading, and writing.

- The requirements were broadly of two kinds: those concerned with language structure and those concerned with language variation.

- Analysis of language is the key to developing pupils' explicit grammatical knowledge, and analysis depends on the ability to name linguistic features, structures, and patterns at word, sentence, and whole-text level. (p. 6)

These requirements were a forceful change from what had been the progressive consensus since the 1975 *Bullock Report*. As the QCA itself noted, "By 1975 most English teaching aimed to integrate the language modes and provide pupils with 'real' purposes and audiences for their language use. In this context, emphasis was placed on pupils' talk and responses to literature. The explicit, discrete teaching of grammar largely disappeared because explicit grammatical knowledge was no longer considered as a necessary precondition for pupils' ability to communicate. Grammar was taught, as the need and occasion arose, in the context of pupils' own work" (p. 12).

The *Grammar Papers* had to deal with the issue of research on grammar teaching. They presented what amounted to a revisionist history of the research on grammar teaching. As noted earlier, the consensus of the 1970s and 1980s, based on frequently quoted research studies on the benefits of learning grammar, was that it did not provide any advantage to pupils' learning to read or write. The *Grammar Papers* reported thorough reviews of this research and found that these research studies were "often referenced but rarely closely examined." The conclusion was that the research was "patchy" and based on narrow definitions of formal grammar. It did not live up to its claims. In some cases the findings were little better than supporting the conclusion that it is not profitable to teach grammar badly. By the 1990s, grammar had moved far beyond the traditional and narrowly prescriptive character that it had up to the 1960s.

TRAINING TEACHERS FOR THE GRAMMAR CURRICULUM

In addition to specifying the school curriculum, the QCA laid out courses that prospective teachers had to take and pass in order to meet the exit requirements for certification. Beginning in 1997, prospective primary school teachers had to complete three required courses: Primary English, Primary Mathematics, and Primary Science. These were not methods courses; rather their aim was to present up-to-date content knowledge about the subjects to help teachers make better instructional decisions.

Institutions that offered programs for teacher training were required to develop these courses and have them accredited. One institution, the Open University (the UK's distance learning institution), developed a course textbook for its program, *Primary English* (Eyres, 2000), which presented an accessible and comprehensive body of knowledge about how language works. Topics included understanding language generally, understanding English at the word level, the sentence level, and the whole-text level. The aim was not to prepare teachers to pass on the explicit knowledge in the course but to help them use the knowledge about how language works. Grammar topics included traditional prescriptive grammar, descriptive grammar, and implicit and explicit knowledge about language rules. The nature of standard English and nonstandard varieties according to regional and social factors were thoroughly treated.

This course nicely sidestepped the question of *what* knowledge about language in the explicit sense should be taught in schools. The answer was that primary level teachers needed to have a thorough and modern understanding of language structure, use, variation, and development. This understanding, enforced by legislation and regulation, was to provide a strong foundational knowledge that would require teachers to be knowledgeable about the primary level English curriculum they were required to teach.

SIGNIFICANCE OF THE CHANGE IN BRITAIN

In many ways the implementation of the new curriculum was a brutally top-down process. Members of the major professional organization for teachers of English, the National Association of Teachers of English (NATE), were deliberately excluded from the process as unrepentant progressives. Government set up the QCA as a powerful administrative body to control the centralized National Curriculum, certification for teachers, and to approve and monitor programs for pre-service and in-service teacher training.

Nevertheless, the implementation was successful. Teachers at last received mandatory training in teaching grammar, knowledge about language, and clear statements about its theory and practice in the curriculum.

The British approach to defining grammar and knowledge about language to be taught in schools represents the reversal of a general trend to reduce and even eliminate grammar's role in the mother tongue curriculum over a two-hundred-year period. In 1800, British children had to memorize the compete contents of grammar textbooks; and they had to parse words in sentences of great complexity. By mid-century the emphasis shifted to sentence analysis. The term *functional grammar* became common usage in the early twentieth century. Progressive ideas about education resulted in calls to reduce and reform the teaching of grammar. Conservative reaction in the 1940s and 1950s brought grammar back into the teaching of English; new ideas from linguistic studies in the 1960s gave it a different face, but only for a short time, as a new wave of progressive ideology swept in from Britain, nearly uprooting the grammar tradition in schools.

Traditionally, in Canadian provinces such a regulation is not possible. A course such as *Primary English* could not be mandated either in Canada nationally or at the provincial level. Programs of teacher training, with only rare exceptions, are offered by universities that determine the program structure and content. Provincial authorities may approve these programs as a whole, but it would be unusual for the regulators to "meddle" with programs to the extent of prescribing particular courses.

Another difficulty in Canadian teacher education is that courses that deal with content, such as courses in linguistics, literature, rhetoric, or even grammar, would normally be found in academic departments, not in professional education departments or faculties. Even though a course such as *Primary English* would be beyond the competence of most academic English departments, there would be internal resistance to attempts to approve a content course in a department or faculty of education. That *Primary English* is required in the training of primary teachers in the United Kingdom is attributable to the massive changes to the training of teachers and the school curriculum brought about by the Thatcher Government in the 1980s. Central control of these matters allowed central decision making.

The Will/Shall Rule

What pupils had to learn under etymology and syntax were three kinds of information, and the word "information" is used advisedly because learning grammar was much more a matter of committing material to memory than of developing skills in the use of the mother tongue. The three main categories of learning were

- the rules of good grammar
- the classifications and inflections of words (parsing)
- the analysis of sentences

Each of these categories will now be explicated to provide an understanding of what grammar teaching was about, what its rationales were, why it was so pervasive for so long, and why it went into the decline that finally led to its virtual demise, at least in official school curricula.

The purpose of this section is not to provide a comprehensive catalogue of the rules. There are many large and heavy books for that. Rather, we will focus on one rule of good grammar, namely the rule that governed the proper use of the auxiliary verbs *will* and *shall*. For most people who completed junior high school after the 1960s, this rule may be a surprise. However, after it was promulgated by John Wallis in the mid-seventeenth century, the rule had a secure position in the grammar books used in schools until about 1950.

THE RATIONALE FOR THE RULES OF GRAMMAR

The eighteenth century was a time of great concern about the state of the English language. Jonathan Swift proposed an academy, along the lines of France's *Academie Francaise*. Samuel Johnson published his dictionary, which helped "fix" the spelling and meaning of words. As far as grammar was concerned, Leonard in his book *The Doctrine of Correctness in English Usage, 1700–1800* (1962) compares two ideological approaches: the *doctrine of correctness* and the *doctrine of usage*.

The **doctrine of correctness** was based on the idea that the English language had once been a perfect instrument of metaphysical origin. It was within the power of logic and reason to restore that purity through the authority of learned men. It was a matter of rooting out barbarisms, solecisms, improprieties, and questions of precision and improving and then "fixing" the language. Learned men (bishops like Lowth, lawyers like Murray, and gentlemen scholars like Priestley) published grammar books in which they presented the rules said to govern correct speaking and writing. Leonard calculated that in the first half of the eighteenth century, some fifty grammar texts were published in England. With the great debates about grammar raging, the second half of the century saw the number exceed two hundred. (pp. 11–13)

The opposing **doctrine of usage**, following Locke and tracing itself back to Quintilian[2], saw language as vastly complicated and dynamic, a haphazard growth of deeply rooted habits. Usage, how people actually spoke and wrote, was the sole arbiter and norm.

---

2 Marcus Fabius Quintilianus (ca. 35–ca. 100) was a Roman rhetorician from Hispania, widely referred to in medieval schools of rhetoric and in Renaissance writing.

In the nineteenth century, the doctrine of correctness carried the day as far as schooling was concerned, although Leonard referred to the ongoing debate between the two doctrines as a "truceless struggle." In times of rapid social change, such as the nineteenth century, people wanted guidance in their use of language. Social status was associated with good character, and character was linked with speech. Good grammar could distinguish a gentleman from a common man. The growing middle class demanded to know the rules of good grammar.

There was a political issue as well. There had been cases in England where petitions presented to Parliament had been rejected because the language in which they had been composed did not meet the standard for propriety. Cobbett wrote his own grammar with a view to assisting the lower classes in writing political manifestos.

In this climate of anxiety about language, the study of English grammar quickly found its way into the curriculum of the common schools. After the basic studies of reading, writing, and arithmetic, grammar became the senior subject in the literacy pantheon. As the colonial governments across the oceans took over control of the common schools in the middle decades of the nineteenth century, grammar texts were approved and prescribed for use in all schools. The memorizing of rules like *will/shall* was required learning. It was not until the end of the century, when the competing doctrine of usage regained popularity, that the prescriptive regime began to be challenged, along with the value and validity of the rules of the grammar book.

Anecdote

The *will* and *shall* rule was featured in Lindley Murray's famous grammar book *English Grammar Adapted to the Different Classes of Learners*, which first appeared in 1795 and was widely used in the Canadian colonies. He told the story of a foreigner who fell into the River Thames in London and cried out, "I *will* be drowned; nobody *shall* save me." Nobody came to his aid because they interpreted the first clause of his cry as an expression of his determination to commit suicide by drowning and the second clause as a warning against any would-be rescue. Had he wished to be saved and had he known his English grammar, his plaintive call should have been "I *shall* be drowned; nobody *will* save me?" Some savvy grammarian could then have jumped into the water to save him.

The presence of this grammatical expertise on the river bank in London might not have been more than fortuitous. The Oxford English Dictionary

(1989) in its discussion of the *will* and *shall* rule, noted an 1837 quotation to the effect that, "Not one Londoner in a million ever misplaces his *will* and *shall*." However, had the river been the Esk, in southern Scotland, the situation might have been more forlorn. According to a commentator in the same source, "Perhaps no Scot ever yet masters his *shalls* and *wills*." On the other hand, a Scottish hero might have saved the poor fellow out of grammatical ignorance!

It is interesting to note that these two sentences illustrating the proper use of the auxiliary verbs *will* and *shall* appeared in at least five other Canadian grammar textbooks between 1795 and 1927. One reason might well have been that, unlike many other example sentences for this rule, the distinction between the meanings of the two sentences is very clear (as well as consequential). *Will*, in the first person, expresses determination as command, threat, or prophecy, whereas *shall* in the same person expresses the simple future. Use in the second and third person switches around so that *will* then expresses simple future and *shall* takes on the role of expressing determination. Thus we had in the first person "I *shall* drown," meaning "I am going to drown and I would prefer not to." The second part in the third person, "Nobody *will* save me," means "I wish they would."

Most people would agree that this little rule is not easy to grasp, and it must have been difficult to teach and to learn. Most readers might say the same about their grasp of the rule as so far presented here. The rule seems to be pointless. The distinction between signaling simple future and the expression of determination is abstract, abstruse, and very fine-grained. In order to make the distinction, one must understand what the writer or speaker intends. For example, the following sentence is taken from an exercise in a late-nineteenth century grammar text, *Lessons in English* (Marshall & Kennedy, 1899) in which pupils were asked to fill in blanks with either *will* or *shall*: "We _____ expect to hear from you often."

The answer could really go either way. You have to be able to imagine the stress in the oral statement before you can decide. If *will* is the answer, the reader assumes that the auxiliary verb is to be stressed and determination is intended (send letters or else!); if the answer were *shall*, it would not be stressed, and the meaning would be that in the normal course of things, letters would be anticipated but not mandated. Unfortunately the stress clue is absent in most cases, so the pupils would have to guess the intent. Incidentally, the sentence about the drowning victim appears as one of the sentences in that exercise.

Dictionary definition

The official dictionary rule governing the use of *shall* and *will* is as follows: "To express a simple future tense, use *shall* with I or we and *will* with you, he, they, etc.; to express permission, obligation, determination, compulsion, etc., use *will* with I or we, *shall* elsewhere." (Webster's Dictionary of English Usage, 1989)

Person	Function: Simple Futurity	Function: Determination
First person: I/We	I/We shall	I/We will
Second person: You	You will	You shall
Third Person: He/She/They	He/She/They will	He/She/They shall

Table 1 Will/Shall

In other words, two functions are involved; one, called "simple futurity," expresses something that will happen in the future, such as "He will be ready for supper soon." The other function is to make a stronger claim related to promising, commanding, determining, or prophesying, such as "I give you my word that I *will* be there."

Lewis Carroll: Through the Looking Glass

"The horror of that moment," the King went on, "I *shall* never, never forget!"

"You *will* though," the Queen said, "if you don't make a memorandum of it." (p. 125)

At first glance one might think that the passion in the King's statement amounted to determination, requiring, therefore, the auxiliary *will*. However, the meaning is that the King will remember the horror despite any wish or attempt to forget it, which makes the simple future expressed by *shall* in the first person the correct choice. The same intent applies to the Queen's barbed response, which expresses the meaning that the King in the normal course of things will not remember. This is a second example of the simple future, being expressed this time by the second person. Therefore *will* accurately expresses the second person requirement.

A fictional grammar lesson

The shall/will rule made its way into a Canadian novel by Jack Hodgins, *The Broken Ground* (1998). The setting was a 1920s rural community on Vancouver Island. Mrs. Seyerstad was the teacher in the one-room school in the village of Portuguese Creek, and Wyatt Taylor, who was trying to win the affections of the teacher, spent time in the classroom helping Mrs. Seyerstad:

> Sometimes she sent Taylor into a corner with just a small group for drill, with English grammar. He made us follow as he read aloud from the text. "Observe the following." He repeated the word 'observe' as though it tasted foreign.
>
> "*I will go to town.*
>
> "*You shall accompany me.*
>
> "*He shall remain at home.*
>
> "*These sentences express desire and resolve.*
>
> He read aloud hesitantly as though this was something he hadn't done for years. You could tell that "desire" and "resolve" were not words he would have used himself.
>
> He read: "*What have you to say about the following uses of shall and will?*
>
> "*I shall be drowned: nobody will help me.*
>
> "*I will be drowned; nobody shall save me.*"
>
> We waited for him to make sense of this. You could see he had no more idea what was expected than we did. His eyes darted to Johanna Seyerstad and back to his book. Eventually his narrow face broke into a grin. Well, I guess if you are drowning it don't matter so much if you get the grammar right so long as somebody's there with a rope.
>
> He raised his voice to read the next example: "I will not remain another minute."
>
> "Oh, but you shall return, Mr. Taylor," said Mrs. Seyerstad.

"Since you promised to help the youngsters build their tree house during lunch."

Mr. Hodgins acknowledges that the grammar text in question was a real book, S.E. Lang's *An Introductory English Grammar* (first published in 1909 and authorized for use in Manitoba). The sentences read by Mr. Taylor are in the section of the book that deals with the rules for the use of auxiliaries *will* and *shall*.

It is interesting how the author of the novel leads from the stiff examples in the grammar book to the impeccable use of the two auxiliaries in the flirtatious exchange between Mrs. Seyerstad and Mr. Taylor. The gap between the formal language of the grammar book and the informal everyday speech of the teacher's assistant is an obvious impediment to an understanding of the material. It is likely that most children's encounters with these fine-grained and abstract grammar rules were no more successful for either teacher or pupils than for Mr. Taylor and his group of young adolescents.

Poetic examples

J. A. MacCabe's *An English Grammar for the Use of Schools*, a textbook in use in 1873, provides a terse four lines of verse of dubious poetic value and doubtful pedagogy, attributed to John Wallis.

> In the first person, simply shall foretells;
> In will a threat or else a promise dwells;
> Shall in the second and third does threat;
> Will simply then foretells the future feat. (p. 39)

Marshall and Kennedy's *Lessons in English* provided a more accessible *aide memoir* in verse.

> Shall with "I" and "we" foretells,
> And will shows our determination;
> With other subjects will foretells,
> And shall denotes necessitation. (p. 76)

Final quiz

Imagine a military victory; the commanding officer of the winning side is making a speech to the defeated nation. The officer knows well his grammar when he says,

1. We _____ help you to build peace and democracy for your people. (promise)

2. You _____ have free elections in six months' time. (promise or prophesy)

3. Terrorism _____ be destroyed. (promise, prophesy, or threat; third person)

Fill in the blanks with the correct auxiliary verb, *will* or *shall*.

The last word is by an American military commander, General Douglas MacArthur. As he was leaving the Philippines war theatre, he intended to commit to return to recapture the Philippines with the promise, "I *shall* return." The rule requires "I *will* return." However, since Americans mostly ignored the will/shall distinction, it would have been unwise to correct the General.

In my collection of school grammar textbooks authorized for use in at least one Canadian province between 1800 and 1950, the great majority includes an explanation, with occasional exercises, of the different uses of *will* and *shall*. The topic also appeared in New Zealand textbooks. By the 1950s, when textbooks for English study had relegated grammar to a reduced topic alongside composition and oral language study, texts acknowledged that the *will/shall* distinction was no longer a strict requirement of writing and speaking, "except in the most formal of situations." For example, *Words and Ideas*, a text for use in Grade 9 classes that was published in 1953, conceded that:

> [Good] speakers and writers do not always make the distinctions even in formal usage. It is indeed quite acceptable to use *will* with any person to indicate either future time, or promise or determination. (Baker, p. 337)

The optional status of the rule was its frequent inclusion as part of an appendix on grammar, to be consulted as needed or according to a teacher's judgment.

As far as modern textbooks for English study are concerned, these rather arcane rules of grammar are not required as formal study. My guess is that few teachers today could explain the will/shall rule, and fewer still will observe it in their speech or writing. After 150 years of compulsory study and of torment to hundreds of thousands of pupils and thousands of teachers, the will/shall issue has suffered extinction, at least in schools and classrooms. A young man from Kosovo told me he had studied the rule in his high school English course in the 1990s, although he confessed that he had never understood it. It is quite likely that in Canada, New Zealand, and Australia the same confession could be heard from fifteen decades of memorization, and the conclusion, as mentioned in the Introduction of this book, could be that this kind of grammar was "more a torment than a benefit."

The status of the will/shall rule

The rule was presented in nineteenth century school grammars as a given and stable prescription. However, in the world outside the school classroom, its actual pedigree was not quite so blue-blooded. Its origin is attributed to John Wallis, whose grammar text was first published in England in 1653 and reprinted at least seven times until 1765. Wallis included a revealing note about the genesis of the rule: "And no other description that I have seen has given any rules for guidance, so I thought I ought to give some." (Kemp, p. 339) Kemp further states in a footnote that, "Shall and will derived from Old English *sceal* and *wile*, expressing respectively obligation and wish or intention. For some centuries there was no clear rule for their use to express the future, and Wallis seems to have been the first to formulate this rule."

Not only did grammatical rules such as *will/shall* owe their formulation to individual and sometimes idiosyncratic opinion, but as Leonard noted, "The will/shall rule has at no time represented universal cultivated usage." (p. 73) The spread of the will/shall rule was mostly confined to the English spoken in England; usage in Scotland, Ireland, and America tended to be less assiduous in following the rule. In fact, *Webster's Dictionary* (1989) draws a clear conclusion about the rule in American usage: "Traditional rules about shall and will do not appear to have described real usage of these words very precisely at any time, although there is no question that they do describe the usage of some people some of the time and that they are more applicable in England than elsewhere." James Thurber made a colourful observation in the *Harper Dictionary of Contemporary Usage* about the status of *shall* in American usage: "Men who use 'shall' west of the Appalachians are the kind who twirl canes and eat ladyfingers." (1975)

From an English-in-England perspective, the case for maintaining the distinction between *will* and *shall* was made by that famous language arbiter and guide, England's Henry Fowler. He acknowledged that modern usage in America, Scotland, and Ireland had made formidable in-roads into the authority of the will/shall rule. However, he regretted this erosion as a loss of a fine distinction. "The English idiom affords a convenient means of distinguishing delicate shades of meaning; and that is a valuable element in a language." Referring to the distinctions between the rules for using *will* and *shall*, Fowler continued, "No formal grammar can be held to have done its duty if it has not stated [the rules]." He went on to say later in the entry on the word *will* that there were still Englishmen who "are convinced that their shall and will endow their speech with a delicate precision that could not be attained without them." (1965: orig. 1926, p. 714) Fowler also admitted that this particular grammar rule had the status of a shibboleth, a means of social class allocation.

George Curme, in his exhaustive two-volume *Grammar of the English Language,* summed up the status of the will/shall rule as he saw it in 1931.

> *Shall* in the first person, singular and plural, is the standard usage in England, though not uniformly observed, and is still the preferred form in the higher grade of the literary language in America, though now not so uniformly used as it used to be … In American colloquial speech *will* is now the more common form in the first person as well as in the second and third. (p. 363)

The will/shall rule received a severe roasting from an Alberta teacher in an article in the *ATA Magazine*, published by the Alberta Teachers' Association. The teacher noted that the question on that year's Grade 8 examination for composition and grammar that caused the most difficulty had asked, "What are the rules for the use of *Shall* and *Will*?" (The question was likely based on the textbook by Cowperthwaite and Marshall, *An English Grammar for Public Schools* from 1925.) The Alberta teacher maintained that *shall* sounded artificial to most people and that in teaching it, schools were "passing on relics from the past which have worn out their usefulness." (p. 11)

CHAPTER 3
Grammar and Good Usage

Provincial Normal School (a school for teachers),
Fredericton, New Brunswick. June 1920.

After forming the child's mind, education's second task was to furnish that mind, in its strengthening powers, with useful information. Grammar had impeccable furnishing qualifications; knowledge of grammar's categories and rules was thought to be essential to the proper use of language in speaking and writing. The early definitions of grammar in school textbooks carried this message very clearly. Lindley Murray (1843, orig. 1795) defined it as "the art of speaking and writing the English language with propriety." The term *art* implied that grammar was a set of classifications and rules that existed in the language, outside the speaker or writer. In that sense, grammar had a normative function as a set of prescriptions for correct usage.

Grammar's normative role was based on two other assumptions, one **epistemological** (concerned with accepted accounts of how individuals learned to control language) and the other **sociocultural** (concerned with the notion

25

of propriety in language use). Linguistic propriety, whereby certain language forms and usages were assigned high status and others were proscribed, was associated with two agendas. One was related to language use as a marker of social standing and the other to the English language as a cultural asset that had to be protected from the corrosive influences of improper speech. Although the issues of propriety grew out of the peculiar social and class structure of Georgian England and out of eighteenth-century attempts in Britain to "fix" the language, their effects on the role of grammar teaching in the schools carried over to the new colonies. First of all, the structures and content of schooling in Canada, New Zealand, and Australia were derivative of those in Britain. Secondly, the question of a standard language took its own form in communities that were distant from what they perceived to be the linguistic centre back in the mother country.

THE EPISTEMOLOGY OF LANGUAGE LEARNING

Throughout the history of Western education there have been two competing answers to the question, what does it mean to know something, such as language? (Groome, 1980) The answer that prevailed in the first part of the nineteenth century was that knowing language was a theory-into-practice matter; knowledge resided in a set of propositions—rules, generalizations, precepts, and categories—that existed outside the learner in authoritative sources such as textbooks and teachers. Acquisition, or mastery, of these propositions was a prerequisite to any proper use of the skills that were related to them.

The key word was *proper*. It would have been readily admitted that people unschooled in grammar were perfectly capable of speaking and reading, and even of writing in a restricted sense. *Proper* use of the refined language, however, absolutely depended on prior mastery of the propositions about language categories and structure that formed the content of school grammar. As William Cobbett wrote,

> Grammar, perfectly understood, enables us not only to express our meaning fully and clearly, but so to express it as to enable us to defy the ingenuity of man to give our words any other meaning than that which we intend them to express. (1833, orig 1817, p. 15)

Moreover, this mastery of grammar was to be achieved by a conscious process of reflection; it was not enough to simply observe the patterns of language that one encountered in, for example, written text. In other words, formal study was indispensable. This was the argument that authorized the memorization of propositions that constituted the theory of proper language. Parsing exercises were designed to apply the propositions to samples of language in order to reinforce their deductive mastery; little effort was made to ensure their application to the real practice of speaking and writing. It was assumed that if the theory was learned, the application to speaking and writing would take care of itself.

The fact that the application did not take care of itself in the classroom or beyond was often noted. An anonymous writer to the *Nova Scotia Journal of Education* in 1871 sums this problem up quite forcibly:

> We have known and still know, pupils who when called upon could repeat without the omission of a word, any of the thirty or forty rules of syntax as readily as give you their own name, and yet could violate every one of them in writing a simple letter. (p. 72)

Inspection reports from New Zealand identified this same failure in 1885. "It would be well," said one report, "for more attention to be paid to its application and less to its technicalities." (p. 28) The whole rationale was a dubious one to another New Zealand inspector, Henry Hill of Hawke's Bay. In 1881, he confessed, "I have yet to learn of what use [are grammatical] rules and definitions to those who cannot … know how to use them to some good purpose." (p. 14) He went on to say that there was such a huge gap between what children had to learn and their own daily experiences that true learning was impossible.

On the other hand, many did not question the potential value of the deductive learning of grammatical concepts and terms for subsequent transfer to speaking and writing. Inspector Goyen, for example, reporting on Southland schools of New Zealand in 1881, expressed his confidence that, "If the pupils are well drilled in the function of words, phrases, and subordinate sentences, there should be little difficulty in teaching them to arrange those parts into a well-ordered sentence." (p. 38) However, Goyen was not speaking about learning as memorization; his use of the term *function* showed his concern that children understand the relationships between grammatical structures and the meanings they represent. The inspection report for the District of Gray for 1888 acknowledged that some progress had been made in the teaching of grammar, but he admitted that the most difficult problem was "How to make the study of formal grammar bear fruit in connection with composition." (p.

29) In the same year, Mr. Hodgson of Nelson reported that although pupils seemed to have a "moderate acquaintance with formal grammar, the technical knowledge thus displayed seems to be of little practical service to them as speaking or writing their own language." (p. 21)

A rare report claiming evidence in support of the theory-into-practice epistemology was offered in the 1889 report of Inspector Gibson-Gow of South Canterbury, perhaps spurred by the forthcoming demotion of grammar from a pass subject in the New Zealand syllabus. "As a rule," the inspector claimed, "I find that when the composition is good, grammar has been well taught." (p. 49)

The alternative answer to the question of the nature of linguistic knowledge was that knowing language lay in—and emerged from—the use of it to express and understand ideas about the world. This "anti-grammar" epistemology had been proposed by several authors of educational tracts long before the nineteenth century. As early as 1570, Roger Ascham had proposed a method of teaching language that placed the emphasis on the study of passages of text, out of which would inductively emerge an apprehension of the rules of grammar. Going beyond this inductive proposal, Joseph Webbe, an early seventeenth-century teacher, in his patent for teaching English and Latin by a double translation method dispensed with grammar entirely (Howat, 1984). Webbe's theory was quite explicit about the superfluous role of grammar in language learning. According to Howat, Webbe's statement from over three and a half centuries ago would be quotable by any recent curriculum guide for English.

> And ere long we will give thee a Grammatical practice upon this book for the further satisfaction of such as are not contented to call custome and authoritie a reason, but will have a grammar rule, the only reason for speaking or writing languages. Though the gravest and most learned judges in this case have already determined that no reason can give rule to speech, but use and custome, from whence all petty rules and reasons are derived: Yes, and though they owne wives, daughters and sisters are found by use and custome to speake as good English as the greatest schollars, and yet never knew Dative or Ablative, Present or Future, Noune or Verbe, or other English Collections or curiosities. ... Let us take heed, lest wee that are so great pretenders in this kind of vulgar learning be not at length out-faced by the arguments of boyes and women. (Webbe, 1627)

In another statement that would find much modern approval, Webbe said that appropriate language teaching leads to the development of "The judgment of the ear … which Grammar cannot help us to; in that it is imperfect and beguileth us." (Howat, 1984, p. 37)

This alternative theory, which might be called an experiential epistemology of language learning, was undermined by the prevailing belief that everyday usage by ordinary people was not only an imperfect language but was virtually a different language from the refined version that gentlemen and scholars were thought to use. Daily experience of language was irrelevant to the mastery of its elevated version. As a consequence, the experiential view received little recognition in the mainstream of grammar teaching that was inherited by the new state education systems in the colonies.

However, some individual voices were raised against the conventional wisdom. In 1862, for example, Inspector Stutzer of the National Board of Education in Tasmania wrote that it was his conviction that "Grammar should not be taught to any but advanced pupils, and should form a superstructure in their knowledge of English instead of being attempted to be formed into its base." (p. 22) In other words, grammar should be built onto an adequate experience of language use.

Generally, though, for Mr. Stutzer's Australian colleagues at that time, any absence of evidence of transfer from formal grammar lessons to speaking and writing was the result of failure in teaching rather than of any failure of the mainstream theory to account for the true nature of language learning. Mr. Stutzer's opposite number in the Tasmanian Denominational Board of Education expressed what seemed to be the Australian consensus of the mid-nineteenth century: "If we 'speak by the book', the leading object of grammar is to 'teach us to express our thoughts correctly, either in speaking or in writing'—an end almost lost sight of amongst us."

A linguistic preoccupation that the nineteenth century inherited from the eighteenth was the quest for a standard for English. By 1700, Latin as the language of the educated elite in Britain was very much in decline. In order for English to take the place of Latin as an exact, dependable medium for the transmission of scientific and cultural knowledge, its status had to be raised. Several literary figures of the early eighteenth century, men like Defoe, Swift, and Dryden, had campaigned for a British Academy that would monitor the language. Dryden had complained that he had to test his English syntax by translating his sentences into Latin. (Bornstein, 1976)

A National Academy did not emerge in Britain as it had in France. There developed instead in the second half of the eighteenth century a prescriptive tradition in linguistic study. From a study of the assumptions underlying school textbooks from 1640 to 1785, Cohen (1977) showed that after 1750 there emerged an implicit conception of language as a socially derived system of communication that had arisen to meet people's needs. This unconscious view replaced earlier epistemes of language as an isomorphic representation of the order of things in the natural world and of language as a representation of the structure of the mind. This new epistemology of language itself gave rise to two opposing views: a liberal conception of language as a changing phenomenon that adapts itself to shifting social needs, and a conservative doctrine seeking to establish more enduring norms of correct usage to achieve the most effective speaking and writing. The latter was strongly motivated by a political agenda, as we shall see.

The liberal intellectual tradition in English linguistics is represented in the later work of Samuel Johnson and in the writings of Joseph Priestley. In the course of his dictionary project, Johnson's original aspiration to "fix the English language" was abandoned when the lexicographer came to realize that a dictionary could not "embalm" the volatile forces of language change. However, Johnson was able to accept that at any particular time a standard could be observed in the usage of the ruling site. Priestley offered an early expression of the liberal doctrine of usage when he wrote, "The custom of speaking is the original and only just standard of any language." (Bornstein, 1976)

However, the prescriptive, utilitarian tradition prevailed in Georgian society and found its way into the schools (largely through the influence of Murray's *Grammar*). His compilation of propositions about the English language made the work of eighteenth century grammarians accessible to pupils in schools and to individuals seeking to improve themselves independently. It was based on sources such as Robert Lowth's *Short Introduction to English Grammar,* published in 1762. Lowth, a Hebrew scholar, professor, and bishop, had regarded the English language as an institution that had declined from a golden age that, to the bishop, had existed at the end of the Elizabethan period. "It is not the Language but the Practice, that is at fault. The truth is, Grammar is very much neglected among us." (Bornstein, 1976) Lowth took written English as the standard and the best authors as his guide. Doubts and discrepancies were resolved by logic or analogy and by an appeal to universal language principles. His aim was to rescue English from the vicissitudes of everyday speech by establishing what good English ought to be. The purpose of his grammar was "To teach us to express ourselves with propriety and to enable us to judge of every phrase and form of construction, whether it be right or not." (Bornstein, 1976)

Latin, a dead language, had not changed for several hundred years because it had not been subjected to the contamination of popular oral forms. In order for English to reach this ideal, static condition, it had to be safeguarded against vernacular usage. This was the mission of the eighteenth-century grammarians that was carried into the elementary school systems emerging in Canada, Australia, and New Zealand, with the aim of elevating both the child as user and the language as cultural asset.

While it was theoretically necessary, according to early nineteenth-century thinking, to teach grammar as a foundation for correct language use, the schoolmaster's mission was given urgency by the critical importance attached to propriety of language at a time when speech was an indelible social marker and when language was used as a political definition. In Britain, respectability, which members of the upper classes strove to protect and to which ambitious members of the lower classes aspired, was defined as following a proper religion, demonstrating refined manners and taste, and speaking and writing proper English. (Prentice, 1977) As Phillipps (1984) wrote about the breakup of the rigid class system in England that occurred during Queen Victoria's reign, exacerbating confusion of rank, "… language was a principal, precise, pragmatic, and subtle way of defining one's (social) position, or of having it defined by others."

For the middle classes, the social upheavals brought about by the Industrial Revolution produced a complex and confusing system of linguistic markings and shibboleths. For example, the use of the term *dinner* for the midday meal became a mark of lower-class status, and it became safer to eat dinner as the evening meal. Under these conditions of complex social change, it was very difficult for the socially ambitious to know what proper language was. Authoritative manuals in the form of grammar textbooks were a solution to the problem, peculiar perhaps to the middle class. In the upper class mind, to care too much about grammar was ungentlemanlike and open to the accusation that real gentlemen studied Latin, not English grammar. Since schools were institutions controlled by the middle classes, it is not surprising that middle-class preoccupation with linguistic propriety showed up in the school curriculum as concern with correct spelling, speaking, and oral reading and with the teaching of the categories and rules of proper English. Neither is it surprising that the same preoccupation was carried over into colonial school systems, where, partly influenced by a perceived threat to linguistic purity from the influence of immigrants from non-English-speaking countries, there was even greater sensitivity to the problem of colonial "twangs" and solecisms.

Respectability also had another face. A respectable person had the emotional side of human nature—passions and feelings—under the control of the faculties of reason and moral judgment, and in such a condition was able to contribute a personal harmony to a stable and decent society. Vernacular, nonstandard speech was associated with the lower orders, who were prone to violence, crime, and disorder, which threatened society and the interests of the propertied middle classes. There was, as a result of this association, a powerful taboo in "respectable" society against colloquial, local forms of speech, which were regarded as signs of personal and social disrepute. Schoolmasters, therefore, taught grammar as a means of eliminating disreputable and even dangerous forms of language that would otherwise impede social mobility and endanger property and the state. There was, in other words, a political motive for grammar.

Linguistic propriety was closely linked with political power in another way too. At the beginning of the nineteenth century, Britain was ruled by a relatively small privileged minority. As Olivia Smith (1984) showed, the attempt made in the second half of the eighteenth century to define a standard for English had, in addition to its cultural motive, a deliberate political agenda. The definition of an elevated literary form of English could be used to mark membership in the ruling establishment and to control access to it and to political power. For example, Smith noted that the British Parliament between 1797 and 1819 rejected petitions from individuals and communities "Because of the language in which they were written." (p. 30)

According to Smith, Johnson's dictionary project and the numerous grammars written by Lowth and others had been part of a successful attempt to engineer an elite form of the language, marked by an abstract and general vocabulary, a complex sentence structure, and a refined style. This elevated form was easily distinguished from the everyday speech of the unlettered masses, the middle classes included, which was crude, vulgar, particular, and primitive. Moreover, this elevated form, so distanced from ordinary usage as to be almost a different language, was difficult to learn. According to the belief of the time, true literacy in refined English depended upon a grounding in the classical languages, as well as upon mastery of English grammar, which texts such as Lowth's were designed to provide to a select group. Linguistic propriety, therefore, had strong overtones of political exclusion, which exacerbated anxieties about language and no doubt helped to build a market for grammar texts and other improving manuals.

The excluding function of polite language was recognized by radicals of the time. Tim Paine deliberately and audaciously flouted the canons of elevated English by writing his famous *Rights of Man* in what Smith called an "intellectual vernacular language." William Cobbett published a grammar text "for the use of young persons, more especially for the use of soldiers, sailors, apprentices, and ploughboys," which was an explicit invitation to them to achieve control over the elite language as a means of exercising political rights. In his *Grammar of the English Language, in a Series of Letters*, Cobbett, who is said to have committed Murray's *Grammar* to memory while on military service in New Brunswick, wrote,

In acquiring a knowledge of grammar, there is one motive which, though it ought at all times to be strongly felt, ought at the present time to be so felt in an extraordinary degree: I mean that desire which every man, and especially every young man, should entertain to be able to assert with effect the rights and liberties of his country. (p. 11)

Cobbett recognized the significance of "literacy founded on correct grammar as a political weapon that conferred power on those who knew how to use it, and undermined those who did not" (Howat, 1984). In doing so, he articulated a strong motive to learn formal grammar on the part of those who wished to advance socially and politically. The sharp polarization of language that Cobbett's project recognized was an important aspect of the context out of which both the content and the epistemology of nineteenth-century school grammar developed. Given the distance that was created between elevated language as the perhaps-mythical instructional target and the ordinary language experience of learners, the mastery of English grammar was endowed with far greater significance than it would possess in more egalitarian times.

GRAMMAR AND PROPRIETY IN COLONIAL SCHOOLS

Faced with two powerful external influences, British and American English, attitudes towards the English spoken in Canada (and thus about the distinctive nature of Canadians) have been plagued with uncertainty. Propriety in speech and writing has been a Canadian preoccupation for a long time. From the beginnings of public schooling in the Maritime provinces, school officials frequently complained about the poor quality of spoken language used by teachers and pupils. In 1845, the Prince Edward Island School Visitors criticized teachers who habitually spoke poor English themselves and who allowed their children to display "indistinctness of articulation and vulgar and provincial dialects." (p. 13) Nervousness about proper English was displayed in the 1851 bylaws of the Durham Nova Scotia Teachers' Association; after the statement that the object of the Association was to hear papers presented by members, another bylaw maintained that it was the duty of members to criticize "in a constructive spirit" any errors of pronunciation and grammar that they noted in the presentations. Fines were specified for members who were derelict in their duties.

For the Reverend G. Geike, who addressed the Canadian Institute on the subject of Canadian English in 1857, the state of Canada's language was a cause for concern. His main argument was that neologisms were rampant in English as it was spoken and written in North America and that these represented unnecessary deviations from the standard established by British usage. The term *Canadian English*, Geike complained, is "expressive of a corrupt dialect growing up amongst our population, and gradually finding access to our periodical literature, until it threatens to produce a language as unlike our noble mother tongue as the negro patua [sic], or the Chinese pidgeon [sic] English." He suggested that common school teachers should correct children under their care "whenever they utter slang or corrupt English, not only in the school, but in the playground and on the streets." (pp. 128-131)

Alexander Munro (1880) of Bay Verte, New Brunswick, wrote an article called "The English Language" that appeared in the *Instructor*, a Maritime publication. He surveyed the many varieties of English: correct English as spoken by the English scholar, then English English, Scots English, Yankee English, "which is abominable, then to crown the whole we have provincial English." He went on to say, "There are few subjects connected with the intellectual well being of the young and aspiring colonies than that of sustaining a pure English. Parents and teachers should endeavour to guide the youth under their charge into the use of correct English and to teach them to avoid on all occasions the use of slang words."

The clergyman's words probably went unheeded by the general curse of usage development in Canada. Writing at the time of the First World War, in the preface to a book of language drills, Ryerson Press editor Lorne Pierce launched a vehement attack on the general standard of spoken language in North America:

The standard of everyday speech in Canada and the United States surely must be the worst in the civilized world. The unmusical huffle, the slurred, strident, ill-bred cackle of most people is hard to bear, but the accompanying vulgarisms make conversation a travesty upon culture (Archibald, 1921, p. 3).

As late as 1940, a Canadian provincial curriculum guide was still referring to children's "vicious language habits" as justification for teaching proper language forms. And an early twentieth-century comment about the effects of grammar teaching on local speech in a Nova Scotia village speaks gently of grammar's futile mission to "civilize" the Maritime tongue:

It is a convention among the pupils to profess that grammar is without value. Yet they do not hate it with especial hatred, and those who reach the dizzy heights of the high school at Fox Brook or the County Academy find its lessons very valuable in their higher studies. But it must on no account influence one's daily speech. There is a mos minorum that requires each and all to speak as the community speak; and the community on the whole, and apart from special occasions of display by licensed speakers, prefers a dialect terse, racy, rather highly figurative, and picturesquely ungrammatical superficially, though not far from correct English idiom in essential structure. (Charyk, 1973, pp. 114-118)

CHAPTER 4
State Grammar in Mid-Century

South Fork School, Caroline, Alberta. 1916

The second half of the eighteenth century saw the growth of permanent English-speaking communities in Nova Scotia, New Brunswick, and Prince Edward Island. Together with the colonies of Upper Canada (Ontario) and Lower Canada (Quebec), these Maritime colonies made up what was called British North America until 1867 when Confederation brought them together as Canada. The Dominion was enlarged by the admission of new provinces: Manitoba and British Columbia created in 1870 and 1871; Alberta and Saskatchewan formed out of the North West Territories in 1905; and finally the former British colony of Newfoundland admitted in 1949. The British North America Act of 1867 assigned full responsibility for education to the provincial authorities with the result that the history of grammar teaching in Canadian schools is, in detail and in management at least, ten different stories, one for each province.

The Australian story is similarly a plural one. European settlement began in 1788 with the establishment of convict colonies in New South Wales and later Van Diemen's Land, or Tasmania. Western Australia was formed in 1829, and South Australia in 1836. Victoria was carved out of New South Wales as a separate colony in 1851, while in 1859 a similar arrangement created the colony of Queensland. Although education in Victoria and Queensland began while they were still part of New South Wales, each of the six colonies or states developed its own centralized educational system. Education in what is now called the Northern Territory, a more recent creation as a separate administrative unit, was operated from Adelaide in South Australia.

In New Zealand, colonial settlement was later, beginning in 1840. Separate provinces—Wellington, Auckland, Nelson, Canterbury and Otago—drawing their identities from the original settlement schemes, controlled education from 1853 to 1877. However, a single national government then assumed authority over state education, so that, beyond the very early tentative period, grammar as taught in New Zealand state schools was under a single system of school administration.

Thus, in all three countries, centralized state systems of education took over the control and management of schooling arrangements originally set up in the scattered settlements by private organizations. These were usually the churches with the assistance of the overseas arms of the various British-based denominations, such as the National Association of the Church of England, the British and Foreign Association of the Protestant nonconformists, the SPCK (Society for Promoting Christian Knowledge) and the London Missionary Society. Since the first schools in these colonies were free enterprise operations funded by fees supplemented by financial support from the churches or other benefactors, what was actually offered as instruction varied in kind and quality. The subjects taught were under the control of each school's patrons, and any textbooks used were published on the free market like any other books and selected, if any choice was available, by teachers, parents, or patrons. In the absence of provision for the training and licensing of teachers, the quality of instruction was also extremely variable. Gradually, however, in each jurisdiction the state began to extend financial support to schools, and, through the power of the purse, statutory authority over schooling at the elementary level gradually followed. By 1880 the principles of universal, free, and compulsory elementary education had been enshrined in legislation in New Zealand and in all extant Canadian provinces and territories.

All jurisdictions had set up centralized administrations to dispense public funds for schooling and to regulate teacher training and certification, curriculum, and textbooks. The supervision of local schools was the responsibility of school inspectors, state-appointed in Canada and Australia, but appointed by regional boards in New Zealand. In theory at least, the machinery of public schooling had taken control of primary or common school education in the scattered settlements and communities of the three colonies. What had been, in the first half of the nineteenth century, largely informal, voluntary, private, and local arrangements for the provision of instruction in the elementary branches of learning—reading, writing, spelling, arithmetic, and, in some cases, English grammar and geography—became a function of the state, operated by departments of education or councils of public instruction.

PRIMARY OR COMMON SCHOOL CURRICULUM DEVELOPMENT

By the 1890s, and much earlier in some cases, this process of state control of primary education was well-established. What was under state control was more than is implied by the term "primary" in its modern usage. In its original meaning, the term "primary school," as used in New Zealand and Australia, and "common school," its synonym in Canada, did not refer simply to an initial level of schooling leading to secondary study. A primary school education was considered to be complete in itself as a program of instruction in basic English literacy and numeracy, with geography and grammar added as useful subjects. Its vernacular program contrasted with classical studies offered by private secondary schools and academies.

Neither did it necessarily constitute a definite number of years of study. Its program was expressed in terms of standards of attainment, which were levels of skill and knowledge to be demonstrated by pupils before promotion from one level to another approved by the school inspector. Standards were closely linked with school reading series, so that references were often made to the "First Reader Class," or "Fourth Reader Class," and so on.

As the nineteenth century progressed, the first four standards of primary or common schooling came to be considered primary in the more modern sense of preliminary study, and, converted into eight year-long grades, constituted what was called in Canada "public schooling," from which pupils could gain access to high school study by passing an "entrance" examination.

Some important points emerge from this discussion of terms. The first is that the term "standard" or "class" is not synonymous with "grade," and that graduation from primary school was not the equivalent of passing Grade 6. The second is that secondary education in its modern sense was not excluded from state control because with Standards V and VI, primary schools included what would be considered secondary levels in today's terms.

Taking centralization to be marked by the assertion of authority over the primary school curriculum, it was a process that began in 1846 when Upper Canada established its first course of studies based on the textbooks of the Irish National Board of School Commissioners. By 1882, all jurisdictions in Canada and Australia and the single national system in New Zealand had put in place mandated courses of study for their schools. This period of centralization occurred in that period in which English grammar enjoyed its highest status and esteem as an elementary school subject. After the foundations skill subjects—reading, writing (handwriting), and spelling—English grammar was the most prestigious and most autonomous of those branches of learning concerned with the native tongue.

This coincidence of administrative growth and subject status meant that the study of English grammar was firmly and almost irrevocably entrenched in the elementary school syllabus for pupils in at least the third standard and above. It was to prove very difficult to either extricate grammar teaching from the common school curriculum or to transform its nature as conceptions of education and language changed later in the nineteenth century and in the twentieth century. In some ways the grammar poltergeist of those mid-Victorian years still rattles its parsing and analysis chains in the teaching of English language arts today.

THE NATURE OF GRAMMAR IN THE COLONIAL PRIMARY SCHOOLS SYLLABUS

The clearest indication of what children were expected to learn as a result of their grammar lessons in the new state schools is found in records of the courses of study, or syllabi, that were drawn up and prescribed by the central authorities. They prescribed what teachers were expected to teach and what pupils were expected to show the school inspector that they had learned when he visited the school to inspect its operation and examine its pupils. In spite of the diversity of geography and the number of different jurisdictions involved, the prescriptions for English grammar that were included in courses of study for all three countries were remarkably similar.

The grammar component of New Zealand's first national syllabus gazetted in 1878 is a good indication of the nature of what was expected across all three countries, although there are some variations in content and level. The syllabus, mandated under the Education Act of 1877[3], was modeled on the Codes of the Board of Education in England, introduced in 1862 and subsequently modified. Inspector-General Hoybens, who had been involved in the design of the earlier Province of Canterbury standards, cast the 1878 New Zealand Standards Regulations in the form of a set of prescriptions of minimum attainments for each subject at each level. Grammar, linked with composition but quite eclipsing it, began in Standard III. The specifications under the heading "Grammar and Composition" were

Standard III

The distinguishing of the nouns (and pronouns used in the same way as nouns) and verbs in easy sentences; also of articles and adjectives (and pronouns used in the same was as adjectives); and very simple exercises in composition, to test the pupil's power of putting his own thoughts on familiar subjects into words.

Standard IV

The distinguishing of all the parts of speech in easy sentences; the inflections of the noun, adjective and pronoun, letter writing on prescribed subjects; the addressing of letters and envelopes.

Standard V

Inflexions of the verb; (the parsing with inflexions) of all the words in any easy sentence; a short essay or letter on a familiar subject, or the rendering of the sense of a passage of easy verse into good prose; analysis of a simple sentence.

Standard VI

Complete parsing (including syntax) of simple and compound sentences; prefixes and affixes, and a few of the more important Latin and Greek roots, illustrated by a part of the reading book: essay or letter; analysis of easy complex sentences. (1878)

---

3 Under the Education Act 1877, schooling was to be free, secular, and compulsory for all children aged between seven and thirteen, with Māori children given the option of attending state or native schools (established in 1867). This occurred after the centralization of government.

A significant feature of the role of grammar in the 1878 standards was its status as a "pass" subject in Standards III through VI. Pass subjects were those in which pupils were examined individually by the inspector in order to ascertain whether the required standard was reached to pass from one standard to the next. In other words, pass subjects were regarded as the core of the syllabus, and the effect of this regulation was to make the teaching of grammar in these standards compulsory. "Class" subjects, on the other hand, were those in which the inspector was required only to test the knowledge of the class of children as a whole.

Grammar, linked with composition, held its compulsory status as a pass subject until 1892, when it was separated from composition and reduced to a class subject in Standards III, V, and VI, but retained as a separate pass subject in Standard IV. This change marked the emergence of composition, which became a pass subject in Standards III to VI in the revised syllabus, officially a more important subject than grammar. Until that demotion, grammar as defined by the 1878 Standards enjoyed a fourteen-year period of ascendancy in New Zealand's national primary curriculum.

Standards issued by Canadian school systems made similar provision for grammar. In 1871, Egerton Ryerson replaced the de facto Upper Canada syllabus of 1846 (which was based on the Irish National textbooks) with a course of study divided into six Standards. Grammar's content in these syllabiwas very similar to its treatment in New Zealand, starting with parts of speech, moving to parsing of words in sentences, and then to the analysis of sentences.

New Brunswick was one of the provinces to follow Ontario in its syllabus policies. A provincial course of study was introduced in 1880. The study of English grammar began in Grade 5 with oral instruction, and in Grades 6, 7, and 8, parts of speech, parsing and sentence analysis were to be completed in a program closely keyed to the prescribed grammar textbook. The textbook-focused pattern was followed by Manitoba in its 1882 course of studies, which was divided into twelve standards, each representing five months' work. Although grammar was not used as a heading until Standard VI, study of the parts of speech and sentence analysis formed a large part of what was called Composition for Standards III through VI, and Grammar for Standards VI through XI. The parsing and analysis requirements were keyed to two grammar texts. Pupils completing Standard VIII were required to demonstrate a thorough knowledge of Mason's 1882 *Outlines of English Grammar* and the ability to carry out full analysis and parsing of extracts.

Grammar was no less important in courses of study implemented by the Australian Boards of Education. In New South Wales, the 1856 National Board of Education's program required pupils in Standard II to be able to give simple definitions of the eight parts of speech and to be able to distinguish the article, noun, pronoun, and verb. South Australia in its 1873 Standards of Proficiency expected the ability to distinguish the article, noun, and verb in Standard I, the other parts of speech being the scope of the next standard. Tasmania brought out a very laconic grammar course as part of its 1869 program: parts of speech in Standard III, parsing in IV, analysis of simple sentences in V, and, rather vaguely, "grammar" for Standard VI. For pupils completing Queensland's 1876 program, at the end of Standard V they would have to "know and apply the rules of syntax; parse and analyze complex and compound sentences." Generally, it was near the end of the century before these requirements were modified in Australia.

It is fair to say that any pupil graduating at, say, the age of thirteen from any of the new state schools in Canada, New Zealand, or Australia would have had a rigorous encounter with concepts and propositions about the structure of the English language. The inspector might ask for the definition of one of the eight parts of speech: "What is a verb?" to which the answer, memorized from the textbook would be, "A verb is a word which expresses existence, condition, or action." (1868) To the question "What are the four parts that comprise grammar?" the pupil would be expected to give the old medieval categories still used in nineteenth-century grammars: Orthography (letters and syllables), Etymology (words and their variations and derivations), Syntax (the ordering of words in sentences), and Prosody (punctuation, intonation, and versification). "Curse o' God on it, isn't it terrible," muttered Sean O'Casey's Irish schoolboy, Johnny, when he read this classification in the 1890s in his grammar book. (1960, p. 289)

Although sentence analysis and other techniques were introduced as reforms in the teaching of grammar (see Morell's sentence analysis in the next chapter), pragmatic schoolmen and textbook authors simply *added* analysis to the grammar course. Thus colonial teachers tried to teach two grammars, each based on different linguistic theories. Pupils were expected to learn to perform two operations on sentences: to parse the words in them and to analyze the sentences' structures. In examinations, the economical approach was to give one sentence or passage and ask candidates to dissect it in both ways.

CHAPTER 5

Parsing versus Sentence Analysis

Class of students at the north door of the Carmangay School,
Alberta (names available in original source). 192-. (Courtesy
Galt Museum & Archives, UID 20091048004.)

Parsing and sentence analysis were the two culminating rituals of the
nineteenth-century grammar class. Parsing emerged from a view of grammar
as an account of individual words and their behavior; the word was the most
significant unit of language structure. Parsing the words in a sentence was
the test of a pupil's knowledge of a complex classification of words and their
inflected forms, whose study began with the definition and identification of
the eight parts of speech and their different subcategories and inflections.
Parsing, adapted as an exercise in the application of etymological concepts
and categories from the study of Latin, had a long history. Sentence analysis,
with its focus on the sentence as the significant unit of language, had only
become popular in the teaching of English grammar after 1852—the year
Morell published his first textbook.

PARSING

To *parse* meant to state what part of speech a word was, to explain its form, so far as inflection is concerned, and to show its syntactical relation in any given connection (Smith O., 1984, p. 143). Some grammars distinguished between "etymological parsing," which was concerned with the form and inflections of words, and "syntactical parsing," which added the relationship between the form of a word and any rules of syntax that governed that form.

The parsing of words in Latin involved making a series of category judgments about each word in a particular sentence so that the word's form, function and relationships to other words in the sentence were fully classified. For example, according to Lennie, the verb *scripserat* (to write) could be parsed as:

> Transitive verb, from scribo, scribers, scripsi, scriptum; active voice; indicative mood; pluperfect tenses; third person, singular agreeing with pronoun of the third person implied in its ending. (1851)

Since Latin was an inflected language with all of the above information coded in its inflections, parsing was a process of making explicit statements about significant grammatical categories. However, as applied to English, which is a word-order language having relatively few inflections, parsing appears a rather artificial activity to modern eyes. Educationists in the early nineteenth century, on the other hand, such as Matthew Arnold, the influential Inspector of Schools in England from 1852 to 1886, strongly supported the teaching of grammar as an exercise of the children's wits. To Arnold, parsing was "the very best of the discipline of grammar" (1880, p. 214); he believed that it was profoundly important. Goold Brown (1832) for example, author of an American school grammar text, asserted the importance of parsing in the learning of grammar in a typically uncompromising nineteenth-century way:

> In etymology and syntax the pupil should be alternately exercised in learning small portions of his book, and then applying them in parsing, till the whole is rendered familiar—The mode of instruction here recommended is the result of a long and successful experience—It is the plain didactic method of definition and example, rule and praxis; which no man who means to teach grammar well will ever desert, with the hope of finding another more rational or more easy (Martyn, 1932).

Although Brown used the word *applying*, the application intended was not in the sense of rules and definitions being related to *actual* speaking or writing but only in the sense of being related to examples of sentences selected by the textbook author or the teacher. The purpose of parsing was to help fix the material being learned and to provide a means of assessing it. In other words, parsing was a technique for the more efficient and thorough learning of the grammar; it was not concerned with the effects on usage of that learning. In the words of Lindley Murray (1843,orig. 1795), it was a means by which "the learners should be exercised, in order to prove their knowledge, and to render it familiar to them." What parsing meant to the older primary pupil is illustrated by an example in Murray's famous grammar, which was first published in 1795. His first specimen of syntactical parsing was a typically moral assertion:

> "Vice produces misery"

> 'Vice' is a common substantive, of the neuter gender, the third person, the singular number, and in the nominative case. 'Produces' is a regular verb active, indicative mood, present tense, the third person singular, agreeing with its nominative 'vice,' according to Rule 1, which says: (here repeat the rule.) 'Misery' is a common substantive, of the neuter gender, the third person, the singular number, and the objective case, governed by the active verb 'produces,' according to Rule XI, which says, etc. (p. 217)

There is no doubt that parsing was a cognitively demanding exercise that depended upon a good understanding of the categories of grammar if pupils were to succeed in this minute dissection of sentences. Teachers were expected to be adroit in parsing and could be given complicated phrases to parse (see p. 150 for an early example).

By the 1870s, parsing questions were a standard part of grammar examinations and remained so for the rest of the nineteenth century and much of the twentieth. The level of difficulty was adjusted through the type of passage chosen for dissection. It could be a straightforward prose passage as short as a sentence (which could nevertheless be tricky, such as "But me no buts"), or it could be tortuous and convoluted, such as the incomprehensible sentence assigned for parsing in the 1881 grammar examination set by the New Zealand Department of Education for teacher certificates, Class E:

> Parse as fully as you can: 'Let me no longer waste the night over the page of antiquity or the sallies of contemporary genius, but

pursue the solitary walk, where Vanity, even changing, but a few hours past walked before me—where she kept up the pageant, and now like a froward [sic] child, seems hushed with her own importunities.'

It was with justification that the August 1881 issue of the New Zealand Schoolmaster complained that this paper had been the hardest one in the examinations that year. (p. 3)

However, it was selections of poetry that seemed to give examiners most satisfaction as a rigorous test of parsing. The three assigned texts for the examination were Book I of *Paradise Lost*, Macaulay's *Essay on Hampden*, and Mason's *Grammar (Advanced)*. Typical was a passage from *Paradise Lost* set in the 1886 Class II Teachers License examination in Prince Edward Island:

Too well I see, and rue the dire event,
That with sad overthrow, and foul defeat,
Hath lost us heaven, and all this mighty host
In horrible destruction laid thus low,
As far as gods and heavenly essences
Can perish. (Appendix F, p. 102)

Eleven- and twelve-year-old boys writing the Exhibition examinations for access to Superior Schools in Tasmania in 1881 faced the task of parsing a piece of lugubrious and atrocious verse:

And when I am forgotten, as I shall be,
And sleep in dull cold marble, where no mention
Of me there must be heard of, say, I taught thee.

In 1862 Tasmania's Southern Board of Education combined parsing with another form of exercise that had been popular in the late eighteenth and early nineteenth centuries: correcting false English. Its Class 2 grammar paper for pupil teachers asked candidates to write out the following passage in correct English and parse the words:

Accordin to obserwashun, moast menn lern weesdom threw sufring. He daely atended two is ordnarry bisnes, butt otherwize waisted nerely all is ours and paide leetle or know reguard too wat ma bee ganed threw conwerashun withe persns off nollege and cense.

Educational journals often gave teachers help with parsing questions, revealing at the same time the level of anxiety that attended this grammatical activity. The *New South Wales Educational Gazette* printed solutions to the parsing question on the previous year's grammar paper in the Third Class Certificate examinations. The treatment of three words from the line 'Watch what thou seest' of a longer passage of poetry indicates the complexity of the answers that were expected.

> Watch. - Trans. verb, 2nd pers. sing., agr. with ("thou") pres., imperative.

> what (1). - Rel. pron. with suppressed antecedent, 3rd pers., sing., neut., obj. governed by "seest."

> seest. - Trans. verb 2nd pers., sing., agr with 'thou' pres., indic. (1891, p. 11)

A South Australia parsing exercise survives within the Class III notebook of a girl called Christina MacKay, who attended a Currie Street School in an unidentified town. On Tuesday, August 29, 1894, under the painstakingly lettered heading, Grammar, and within a carefully drawn frame for the page, Christina had parsed the nouns in the sentence, "The girl's brother broke his arm."

> Girl's—Possessive case governed by the noun 'brother';

> brother—Nominative case to the verb 'broke'; arm—Objective case governed by the verb 'broke'. (School notebooks, South Australia Department of Education Library).

The teacher had initialed the page the next day without comment.

SENTENCE ANALYSIS

The practice of breaking simple sentences up into their parts and of complex and compound sentences into their clauses is so familiar to anyone who studied English until the 1960s that it is hard to imagine a time when it was not part of the repertoire of grammar teachers.

Sentence analysis (which, after 1875, became known by the term familiar up to the present day, **clause analysis**) did not become an established part of the school curriculum until after 1850. Although the term *analysis* was used earlier, it referred to little more than identification of the parts of simple sentences. Terminology was variable, and the concept of subordination, the key to sentence analysis as taught by generations of school teachers after the middle of the century, was missing. The early part of the nineteenth century saw language as a kind of mosaic, constructed by putting together the separate parts of speech (Woods, 1985). Grammar study, under this conception, was the scientific body of knowledge about the relationships among individual words. Thus the focus of study was upon the word, its different classifications and its inflections, giving rise to the primacy of etymology over syntax as content and of parsing words as an exercise.

By the mid-1800s, a new concept was taking over, one that saw language as an instrument of communication and thought. This brought about a shift from the word and etymology to the sentence and analysis of its different parts. There was also a related shift within the mental discipline theory that supported grammar teaching. No longer was the emphasis on exercising the separate faculties; intellectual training referred to the teaching of thinking through analysis of language, as what Morell (1852) called "the great complex organ of human thought."

An inspector of government training schools for teachers in England, John Daniel Morell was credited with introducing into England what became the standard form of sentence analysis, including subordination as the key to the analysis of complex sentences (Michael, p. 370). His first grammar text, *The Analysis of Sentences Explained and Systematized*, was published in 1852 as a text for grammar instruction in teacher-training schools.

As an inspector, Morell had found that the prevailing variation in grammatical analysis was a handicap in his examination of pupil teachers' knowledge of the subject: "Beyond the ordinary modes of parsing I found it almost impossible to give out any questions on Syntax and the Analysis of Sentences to which a common meaning was attached by pupils ... or any number of distinct answers returned." (p. iii)

Morell found a coherent and systematic analysis in the work of the German grammarian Karl Ferdinand Becker, which Morell then applied to English. He argued the shift from the study of the word to the study of the sentence.

> The chief advantage I look for in pursuing grammar on these principles is, to avoid the folly in education, of putting Etymology before Syntax, and of inculcating the mere study of individual words, and of their structure, in preference to the investigation of language as the great complex organ of human thought. I have long been convinced that the proper study of language is the preparatory discipline for all abstract thinking, and that if the

intellect is to be strengthened in this direction, we must begin the process here. (p. v)

The advantage Morell claimed for the sentence analysis approach was intellectual. He claimed that to some extent the study of English grammar would bestow the same benefits as the study of the ancient languages, "without departing from the usages and idiom of our own tongue," namely insights into the structure of language and an understanding of the "laws of thought."

MORELL'S SENTENCE ANALYSIS (1852)

Morell's text began with an analysis of the parts of a sentence, which he defined as "the complete utterance of a single thought." A sentence consisted of a subject and a predicate, and the predicate could take a completion (object) and an extension (adverbial elements). Part II dealt with the analysis of complex and compound sentences. The analysis of complex sentences was into principal and subordinate "sentences," not yet called clauses. Subordinate sentences, which contained a subject and a finite verb, could be of three types: a substantive sentence—what would be called noun clauses in more modern terms; an adjective sentence; and an adverbial sentence. The last category was further broken down into the familiar types: time, place, manner, cause, and effect.

Morell recommended a definite set of steps for pupils to follow in analyzing complex sentences: "Divide the complex sentence into as many portions as there are finite verbs; keep the same order as nearly as possible as in the passage to be analyzed; prefix a letter to each and then arrange them in a column and opposite each write the kind of sentence, determined according to the explanations given in the preceding sections of the text." Several examples were given.

a. *We are now treading that illustrious island.* Principal sentence to b. and c.

b. *which was once the luminary of Caledonian regions.* Adjective sentence to a.

c. *and whence savage clans derive the blessings of religion.* Adjective sentence to a. coordinate with b.

Part III of the text dealt with the laws of syntax, seven in all, which were exercised by a system of parsing based not on inflections but on the relationships between words. Each word in a sentence was merely put into its class and subcategory as a part of speech and its relation to another word in the sentence stated. Thus in the sentence, "Alfred, King of England, having inspected the enemy's position, shortly routed them with great slaughter," *Alfred* was parsed as "Proper noun, subject to 'routed'" (rule i) and *king* as "Common noun, attributive to 'Alfred'."

The final section of the text was a short explanation of punctuation, not for the purposes of composition but as an aid to the parceling up of the various parts of difficult sentences. In other words, punctuation was in the service of grammar.

Two years later Morell brought out a second text, *The Essentials of English Grammar; and Analysis*. He claimed that in response to many requests, this new, simpler book was an attempt to make the system of analysis accessible to pupils in the higher primary grades. One can imagine the graduates of the training schools going out into their classrooms and finding that their own study of Morell's earlier text was inadequate preparation to teach the new grammar to their pupils and turning to their former inspector for assistance.

Despite his earlier criticism of putting etymology first as "folly," he must have realized that his system depended upon a prior knowledge of the parts of speech, for the first section in the new text was "On Words," and the second was on inflection as an expression of relationships in sentences. This knowledge was to be exercised by a system of parsing almost as extended as the traditional systems. For example, the sentence "Now I climb the mountain" yielded the following:

Now	Adverb of time
I	Per. pron. 1st per. sing. nom.
climb	Verb reg. ind mood pres. tense 1st per. sing.
the	Adj. limiting 'mountain'
mountain	Noun com. sing. simple form.

This was followed by a condensed form of the analysis system, culminating in an outline form for written practice exercises with the headings: Kind of sentence, Subject, Predicate, Completion of predicate, Extension of predicate.

a. *That man is blessed indeed.* Principal sentence to b, c, d, & e.
   Subject: that man
   Predicate: is blessed
   Completion of predicate
   Extension of predicate: indeed

b. *who noble ends by noble means obtains.* Adjective sentence to a.
Subject: who
Predicate: obtains
Completion of predicate: noble ends
Extension of predicate: by noble means.

The end paper of the 1854 book carried this note: "This work is now used in most of the training schools under Government inspection and as a text book for aiding in the examination for the certificate of merit." (Also offered for sale was a portrait of Morell for seven shillings and six pence.)

In both of Morell's texts, the teacher was given an important role, as one would expect from someone involved in the training of teachers. In his 1852 text he noted that his presentation included only a brief treatment of the general principles "that may be expanded by the intelligent teacher into innumerable examples and illustrations." Throughout the text appeared items of advice to the teacher, for example, "Let the pupil select passages from any author containing complex sentences ..." When it came to his second, simpler text for primary pupils, Morell made much of this virtue.

> Use of this book implies a great deal of explanatory teaching on the part of the master. This I have not been anxious to avoid, but rather to encourage; the more so because the whole use of grammar in the primary school arises from its being made an instrument of intellectual training. Unless this end be accomplished, the whole of the time and trouble employed in learning it had much better be spared and devoted to other objects.

The format of both books was similar. A point of concept would be defined and explained, and then there would appear several illustrations and exercises for the pupil to complete, including identifying particular elements in sentences and expanding elements into complete sentences. In this respect the books were well suited for classroom use.

With Morell's texts available, and with other popular authors such as C.P. Mason following his lead, analysis seems to have spread quickly to all the colonial school systems. By the 1870s and 1880s, it was included in all the mandated syllabi as an examinable outcome of primary school grammar teaching. The record indicates that educationists in some systems were enthusiastic about analysis. In Nova Scotia, for example, where Morell's easier text, *Essentials of English Grammar; and Analysis,* was prescribed in 1865 as a replacement grammar text for Lennie's, school inspectors endorsed its adoption and anticipated success in its classroom use, even going so far as to say that it would remedy the imperfections of Lennie's *Grammar*. There were scattered references to its use in the province over the next eight years, until it was replaced by a locally published grammar text by MacCabe.

There are also references to its use in Prince Edward Island and New Brunswick, with a particularly enthusiastic supporter in PEI in the person of School Visitor John Arbuckle, who in 1861 said he had given demonstrations of the method to teachers and distributed printed material explaining it. Arbuckle explained that the system replaced the emphasis on the word under the old formal method of parsing with a focus on the sentence as the fundamental starting point, keeping the development of the sentence as the guiding idea of all grammatical teaching. Only two years later, Arbuckle seemed to be rather discouraged by a lack of progress in encouraging teachers to give up Lennie's system and turn to Morell's, although he was consoled that sentence analysis had been introduced to the program of teacher training at the provincial Normal School. (He must have abandoned his attempts to have analysis introduced into the schools, for in 1863 he recommended the adoption of Currie's *English Grammar*.)

Although New Zealand's Department of Education did not prescribe textbooks, as was the Canadian practice, sentence analysis was represented on the list of sixteen approved grammars in 1878 and ten approved texts for grammar and composition in 1887. Morell's 1854 text was approved for use in New Zealand primary schools in 1878, while the 1887 list included one text referred to as "Morell's English Grammar and First Book of Composition." Other texts that included sentence analysis, notably by Allen and Cornwell and by Mason, were also included in 1887.

In Australia, Morell's texts were available from at least 1859. In that year the National Board of Education for New South Wales listed "Morell's Analysis" as one of the grammar texts recommended for teachers studying to take their certificate examinations. Morell's texts were in use in Victoria schools by the 1860s, and by the 1870s both of his texts were included on the Tasmania book order forms for schools. The Queensland record showed that by 1880 "Morell's Analysis" was an approved text for primary school grammar and composition.

The legacy of analysis reached right into the twentieth century. Fourteen-year-olds in the Prairie province of Alberta, writing the 1906 public examination in English Grammar for Standard V, would have found their ability to dissect sentences tested by Question 1:

> Analyze fully, showing clearly the kind and relation of the subordinate clauses:

> "On the top of a windmill, of which the solid tower is still to be seen on the ridge overhanging the field, the king, who had his head quite bare, remained in absorbed silence, whilst the young Prince, who had been knighted a month before, went forward with his companions in arms into the thickest of the fray."

In 1936, Grade 9 pupils in the colony of Newfoundland, not yet part of Canada, faced an analysis question on their public examination in grammar that asked them to pick out the subordinate clauses in a passage of poetry that the examiners later admitted had been difficult.

> 'Tis a common proof

> That lowliness is young Ambition's ladder

> Whereto the climber upwards turns his face;

> But when he once attains the utmost round,

> He then until the ladder turns his back,

> Looks into the clouds, scorning his base degrees

> By which he did ascend. (1936, Report of the Examinations conducted by the Council of Higher Education, St. John's, Newfoundland, p. 27)

Clause analysis questions on the Newfoundland public examinations in English lasted until 1970, although with considerable moderation in the difficulty of the passages to be analyzed. Notebooks that have survived to be stored in archives tell the story of a hundred years of analysis activities in classrooms all over the colonies: errors, crossings out, and repeated exercises. Many teachers of English would probably admit to having had but an indifferent knowledge of subordinate clauses until they found themselves having to teach them to the next generation as a kind of penance.

SENTENCE DIAGRAMS (1877)

A remarkable little book by two Brooklyn professors, Reed and Kellogg's *Higher Lessons in English* was published in the United States in 1877. Replacing Morell's tabular system, it introduced a new method of revealing the grammatical structures and relationships among the parts of a sentence. First copyrighted in 1868, Reed and Kellogg's diagramming system was widely available from 1874 onwards. The system was developed out of experience in teaching in American polytechnics. Kitty Burns Florey claimed that this diagramming system "swept through American public schools like the measles, and was embraced by teachers as the way to reform students who were engaged in 'the cold-blooded murder of the English tongue.'" (2006, p. 23)

The two authors went on to publish an elementary grammar text, *An Elementary English Grammar* (1884), and *A One-Book Course in English* (1895). The sentence diagramming system presented in these books was based on a sophisticated and insightful pedagogy that claimed the following features, as described by the authors in the prefaces to their textbooks:

1. minimizing memorization
2. using oral instruction
3. using inductive learning techniques
4. making the sentence the central unit of analysis
5. grading materials to meet the needs of different levels of learners
6. encouraging students to build their own sentences
7. actively engaging students in their own learning
8. presenting textbook material that helps teachers to provide step-by-step guidance for their students

In many ways this was the antithesis of conventional nineteenth-century practice in the teaching of grammar. Unfortunately, there is only scant evidence in the records that sentence diagramming was widely used in schools in Canada, New Zealand, or Australia. Grammar texts published in Canada from about 1880 until 1930 did not even refer to sentence diagramming. Perhaps one reason for this was that colonial school administrators looked more to England and Scotland than to the United States for their inspiration.

One Canadian textbook, first published in 1937, did incorporate diagramming. This was a high school text called *Mastering Effective English* (Tressler & Lewis). Grammar, including the fourteen pages devoted to diagramming, was an appendix in a broad treatment of reading, writing, listening, and speaking. This was a Canadian book widely used throughout the Dominion schools; many Canadians remember lessons in diagramming sentences from their schooling in the 1950s and 1960s.

EXAMPLE OF SENTENCE DIAGRAMS

The purpose of this book is not to provide instruction on sentence diagramming; there are many available resources, both in text and online, that do so. However, I have included the following diagram and explanation, both taken directly from Gene Moutoux's website called "German-Latin-English.com":

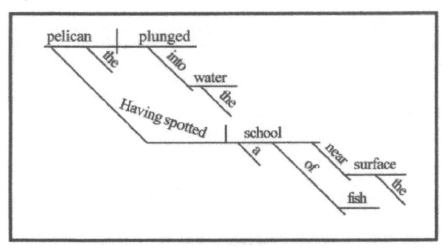

Sentence 46: Having spotted a school of fish near the surface, the pelican plunged into the water. (Used with permission of the website author, Gene Moutoux.)

The verb *spot* (to catch sight of) has five participial forms: *spotting* (present active participle), *being spotted* (present passive participle), *having spotted* (present-perfect active participle), *having been spotted* (present-perfect passive participle), and *spotted* (past participle). **Participles** are verbal adjectives; they are diagrammed like *having spotted* in this sentence. As adjectives, they modify nouns and pronouns; as verbs, they can take direct objects or predicate nominatives. (Sentence Diagramming)

DASHWOOD-JONES' PATTERNS OF WRITING

The early 1950s brought a severe critique of school grammar from American linguists such as Charles Carpenter Fries and Nelson Francis. They argued that traditional grammar was flawed and that its concepts and pedagogy, such as sentence analysis and parsing, were based on a false science; it was an inadequate theory on which to base instruction. These critics, known as *structural linguists*, proposed an alternative theory based on real data obtained from large samples of speech and writing produced in normal situations. They rejected the traditional definitions of parts of speech and grammatical categories based on written language and, in many cases, derived from Latin. The new structural model was based strictly on accurate description of how people actually used language.

In the mid-1960s a new series of grammar textbooks was approved for use in the junior high school language arts program in Alberta. Written by Donald Dashwood-Jones, a teacher in British Columbia, *Patterns of Writing* was intended as a new way of looking at grammar as a way of helping students use grammar to improve their written skills. The author indicated that his texts were derived from the work of Paul Roberts and Charles Fries, both associated with the structural linguistics movement of the 1950s and 1960s.

One principle of structuralism was that linguistic categories, such as noun and verb, should be defined based on their role in sentences, not with reference to their meaning. For example, a noun should not be defined as a "person, place, or thing." Rather, it should be considered from the point of view of its behaviour in sentence patterns. Thus, these are the following tests that can be applied:

1. a noun can fill the blank in a sentence such as "I saw the _____."

2. a noun can have the letter *s* added to it to indicate plurality.

3. a noun can be preceded by *a* or *an*.

4. a noun can have added to it an *'s* indicating possession.

These attributes can all be tested in the classroom, allowing for inductive learning activities that encouraged students to trust their ears in judging and confirming the classification of words.

Dashwood-Jones' program taught that sentences in English had four basic patterns, or skeleton sentences. Students were taught that each basic pattern could be represented as a formula:

Pattern 1 (Somebody does something)
    Cats purr. Noun + verb; 1 + 2
Pattern 2 (Somebody does something to someone)
    Cats catch mice. Noun + verb + Noun; 1a +2 +1b
Pattern 3 (Somebody is described)
    Cats are clever. Noun + Verb + Adjective; 1 +2L + 3
Pattern 4 (Somebody is identified)
    Cats are characters. Noun + Linking Verb + Noun; 1a + 2L + 1a

In addition to the sentence pattern formulae, students were taught the parts of speech so that, given a formula, they could compose sentences that fit the pattern. Some changes in the traditional names for the parts of speech were made, arising out of structural linguistics: **determiner**, which includes articles, possessive pronouns, demonstratives, and other forms which "determine" or constrain the subsequent noun; and **intensifier**, which refers to words like *very, quite,* and *somewhat*. In other words, intensifiers form a special class of adverbs that modify another adverb adjective. **Linking verb** was the name given for the subset of verbs that can stand between two nouns that refer to the same person or thing, or between a noun and an adjective that refer to the same person or thing.

Each part of speech was given a code number or letter:

Part of Speech	Code
Noun or pronoun	1
Verb	2
Linking verb	2L
Adjective	3
Adverb	4
Determiner	D
Auxiliary	A
Intensifier	V

Students with an understanding of the basic patterns and the parts of speech would be able to turn sentences into codes, such as:

He ran very quickly	1 2 V 4
He was very happy	1 2L V 3
The old carpenter was fixing the roof	D 3 1a A 2 D 1b

Patterns for Writing had some useful features. The shift toward how words behaved in sentences, away from their meaning, was useful. This allowed teachers to show students that their own ear was a good judge of whether or not a word could be fitted into a particular slot in a sentence. "Give me a word that would fit into this blank: The old man was _____tired. Suggestions: very, quite, somewhat, terribly." Each suggestion could be tested with the questions, "Does it sound right? Can we say that?" The idea that grammar is something we know how to use through the judgment of our ear based on years of experience of speaking and listening is better pedagogy than classifying and parsing.

However, the problem was that *Patterns for Writing* inevitably threw up another set of concepts *about* writing that students had to learn as an assumed foundation for writing. It was hard for teachers to learn how to use these books, and not a great deal of help was provided. I recall an in-service session with Mr. Dashwood-Jones himself in 1966, when I was teaching in a junior high school in Edmonton, Alberta. As a relatively young teacher, I failed to grasp what it was all about. I used Book 2 with my Grade 8 classes in language arts. Neither my students nor I drew much value from it.

CHAPTER 6
The Rationales Supporting State Grammar

Classroom, around 1910.

Grammar's high status as a school subject, cast into the new form of state syllabi but defined (as far as children's experience of it was concerned) by conservative textbooks and teaching methods, drew its strength from an ideology of schooling that arose out of certain nineteenth-century assumptions about the nature of learning, language, and social organization. Not that these assumptions formed any consensus at the time, for the nineteenth century was one of vigorous philosophical controversy and profound social change. However, it seems to be a characteristic of education that as it grasps philosophical ideas as its theories and rationales, it simplifies and reifies them as rather static justifications. Three propositions, explicit and implicit in much of early nineteenth-century education, all bearing on grammar teaching, seem to have enjoyed a long acceptance in the practice of early colonial schooling.

The first, drawn from popular as opposed to scientific psychology, was that the mind consists of separate faculties whose individual training and exercise is the function of the school curriculum (Leahey, 1980). Under the label of faculty psychology and its attendant educational corollary, mental discipline, this popularly accepted theory, already rejected by serious philosophers of the human mind before the end of the eighteenth century, provided the dominant psychological rationale for classroom practice until the end of the nineteenth century (Kliebard, 1986).

The second proposition was epistemological, asserting that good speaking and writing depended upon the prior mastery of the categories and rules of language, a belief that withstood much classroom evidence to the contrary.

The third, sociological in origin, maintained that social harmony and individual respectability were undermined by improprieties in speech and writing, an idea not entirely dismissed from educational debates even into the 1980s.

These interconnected assumptions justified the particular practices of schooling in the nineteenth century. They formed an "ideology" of primary education in the broad cultural sense of the term, which refers to the inevitable "general ideas potent in specific situations of conduct" (Geertz, 1964). This ideology gave authority to grammar's inclusion in the school curriculum as worthwhile knowledge and authority to the methods and texts that teachers used to instill that knowledge in their pupils. It authorized two convictions that were frequently expressed in the reports of colonial educators: that the intellectual exercise involved in learning grammar was valuable, generalizable training for the mind; and that a formal, propositional knowledge of the categories and rules of the English language was an indispensable prerequisite for proper use of the language in speaking and writing. These convictions, shaping the content and form of grammar teaching, generated its rationale.

Mental discipline

For most of the nineteenth century, the traditional answer to the question of what schools should teach and how they should teach it was provided within a speculative theory of the human mind and how it learned: **faculty psychology,** with its educational derivative **mental discipline**. According to the assumptions underlying these views of the human mind and its proper training, the mind was composed of a hierarchy of separate powers, or faculties, such as the will, reason, memory, taste, moral feeling, sensation, perception, and belief. Moreover, it was believed that these faculties, or powers, were innate and equally available to all. Their proper development required that each be exercised without any regard for the possibility of individual differences in intellectual endowment.

One major function of education was to provide this exercise, so that each faculty could be strengthened in much the same way that calisthenics builds muscles. Since each faculty was assumed to be responsible for a general capacity, a particular mental activity, such as memorizing the inflections of nouns and pronouns, could produce generalizable benefits to the memory, allowing the individual to develop a sound grasp of details, even a "head for business" (Woods, 1985). From a mental discipline point of view, the curriculum could be defined as a set of mental activities designed to exercise the full range of the mind's faculties, and the case for a particular subject could be made in terms of the particular faculties that it exercised in all pupils.

With roots in the educational practices of the Greeks and Romans and passed on via medieval scholasticism, the doctrine of mental discipline was formulated as an educational theory in the seventeenth century, especially by Locke. It was well suited to the defense of an education in the classics, which was coming under increasing attack in the eighteenth century on the grounds that learning Latin and Greek had no direct connection with the practical demands of the times. The principles of mental discipline reassured teachers of the dead languages that what mattered in education was not the thing to be learned but the process of learning.

From this perspective, grammar's contribution to the school curriculum lay first of all in the rigorous exercise of the mind's faculties. **Memory**, the faculty on which all others relied and on which a successful education depended, was disciplined in learning grammar's complex and abstract classifications; others, including the highest-order faculty, **reasoning**, were strengthened in the application of these categories in parsing exercises. Goold Brown, a mid-century American grammarian, said,

> Parsing is … an exercise for all the powers of the mind, except the inventive faculty. Perception, judgment, memory, and method, are indispensable to the performance. Nothing is to be guessed at, or devised, or uttered at random (Woods, 1985).

The doctrine of mental discipline explains why school grammar in the nineteenth century (as revealed by Lennie's text, for example) appears to modern eyes to have been so difficult in its density, abstractness, and complexity, and why so few concessions to ease of comprehension were made in the sentences used in the examples and exercises. The terms *rigour* and *precision* were key words in this theory of learning. Difficult material was better mental exercise. As Monroe said in 1905, "The best training for the memory was afforded by the mastery of material which had no inherent interest for the child" (Heck, 1912). Interest, relevance, and motivation were not part of this psychology. The focus was upon the matter to be learned, not upon the learner. Grammar would have been a favorite subject of a schoolmaster in England, who is reported to have said, "If once you interest boys in the work, you lose half of its disciplinary profit" (Murray, E. K., 1977).

By mid-century the doctrine of mental discipline was undergoing a shift. The Romantic idealism of Pestalozzi[4] was emphasizing that the mind was not like a blank slate on which subjects such as grammar were inscribed by memorization and recitation, but that it was an active agent in learning, responding to its own interests. While the framework was still mental discipline and the mission still to "form the mind" in order that it might then be properly "furnished," the old focus on **memory** as the basic faculty was being replaced with a new emphasis on the faculty of **reasoning**. In this new version of mental discipline, it was essential that the material be understood in order for this intellectual power to be properly exercised.

This shift to reason and comprehension was reflected in the rationales of the grammar textbooks. Even Lennie's *Grammar* and the Irish *Grammar* had urged the importance of understanding what was committed to memory, and both had employed exercises in false grammar and parsing to intellectually engage the pupil in grammar learning. As suggested above, however, in Lennie's case at least, this intention was probably frustrated by the difficulty of the material and exercises. The new wave of grammars that replaced Lennie's and the Irish grammars in the 1860s and 1870s were generally much more accessible to younger pupils, written in a simpler style, using examples more familiar to children, and containing more exercises and activities. For example, one of the state-commissioned grammars published in 1868 as part of the Canadian National Series of School Books was Davies' *An English Grammar for the Use of Junior Classes*[5]. This text contained an introductory section to

---

4   Johann Heinrich Pestalozzi (1746–1827), considered by many to be the founder of modern pedagogy, was one of the first advocates of a holistic education for all.

5   Authorized in 1868 for Ontario common schools. Pupils would then go on to the second level grammar, *An Analytical and Practical Grammar of the English Language*, 1868.

"render the study more congenial to the younger pupils" and to "serve as an example of the simple language in which children may be taught Grammar" (Davies, 1882).

The shift was also reflected in the growing interest after 1852 in sentence analysis. The older "grammar of the word" had been compatible with the primacy of memory and a theory of language as a mosaic of individual words, but it did not easily take account of the *context* of the word from which it took its meaning. The need to consider meaning in grammar teaching was acknowledged by Morell's system of sentence analysis, which placed the focus on the sentence as the unit of language and as a means of communication. The grammar of the sentence was an analysis of how meanings may be assembled as language structures; to learn this grammar was to exercise the power of reason.

School inspectors under the new state systems were aware of the enhanced intellectual role for grammar teaching in training the faculty of reason, although they did not seem able to articulate the shift that had taken place in the mental discipline rationale for grammar. They seemed to define the problem as simply one of teachers who, because of inadequate training or knowledge, failed to teach grammar as it should have been taught. Most of their comments about mechanical teaching, rote memorization, and the failure to engage pupils' understanding of the grammar being taught were critical rather than sympathetic. It was as though the classroom became the site of a struggle between conservative teachers holding on to the old conception of grammar (the exercise of the faculty of memory) and inspectors who wanted them to teach it as an exercise of reason.

The record of grammar teaching under New Zealand's national syllabus of 1878 illustrated this struggle clearly. The very structure of the course of study for grammar and composition revealed the influence of the older emphasis on memorization and the isolated word as the key or grammatical unit. Although sentence analysis was included, it did not begin until Standard V. The first two years of grammar were concerned with words as parts of speech and with their inflections.

As many inspectors pointed out in their later reports, the effect of this logical order of grammar topics was to require children to master the grammar of words before they learned the grammar of sentences. This sequence of grammar topics discouraged attention to the meanings that words represented and fostered instead the memorization of words as forms or things in their own right. In 1868, Davies' new text showed that it was not necessary to defer sentence analysis until a foundation in the parts of speech had been laid down; instead, analysis was introduced early in the course, presenting it alongside the work on etymology.

The position of the New Zealand inspectorate on the rationale for grammar was expressed by a team of school inspectors from North Canterbury in 1888, when they wrote,

> For the grammar itself, clear ideas of the duties performed by words, phrases, and clauses in a sentence are, both in themselves and in the mental training received from the study, of sufficient value to the business of life to warrant a high position in an education scheme. (p. 35)

These sentiments were shared by school inspectors in other jurisdictions. Inspector Wood of New Brunswick, commenting in 1869 on the scholarship examination results, observed that, "Some of the papers in Grammar too give evidence that the mind of the writer has not been trained to the practice and power of discriminating—that mental discipline, the great advantage of grammar as a study, had been neglected." (p. 31) William Wilkins, inspector and superintendent of education for the National Board of Education, referred in 1859 to one of the purposes of grammar teaching "as a mental discipline of the highest kind." (p. 13) Later in 1865, commenting on parental opposition to the inclusion of grammar in the primary school course, Wilkins lamented, "Its powers of assisting in the processes of mental development have never been recognized by parents in the country." (p. 14) In New South Wales, the 1887 Annual Report on National Schools commented on improved teaching resulting from more intellectual methods, which led to a "strengthening of the mental faculties." (p. 8) Comments supporting the mental training rationale were seen right up to the late 1890s, including some in British Columbia.

Inspectors tried to help their teachers adapt their instruction to the recommended intellectual rationale for grammar. Mr. Lee of Wellington reported in 1901 that he had sent out a circular to his teachers urging them to "use every available means of rendering the instruction less monotonous in character, less an exercise requiring mere imitation or the remembering of sets of dry facts, and more a process of mind-building and thought forming." (p. 10) Since the New Zealand inspectors' views were backed by their control of the examination of pupils for promotion and school leaving certificates, teachers had to listen to what they said. By the end of the century and after the syllabus revision of 1891, some of the inspectors' reports were indicating progress. For example, in 1893 the Southland inspectors reported:

> The more intelligent teachers, proceeding on the line of the syllabus when it describes grammar as 'school logic' have made the subject a means of sound mental discipline. (p. 37)

The expression *school logic* was becoming popular in the discourse of grammar teaching by the end of the century. Its use by New Zealand educationists indicated that they were well aware of a further transformation of the mental discipline rationale for grammar was taking place elsewhere, one that was bringing it into the tradition of nineteenth-century liberal humanism. After 1880, William Torrey Harris, United States Commissioner of Education and former school superintendent in St. Louis, was Influential in this transformation. In the face of a growing movement for reform, Harris redefined a conservative humanist theory of the curriculum, in which the aim of schooling was to transmit the culture of the race through the "five windows of the soul": grammar, literature and art, mathematics, geography, and history (Kliebard, 1986). Education's task was to initiate children into these disciplines to engender their command of the resources of civilization. Harris made the case for grammar teaching in the strongest terms.

> In the language of a people are revealed the internal logical laws of structural framework of its intellect and the conscious realization of the mind of the race, as they appear in the vocabulary, grammatical laws, or syntax. Grammar opens to the child his view of the inner workings of the mind of the race, and helps him in so far to a comprehension of his own spiritual self. (*Psychological Foundations of Education*, 1898)

Grammar, for Harris, was not studied as an intellectual discipline in order to transfer the benefits of the exercise to other activities; its content was important in its own right as a resource of civilization. To this extent Harris had distanced himself from the traditional theory of mental discipline, even the version that had emphasized the power of reasoning as the most important faculty.

However, this distinction between learning grammar as the *exercise* of reason and learning it as the *study* of reason was one that neither Harris nor those school officials who used his authority to support their recommendations consistently maintained. As a result, there was perhaps more continuity between mental discipline and Harris's ideas than he'd intended, insofar as they influenced grammar teaching in the colonies. For example, New Zealand inspector Strachan in his 1906 report quoted from one of Harris's monographs:

> The categories of the mental operation are the categories of grammar, and appear as parts of speech. The child, by the study of grammar, gets some practice in the use of these categories, and acquires unconsciously a power of analysis of thoughts, motives, feelings, which is of the most practical character. (p. 30)

The word *unconsciously* betrays the survival of the older doctrine. Nevertheless, the influence of Harris's view of grammar in New Zealand was evident when grammar was reduced to a class subject in the 1891 syllabus revision.

Harris's view of the intellectual value of grammar study was compatible with the cultural rationales for schooling that were promoted by one of the most influential British educators of the nineteenth century, Matthew Arnold. Arnold saw the curriculum of the elementary schools making the best ideas of the time available to the children of the lower classes. The 1895 report by the Wanganui inspectors quoted Arnold's view of grammar as a school subject: "I attach great importance to grammar as leading the children to reflect and reason, as a very simple sort of logic, more effective than arithmetic as a logical training, because it operates with concretes, or words, instead of with abstracts, or figures."

By the turn of the century it was common to find references in all three countries to grammar as "the logic of the elementary school" or "the Euclid of the elementary school." One such reference came from Victoria State, in a curriculum document of 1943, which noted that "grammar has been defined as the 'logic of speech,' and for that reason it was formerly taught as a mental discipline, and was accorded a very important place in the course of study" (Ellwood, 1943, p. 117).

The New Zealand school inspectors seemed to accept this revised rationale for grammar as a school subject. Their comments suggest that their task as supervisors was to rescue the teaching of grammar from the worst excesses of the older version of the mental discipline theory and transform it into a genuine tool for the development of the intellect and thought processes. Their reports made frequent approving references to grammar as one of the "most truly educative subjects in the primary course of instruction" (Verekker-Bindon, 1895, p. 13). In the same year, Petrie of Auckland referred to the "fine logical training that a skillful handling of the subject is so well fitted to give," and to its role in "training and enlightening the mind." In 1893, the Southland inspectors had noted approvingly that "the more intelligent teachers, proceeding on the lines of the syllabus when it describes grammar as 'school logic,' have made the subject a means of sound mental discipline." In

1908, the Wellington inspectorate was calling for the restoration of grammar on the grounds of its value as a mental exercise and as a tool for the analytical and critical study of language.

An interesting postscript to the doctrine of mental discipline was contained in a statement made by the New Zealand minister of education, Mr. Hanna, in a memorandum laid before the House of Representatives in 1916. Under the heading "Mental Discipline and Culture," the statement seemed to pronounce the demise of the doctrine when it maintained:

> The argument for formal, abstract, unapplied study—that it provides good mental discipline and culture transferable to other activities—is now fighting in the last ditch all the world over. Such production of chaff for a grain of wheat has as much justification as would the pounding of the earth with one's fist for several hours a day to develop muscle when that purpose, and a much greater one, could be secured by getting a blacksmith's hammer and doing something. Surely if the proper methods of teaching are used and the powers of thought developed, an even greater mental discipline and culture can be secured by studying real things in a practical manner. There is no real antithesis between culture and vocational study. That false distinction is merely a relic of old class barriers and an age when the best educated people were not expected to be or do anything outside a very limited sphere (Hanna, 1916).

CHAPTER 7
Purity of Language

Fleetwood School, Lethbridge, Alberta. 1911. (Courtesy
Galt Museum & Archives, UID 19760231288.)

THE SURVIVAL OF FORMAL GRAMMAR IN THE PRIMARY SCHOOL

In 1908, Inspector Williams of Broken Hill in New South Wales made
an interesting observation about an effect of New Education changes in
teaching English. "The new emphasis on composition," he remarked, "had
revealed what the older methods had hidden, namely errors in sentence
structure and pronunciation." (p. 308) The inspector did not elaborate,
but it seems reasonable to suppose that as long as children were confined
to reciting memorized text and responding with learned answers, and as
long as their written work consisted of reproducing and paraphrasing set
material, deficiencies in speaking and writing would be less visible than under

a regime that encouraged them to talk and write out of their own ideas and experience.

Whatever the truth of Inspector Williams' claim, in Australia, as in New Zealand and Canada, the nineteenth-century preoccupation with propriety of usage intensified into a campaign, and occasionally into a crusade, against linguistic error in the speech and writing of citizens and school children. As educators participated in and responded to campaigns in their communities—often conducted under the banner of "pure speech"—the eradication of error in speech and writing became an important objective of the English studies syllabus. Since the issue involved standards, and since grammar was concerned with standards in language, the pure speech movement lent support to the rehabilitation of formal grammar in the primary school.

Poor usage in colonial society was a popular topic in educational journals around the turn of the century, and some strange theories were advanced to account for deviations from pure speech in colonial societies. In 1906, E. Burgess, a school principal in Manitoba, blamed the cold northern climate for problems in the Canadian accent. "In cold countries," he claimed, "the vocal chords are tense, in warm countries, relaxed; consequently a Northerner is bound to speak more harshly than a Southerner, a Canadian more harshly than an Australian." Mr. Burgess's experience of the Manitoba winter might excuse but not justify his theory. Over in Nova Scotia, an equally unusual theory was advanced by the Department of Education for the prevalence of dialect speech in the damper and milder climate of the Atlantic seaboard. Teachers were advised that dialect features were caused by the "lack of some muscular throat development and not to any want of intelligence" (*Journal of Education*, 1910).

An unnamed commentator in the *Western School Journal* lamented the stridency of Canadian speech. The absence of a mellow tone was attributed to environmental factors: "Our forefathers hollering across the fields in the bush"; "The habit of shouting at the telephone"; "Yelling on the street car"; and "Shrieking to be heard" on the noisy streets (*Canadian Musical Speech*, 1914).

More plausibly, A. E. Cross, a Quebec advocate, maintained that a general relaxation of care had occurred in people's use of language, to the extent that slang was even invading the pulpit. One effect, he claimed, of the loss of linguistic precision was that since no one could rely anymore on a man's careless word, businessmen were more and more forced to resort to warily written contracts. Another was that popular newspapers were printing whatever they wanted, failing to acknowledge that "words spoken and written are important things and may have far-reaching consequences" (1915, pp. 357–366).

The link between quality of language and quality of thought was invoked in an 1895 editorial in the Educational Record of Quebec. Referring to an early "campaign for better English in schools," the writer suggested that schools adopt the motto, "If we wish to think correctly we must learn to speak correctly and to write correctly."

Mr. Burgess, that Manitoba principal, might have been surprised to learn that in spite of Australia's warm climate, there was a similar concern in that country about the quality of spoken language. A Sydney clergyman in 1920 advanced the argument that intellect and character were at risk if poor speech were to be tolerated. The Reverend Tait thought that pure speech was undermined in Australia by the tendency to speak too quickly, which led "to the mauling of syllables and words, sometimes beyond all recognition," and by the national "instinctive preference for the easy and lazy way of doing things," which led to the "indolent action of the jaw, and the organs of speech generally." The seriousness of these tendencies arose because "the very language one uses tends to coarsen the feeling and degrade the character" (1920, pp. 132–133).

Concern about the development of a distinctive Australian accent was one of the topics included in an address to the New South Wales Teachers' Federation Conference in 1926 by the Director of Education. He disapproved of this divergence from standard English; cultured speech was the birthright of everyone, and the "careless happy-go-lucky speech of Australia" should be checked. He wanted teachers to train children to speak more musically and more clearly, and he hoped that, as a result of their efforts, New South Wales might someday provide a standard of spoken English for the rest of the country.

Another concern was the "excessive use of expletives in Australian English." E. H. Dunlop, a Brisbane school inspector, gave an address to Queensland teachers on the subject, which was reprinted in the *New Zealand Education Gazette* in 1929. He recounted an item from *Punch* in which an old lady in London, upon being asked politely for directions to the Bloody Tower, assumed that her interrogator was an Australian. Then, quoting from Sampson, Dunlop recommended that since "a man's speech is usually his label for life ... it is a teacher's work to see to it that boys are not wrongly labeled." (p. 145)

In New Zealand, a manifestation of the pure speech issue came in some of the evidence presented to the Cohen Commission in 1912 and in one of its recommendations. Several witnesses who addressed the Commission, which was set up to inquire into the system of education in New Zealand, expressed their concern about the quality of English spoken in the Dominion. Mr. Louis Cohen, a barrister (a witness, not the chairman of the Commission) claimed that on the basis of his legal experience with witnesses and clerks and of his everyday contacts, he believed that the English spoken in New Zealand had become degraded. Although it was not yet in such a serious condition as it was in Australia, New Zealand English had become what he called "characteristically colonial." (1912, p. 460)

His criticisms centered on pronunciation, not dialect of grammar, and he gave as examples of the problem: *merit* pronounced /murit/, *impossible* /umpossible/, and *justice* /jestice/. His objections to New Zealand pronunciation were based more on what he regarded as its aesthetic offence than on its interference with communication. He seemed to regard the English language in its pure form as a national cultural asset that should not be squandered, and he placed the responsibility for the protection of this asset on the shoulders of teachers, whom he hoped could be encouraged or required to present better models to their pupils.

Another witness, A. Heine, an English teacher and acting headmaster of Wellington College, also complained about declining standards of pronunciation, using the term "objectionable colonial dialect," which, he claimed, he had noticed becoming worse in the previous ten years, especially in a carelessness in pronouncing vowels: *house* pronounced as /heouse/ and *oh no* as /ow neow/, for example. On being asked to give other examples of colonial pronunciation, Mr. Heine gave this list: *fine*-foine; *lady*-lidy; *make*-mike; *lake*-like. Commissioner Pirani then noted that two of the principals of the largest secondary schools in New Zealand, in giving evidence to the Commission, had used pronunciations such as taime for *table*, Ai for *I*, may own for *my own*, bay for buy, Ingland, nainteen, faive, naine, naight, laike, gairls, supervaise, laines, advaise, taimes, provaided, laife. "Have you ever heard a primary school teacher do worse than that?" asked the Commissioner. (p. 624) Hogben challenged Mr. Heine's conclusion as being based only on his own impression of a decline, but the acting headmaster refused to back down, claiming that his memory was very good.

Apparently impressed by this kind of testimony, the Commission included in its report a recommendation that particular attention be paid to teaching correct speech in the primary school. In the following year the recommendation was incorporated into the syllabus in the form of statements about the importance of "purity of speech."

The fact that the influential *Newbolt Report on the Teaching of English in England*, published in 1921, emphasized this link between language and mind helped to authorize concern in the colonies about the mental consequences of poor speech for both individuals and the nation. Leading colonial educators kept in close touch with developments "back home." The *Newbolt Report* quoted from the testimony of one witness who had spoken of that "refinement of speech which, in a subtle manner, is an index to the mind, and helps to place it beyond the reach of vulgarity of thought and action." (1921)

The connection between quality of language and quality of thought was also emphasized by a New Zealand teacher in a 1926 article. Mr. Denny quoted from a "very successful business man" who judged potential employees by their ability to speak and write well. His hiring policy was based on the conviction that "if we speak neatly and accurately it is because our thinking is orderly; if our expression is forceful, the thought at the back of our mind must be forceful. If we blunder for words, punctuate incorrectly, spell incorrectly, and express ourselves clumsily, our minds are cluttered and ill-disciplined" (1926).

The language panic

While the concern about language decline was indigenous to these three colonial countries and arose from some linguistic insecurity about life so far removed from the cultural and linguistic centre back in the Old Country, it no doubt received some extra support from excitement in the United States about what Daniels (1983) called the "language panic" after the Great War. In Daniels' view, this intensification of what has really been a recurring crisis, both in America and in other parts of the English-speaking world, was a result of rapid immigration and based on fear of foreign accents and races. Ex-president Theodore Roosevelt expressed this fear in a 1919 speech: "We have room but for one language here and that is the English language not a polyglot boarding-house" (Daniels, p. 54). The neophyte National Council of Teachers of English joined with other groups to sponsor an event known as "Better Speech Week" with posters, parades, contests, slogans, skits, newspaper articles, and school competitions. Some American schools organized an "Ain't-less Week" or a "Final-G." Some had "Tag Days" when students committing solecisms such as "It's me" or "I have got" had reproving slogans hung around their necks. Students had to pledge:

I will not dishonour my country's speech by leaving off the last syllable of words; I will say a good American 'yes' and 'no' in place of an Indian grunt 'um-hum' and 'nup-up' or a foreign 'ya' or 'yeh' or 'nope.' (Daniels, p. 57)

A Nova Scotia crusader

In Nova Scotia, a rather colorful campaign for better speech was mounted by a teacher from Wolfville, Miss Rosamund de Wolfe Archibald. Her work was brought to popular national attention by an article in *Maclean's Magazine* (Shaw, 1924) under the title, "Rosamund de Wolfe Archibald Crusades for Better English." Ms. Archibald's reputation as a language crusader came from her popular book of English exercises, called *The King's English Drill* (1921), and from her lecture tours throughout the Maritimes and Ontario.

Her book, which was published in a sixth edition as late as 1948, consisted of a series of drills for use at any grade level. Drills I to XI, for example, were designed to establish the proper case of the personal pronoun as complement of the verb "to be"; in other words, their purpose was to get rid of expressions such as "It's me" in favor of "It is I." Drill V(b) went:

It might have been I.
It might have been we.
It might have been he.
It might have been she.
It might have been they.

The author's recommended method for the early grades was as follows:

Let the pupils stand. Open the windows, and give a few head and arm calisthenics. Let the pupils recite in unison the Motto and the Creed. Let the honour pupil of the day recite the Drill that has been explained by the teacher and memorized the day before. Then let the whole school say it in unison just as they do their tables, slowly and emphatically at first, and then gradually more quickly, but always distinctly. (p. 5)

The moral fervour of the campaign—which truly was a crusade—was suggested by the wording of the Motto and the Creed: the former was "To think clearly and to speak the King's English," and the latter, "We believe in our flag, our country and our mother tongue." A retired teacher who had known Miss Archibald recalled that the author would take her pupils from the Acadia Ladies' Seminary to hear visiting lecturers at nearby Acadia University.

They would sit in the front row with notebooks and pencils at the ready. The speaker would think they were taking down the words of wisdom, but actually they were like little hawks watching for poor grammar. Any lapses noted would be the subject of gleeful discussions back in the classroom.

CHAPTER 8
The Nature of Formal Grammar Instruction

"Name the prepositions!"

Parsing words and analyzing sentences were what would today be called *instructional outcomes*. The other aspect of the grammar curriculum was how teachers set about achieving these outcomes—the methods that they used to teach. As with the content of the grammar course and its objectives, instructional techniques were inherited from the earlier experience of teaching under the voluntary system of schooling. Indeed this inheritance was a challenge for many, because as better methods of instruction were developed and advocated, many teachers clung to the older methods, often to the despair of their inspectors. A theme that runs through the history of grammar teaching is the way indelible residues of older methods and rationales are deposited in the English classroom. The use of memorization as an enduring method of teaching grammar is a good case in point.

SURVIVAL OF MEMORIZATION IN GRAMMAR

Since both parsing and analysis were exercises in the discrimination of grammatical categories, a necessary first step was to learn the categories. To state that a verb was in the subjunctive mood, active voice, past tense, third person, and plural number involved knowledge of a range of rather complex and abstract terms. To many of the colonial school teachers, acquisition of this prerequisite knowledge could only mean that their pupils had to memorize these grammatical terms and their definitions. According to the reports of school inspectors who, by the time or perhaps by condition of their appointment, seemed to know better than their teachers, memorization was a major source of dissatisfaction over the state of grammar teaching. Memorization in textbooks is discussed later in this book.

The New Zealand inspectors made frequent disparaging mention of teachers who relied on memorization. For example, Westland's Inspector Smith in 1881 reported, "Each child being required to repeat the whole of each lesson word for word, while few or no questions were asked to ascertain how much was understood of what was then gabbled over." (p. 29) Other inspectors reported "mechanical teaching," "monotonous drills," "parsing by guess," and grammar taught as though it were a Chinese puzzle (1896, p. 32). In his 1891 report, Inspector Verekker-Bindon of Wanganui illustrated this kind of grammar teaching with an account of a teaching episode:

> What part of speech is *that* in this sentence?
>
> Answer (shouted by several pupils here and there in the class):
>
> "Relative pronoun."
>
> Teacher: "Nonsense! How could it be?"
>
> Answer (shouted immediately by several pupils): "Conjunction."
>
> Teacher: "Right. Now, whole class together, what part of speech is *that*?"
>
> Answer: (in one great shout, some pupils looking amused or supremely self-satisfied, others gazing about in absent-minded manner): "Conjunction." (p. 13)

Canadian inspectors were finding the same thing. In 1869, Inspector Duval of New Brunswick commented that the advanced branches, such as grammar, geography, and history, were taught in most of his schools, but he reported, "Too often they are learned merely by rote, not being accompanied by oral instruction to such an extent as to make the studies interesting and permanently useful." (p. 23)

Oral instruction referred to the newer method of group or class instruction by the teacher using explanation and questioning as opposed to the old method of assigning individual passages to be "got by heart" or "without book." As far as grammar was concerned, the old method still prevailed in Cumberland County in Nova Scotia in 1865. In that year's Annual Report, Inspector Christie noted, "In most schools most of the time is spent defining parts of speech, committing rules to memory, and parsing by guess." (p. 95)

Twenty-six years later (1891) in Lunenburg and Queens counties, inspectors were still finding the same emphasis in the teaching of history, geography, and grammar. Inspector MacIntosh claimed, "Too much time is spent in these subjects in the way of home lessons, requiring the child to commit page after page to memory without any explanation." In the same year, his colleague from Pictou and South Colchester complained, "At present the schoolroom is regarded in most cases as a place for listening to recitations, the home is a place for memorizing words, which, too often, are forgotten shortly after they have been 'said'." (p. 107)

Similar comments continued to be made throughout the years. In 1862 (thirteen years later), PEI School Visitor Arbuckle was still making the same observation: "Reason is superseding rote-work. Parsing is now seldom attempted without an effort to associate the grammatical connexion [sic] of the words with the sense of the passage." Even in 1874 visitors' complaints about grammar continued. "One would be inclined to think, by the manner in which it is generally taught, that it is the art of repeating definitions and rules with readiness, without the ability of making a practical application of them, and not the art of speaking and writing with propriety" (1874, p. 89).

The Annual Reports of Australian inspectors also include references to memorization. In Victoria in 1871, Inspector Gilchrist observed that textbooks such as those by Lennie and Morell were being learned by rote. Tasmanian Inspector Stutzer noted that children were proficient in grammar as far as "knowledge of the contents of the books on the subject can be considered satisfactory." He went on to say, "I cannot, however, help thinking that if they were taught less out of books and more viva voce, they would make more real progress. At present their knowledge is too much a matter of rote, and not sufficiently intelligent." (p. 26)

Inspector Stephens of Tasmania had a number of suggestions. One of his themes was that, as a means of preventing rote learning, teachers should not use textbooks in the teaching of grammar. His 1859 report said that grammar textbooks should be entirely discarded from public schools. He observed that teachers often forget the ultimate purpose of teaching grammar, being too content to "ram their pupils' memories with a host of abstract rules and definitions." Then in 1863, using a more positive psychology, he noted,

> Grammar is best taught when it is taken in connection with the reading lesson, or the passage which has been written to dictation. The teachers who understand their business seldom allow textbooks to be used except for home lessons. (p. 21)

Perhaps this recommendation (which Stephens was still making in his reports as late as 1871) was borne out by the 1861 New South Wales National Board of Education report when it offered the following reason for the success that its schools were reportedly enjoying in the teaching of grammar, a "most difficult subject" and one of the "tests" of a good teacher: "Generally speaking books are not used in teaching grammar, and these circumstances, by necessitating previous study on the part of the teacher, assist in bringing about the superior character of the instruction." (p. 10) It is worth noting that this official satisfaction in New South Wales had evaporated four years later in 1865, when grammar was referred to in more familiar negative terms as "a defective subject." (p. 14)

Teachers

When the colonial school systems were established, there was an inadequate supply of well-educated and properly trained teachers to staff the rapidly increasing number of classrooms. Thomas Arnold, inspector of schools in Tasmania in 1855, put it bluntly when he recommended that candidates for teaching should be required to write a preliminary test "to keep out the duds." (p. 6)

It is hardly surprising that many teachers could not teach grammar as their inspectors would have liked. Their own knowledge of the subject was sometimes so weak that the textbook was the only source of authority on the subject and its memorization the only method of instruction they knew.

In England, the first training colleges for teachers were not established until the 1840s, while in the far-flung colonies finding people capable of teaching the new, often ambitious courses of study was an enormous problem for the educational leaders. Children as young as thirteen years of age were taken on as pupil-teachers and, under the supervision of a regular teacher, taught as best they could and studied for their own examinations. By the 1850s in New South Wales, teachers' salaries were linked to levels of certificate, determined by inspection and examination; included in the latter were papers in English grammar (1855, Report of the Commissioners of National Education).

Grammar was a particularly difficult subject for poorly educated, poorly trained, and poorly paid teachers to handle. In order to preempt any charge that colonial education was inferior to that offered in the Old Country, the new syllabi sometimes deliberately went beyond the requirements of the Standards in England upon which they were modeled. In New Zealand, for example, the fact that grammar was a pass rather than a class subject (unlike the situation in England) made the teaching of the subject a much more stringent demand upon teachers than it was in the Old Country; the 1878 course of study was severely criticized by many contemporaries on the grounds that it was unrealistically demanding on teachers and pupils. The State of Victoria's Board of Education acknowledged in 1864 that grammar and geography had been "super-added" in its adoption of the English Standards (1864, Annual Report of the Board of Education).

In New Zealand, the general impression given by the inspectors' reports between 1881 and 1908 was that grammar was not only a subject that was difficult to teach but also, on the whole, disliked by both teachers and pupils. In 1892 the Marlborough inspector reported that the relegation of grammar to a class subject at the beginning of that year had come as a very great relief to teachers. In discussing the same change, the North Canterbury report for 1893 noted that grammar had been a "stumbling block that teachers had little taste for and knowledge in." (p. 27)

Not surprisingly, the results of such reluctant instruction were not very impressive. For example, the inspector for Wanganui included in his 1888 report the percentage of passes he had awarded in the different subjects, and grammar, with composition, showed a lower success rate than any other subject. The Southland inspector declared in 1881 that grammar was "the worst taught subject on the syllabus." (p. 38) In the same year, Henry Hill of Hawke's Bay (New Zealand) reported that whereas two pupils in five could read and write and two in seven could add simple numbers, only two in twenty-one could distinguish the parts of speech. Four years later

Hill's reported pass rates were 69 to 84 percent in reading, writing, and arithmetic, but only 23 percent in English grammar. (p. 23) And in 1903, the Wanganui inspectors commented that grammar was the "most ill-used and misunderstood subject in the syllabus." (p. 13)

Canadian inspectors sometimes made rather scathing comments about teachers' grasp of the grammatical terms they were trying to teach. In New Brunswick, for example, where one inspector later found English grammar "to be but rudely handled," Inspector Wood made notes on his 1860 inspection of the Superior School in Kingston in the Parish of Richibucta. Under "Grammar," he wrote:

> Teacher thinks 'a' or 'an' are demonstrative pronouns, and maintains that verbs, with a single exception, express 'doing something.' (Report of Examination of Schools in Kent County, summer term, 1860)

In Inspector Morrison's 1859 notes, he writes, "Grammar II, Parsing, but it is not at all up to the mark. Doubtful if the teacher be thoroughly posted up herself." In another school, Morrison had examined two pupils in grammar, using a sentence showing false syntax for correction and parsing. He reported,

> Sentence read at first by correcting which both pupils do inaccurately. Both parse improperly. This is when they have liberty to say what they have learned with none of the master's interference. Then the sentence is tried again under master's care, neither accurately corrected nor parsed, but are allowed to pass by the teacher who has a want of grammatical knowledge reflecting no credit upon his examiners in the training school … nothing but one blunder after another. (p. 843)

Morrison must have found this 1859 tour inspection rather trying because his only note about one school was, "This school is nothing but a slaughter house of the intellect." (p. 810)

Classroom design

The inspectors in the new colonial school systems might have wanted to see more oral teaching and more attention to comprehension in grammar lessons, but these expectations had not been part of the tradition of schooling, which the state systems had taken over. This tradition, based on a regime of memoriter work, was reflected in the design of early schoolrooms. Take, for example, the furnishings of an early log-cabin school in Nova Scotia. Instead of having desks facing the front of the room, it was equipped with individual writing shelves of sloping boards attached to the walls. Children therefore faced the wall as they sat on rough benches copying or learning passages off by heart to be heard by the master at his desk near the stove (Eaton, 1910).

The assumption behind this design was that learning was an individual matter of pupils working silently at their textbooks, and that the teacher's main instructional task was to hear pupils "say their lessons": that is, to listen to their recitations of material committed to memory. In some cases this recitation took place while the teacher busied himself at some other activity, such as sharpening goose quill pens. Asaph Marshall, a teacher in Paradise, Annapolis County, Nova Scotia, around 1850, was said to "sit before the fire and weave fishing lines out of horse hairs, [and] make split brooms from yellow birch saplings" (Morse, 1938).

In those early schools there were many constraints against the ready adoption of newer teaching methods, such as the viva voce technique, or oral teaching, as Howat (1984) pointed out: expensive textbooks, scarce paper (even of the roughest kind), and limited slates. Another was the "miscellaneous" class, the single classroom containing a large range of children of different ages. This arrangement must have encouraged the use of memorization; the teacher would have been able to survey the whole class while particular individual pupils or groups were reciting at the "line." Hearing recitations was a task that could even be delegated, as shown by the following recollection of grammar teaching in the United States:

> In those days [1850s] we studied grammar by committing a portion of a small book to memory and reciting it to the teacher. If he was engaged, the lesson was recited to one of the highest class ... and, as no explanation was ever made of any principle, the pupil was as well qualified as the teacher to hear the words (Lyman, 1922, p. 114).

Grammar lessons

One recollection of a New Zealand school suggests how the memoriter regime worked. William Fennimore, who opened his Wellington school in the mid-1840s, had a reputation as a thorough teacher and rigorous disciplinarian, and he was particularly noted for his teaching in the "strong subjects, English grammar, mental arithmetic and writing." Grammar might have been one of the subjects of the lessons his pupils had to recite at "the curved chalk line" on the floor in front of the teacher's platform, where, "seated on his chair—his regal chair—erect, clean, keen-eyed, sharp-eared, precise in dress and manner, with a long yellow cane in his hand," Mr. Fennimore heard the lessons of his classes in rotation (McMorran, 1900).

Agnes Deans Cameron graphically recalls, more than thirty years later, what it was like to learn grammar in a school in Victoria, British Columbia, just before that part of Canada joined the Confederation in 1871.

> Lennie's Grammar was a more indirect good as old Mr. Scottinger expounded it. His method was very simple. We learned the book off holus bolus from preface to postscript, rules, examples, fine print, footnotes, with a large contempt for the claims of any one part to paramount importance. The reasoning was very plain: grammar is 'the science which teaches us to read, write, and speak the English language correctly.' If we learned all the grammar there was, could we miss it? Hold up any of the boys or girls of that school at midnight on a lonely highway with, 'Name the prepositions!' and out of the darkness will come, 'About, above, according to, around, at athwart, before, behind, below, beyond, by, concerning, down, during, except, excepting, for, from, in, into, instead of,' etc. Ask him for the example to the pluperfect tense, and you will learn that 'All the judges had taken their places before Sir Roger came' (Cameron, 1902, p. 137).

Mr. Scottinger was no doubt an extreme practitioner of learning through memorization. However, as Michael (1987) noted, "In the seventeenth and eighteenth centuries, and until 1870 at least, some pupils were expected to learn the grammar by heart." Reading and spelling were taught in the same way. Children had to commit to memory the names of the letters, followed by words of one syllable in list form, words of two syllables, and so on. J. B. Calkin's account of an early nineteenth-century spelling lesson in a Nova Scotia school illustrates the method:

> Perhaps the most unique feature of the old-time school was the spelling lesson. The last twenty minutes of the day was devoted to the preparation of this lesson. The class, including all who could read, sat on the high seats, facing inwards, with full room between their feet and the floor for the free play of their legs. All studied aloud and they did so with emphasis. As they pronounced each letter and syllable and word, they swayed to and fro, keeping

time in their bodily movement with the rhythm of the voice: 'Big a, little a, r, o, n, ron, Aron; H, a, b, hab, e, r, er, haber, d, a, s, h, dash, haberdash, e, r, er, haberdasher.' When time was up, all took their places, standing in a long row, in order from head to foot. The first part of the exercise was the numbering, to see that each had his proper place, for there was 'going up and down,' and every pupil was jealous of his place in the line. Then the spelling began (Eaton, 1910).

This lesson in the New World recalls Dickens' caricature of Yorkshire schoolmasters in the Old. In the novel *Nicholas Nickleby,* Mr. Squeers demonstrates his teaching method to Nicholas with the help of the first class in English spelling and philosophy, "Half a dozen scarecrows":

> "We go upon the practical mode of teaching, Nickleby; the regular education system. C-l-e-a-n, clean, verb active, to make bright, to scour. W-i-n, win, d-e-r, der, winder, a casement. When the boy knows this out of the book, he goes and does it … B-o-t, bot, t-i-n, tin, bottin, n-e-y, bottinney, noun substantive, a knowledge of plants. When he has learned that bottiney is a knowledge of plants, he goes and knows 'em. That's our system, Nickleby." (pp. 91–92)

Memorization as a classroom practice was not simply an expedient of ill-trained, low-status schoolmasters. Its value was affirmed by expert authority. For example, Goold Brown, American author of several school grammar texts in the 1850s, asserted the importance of memorization in the learning of grammar:

> The only successful method of teaching grammar is to cause the principal definitions and rules to be committed thoroughly to memory, that they may ever afterwards be readily applied. Oral instruction may smooth the way, and facilitate the labour of the learner; but the notion of communicating a competent knowledge of grammar without imposing this task, is disproved by universal experience (Martyn, 1932).

Brown's advice on method was consistent with that given by most grammarians. Joseph Priestley (1761) in the preface to his grammar text, *The Rudiments of English Grammar,* simply said in a note: "What the author judged less proper to be committed to memory … he hath thrown into the notes." Even William Cobbett, author of an 1819 grammar book and by no means a conventional thinker, had taught himself the subject while on military service in Canada by memorizing Bishop Lowth's 1762 text (Howat, 1984).

It would seem that when memorization attached itself to oral teaching as a residue of the old method deposited on the new, the resulting instruction was not always scintillating. The late Nova Scotia novelist Ernest Buckler left a poignant anecdote about his own school days in the Annapolis Valley. Recalling how he was taught grammar in the early years of the twentieth century, he wrote:

'What did we learn?'

'Well, in grammar we learn that "the subject is?"'

'What are we talking about?' (The teacher would start the question off and everyone would chorus the ending.)

'The predicate is?'

'What we say about the subject?'

'The object answers the question?'

'Who or what?'

No matter that in the face of a concrete example anything but the simplest sentence would trip us up. In 'O, when will the rain unleash the buds?' *O* was named as subject almost every time. Whereas 'analyzing' a complete sentence or parsing its nouns was a problem that found the teacher herself on such shaky ground that she'd move on quickly to figures of speech.

'Synecdoche is?'

'Using the part for the whole.'

'As in?'

'All hands to the pump!' we would shout as one man (Buckler, 1968, p. 62).

Textbooks

The absence of uniform textbooks also encouraged memorization. Jeremiah Willoughby recalled this aspect of his early teaching career in Lunenburg County, Nova Scotia, in the 1850s:

> In the schoolroom the children, some with parts of spelling books, some with a few leaves of the New Testament or some forgotten author, some with old almanacs and some without a printed page of any author, conned over their lessons aloud. (Progress of education in Nova Scotia during fifty years, 1982–3 (orig. 1884))

Egerton Ryerson, appointed as assistant superintendent of education for Upper Canada in 1844, regarded the chaotic textbook situation as one of the most serious deficiencies of the old system. In his report of that year he argued the importance of the issue:

> The variety of textbooks in the schools, and the objectionable character of many of them, is a subject of serious and general complaints. All classification of the pupils is thereby prevented; the exertions of the best teachers are in a great measure paralyzed; the time of the scholars is almost wasted; and improper sentiments are inculcated. (Parvin, 1965, p. 22)

In New Zealand textbooks were sometimes provided by parents, sometimes by school committees, and occasionally by the teacher. An 1865 report noted that in one New Zealand school, twelve pupils of approximately the same age each had a different textbook, depending upon which ones their parents had brought over from England (Ewing, 1960, p. 36). Since to memorize was to learn, no matter what texts children brought to school, often handed down through a line of older brothers and sisters, the teacher could set them to work.

The school textbook has almost always exerted a powerful influence on the curriculum and on teaching methods. In the years before formal syllabi were available as statements about what teachers should teach, the textbook inevitably defined the course. In these circumstances it was natural that grammar teaching should be influenced, if not defined, by the grammar texts that were used.

Four early texts, used in the period immediately before the transition from voluntary to state control of primary education, can be considered to have contributed to memorization in the teaching of grammar in all three countries. Two of these books served the new state syllabi as interim texts in some jurisdictions. All four assumed that memorizing at least some of their grammatical definitions and rules was a necessary part of their use. These four texts are artifacts that speak to the nature of grammar teaching as inherited by the new colonial state systems of primary schooling, particularly as they reveal the regime of memorization. Evidence of their use in the early colonial schools is followed by an interpretation of the rote learning they promoted and illustrated.

1. Dilworth's Speller

The first and earliest in use was Thomas Dilworth's *New Guide to the English Tongue*, first published in England in 1740 and widely reprinted in the United States—including a 1747 edition by Benjamin Franklin—and in the Canadian colonies. Dilworth's slender little volume was mainly a speller, consisting of lists of letters, syllables, and words for instruction in reading and spelling. To this, in at least some editions and printings, was added a twenty-page section on English grammar, a collection of moralistic sentences and short fables, and a set of prayers.

Calkin noted that Dilworth's speller was commonly used in the schools of early Nova Scotia as the single textbook for all the studies a child might encounter in school (Eaton, 1910). Jeremiah Willoughby also referred to the Dilworth text in his account of his life as a Nova Scotia teacher. He had graduated as a member of the first class of the Nova Scotia Normal School with three other teachers in 1855. He recorded the use of Dilworth in Nova Scotia earlier in the century with a newspaper account of schooling near Cornwallis:

> We all had Dilworth's spelling book and the primer as our only textbooks. At first only two of our number could read without spelling out the words, and most of us had to begin at the letter 'A'. We all thought the spelling book contained the stores of all necessary knowledge of a secular nature—quite sufficient for the most aspiring mind. The last part of the book, i.e., the grammar, was what we emphatically called hard reading. Anyone able to read it readily was regarded by us with wonder approaching reverence. (1982–3, orig. 1884, pp. 10-11)

He also recalled an incident in which pupils were engaged in learning Dilworth's list of harder monosyllabic words. When they came to the word *aisle* they were stuck. They referred the problem to "headquarters," and the teacher puzzled over the word for a long time, finally declaring that *aisle* was a two-syllable word that by mistake or trick of the printer had found its way into the wrong list. What the stubborn little word was she never told them. (The word *aisle* is found on page nineteen of Dilworth among the "words of five to six letters with a diphthong and the rest consonants ... Daunt, haunt, taunt, pause, cause, etc.")

A copy of Dilworth's text in the collection of school textbooks at Acadia University in Wolfville, Nova Scotia, was printed in Halifax, likely indicating widespread use of the text in the colony. Called the "new Edition" and undated, it includes in its verse sentences section a note in honour of Queen Victoria, which dates that printing after her accession to the throne in 1837—nearly a hundred years after the book's first appearance.

There is no surviving evidence that Dilworth's book was used in Upper Canada. Neither the New Zealand nor the Australian record mentions it either, although it would be surprising if some copies of such a popular and widespread text had not made the journey to the South Pacific in the baggage of immigrant teachers.

2. Murray's Grammar

The second book, Lindley Murray's famous grammar text *English Grammar Adapted to the Different Classes of Learners* (1843, orig. 1795), definitely found its way into schools in the Maritime colonies and Upper Canada. Murray's text was the preeminent school grammar textbook of the century in Britain and North America. Over fifty editions were published, and in 1816 an abridged version was produced that went through more than 120 editions, with sales exceeding ten thousand copies per edition. Not only was it a bestseller, but "more than any other influence, perhaps ... it fixed the form and nomenclature of modern English grammar" (Martyn, 1932, pp. 9-10).

Parvin (1965) noted that on an 1838 list of texts used in the common schools of Upper Canada, the Bible and Murray's text appeared on the inventory of almost every school. The report of the Chief Superintendent of Schools for Upper Canada for the year 1847 stated that Murray's text was used in 321 schools in that colony (Martyn, 1932). In the 1851 Annual Report, that figure had declined to only 92. (p. 34)

On the question of whether Murray's *Grammar* ever reached New Zealand and Australia, the record is sporadic; there is no mention of it in New

Zealand, and in Australia there are some notes that it was used in New South Wales. Surprisingly, the secondary syllabus for 1914 for that state listed "Murray's English Grammar Revised by Morgan" as one of three grammar texts authorized for use.

3. Lennie's Grammar

Lennie's *Grammar* appeared very early in the nineteenth century. It was already in its third edition in 1815, published for the author by Oliver and Boyd in Edinburgh, and its last edition was printed in 1894. In the course of the century it went through several revisions, and a key to the exercises was added. It was used as early as 1835 in some Upper Canada schools and probably continued in use there until the late 1860s (Martyn, 1932). Egerton Ryerson, appointed assistant superintendent of education for Upper Canada in 1844, included it on the Board of Education's list of approved textbooks for common schools in 1846, even though Ryerson was moving to adopt the Irish Board of Education's texts in the interests of uniformity (Parvin, 1965). In the following year it was the most popular grammar textbook in Upper Canada, being used in 717 schools (Martyn, 1932). According to the 1851 Annual Report on Education, it was still the most popular text, being used in 1040 schools, almost as many as the total number of schools using the alternative grammars that were authorized.

When its use was first officially approved in Nova Scotia in 1850 by the first superintendent of schools, John William Dawson, the wording of the approval indicated that the use of Lennie's text was well established by that date. He "sanctioned" the use of the text, "being unwilling to interfere with a useful work so very generally in use." (p. 60) He also referred to the enforcement in some school districts of regulations governing teachers' qualifications that had led to "many teachers" having been rejected on the grounds of their inability to teach grammar. According to the reports of school inspectors in Nova Scotia from 1850 to 1865, this text was in general use throughout the province. Even as late as 1875, Inspector Most of Annapolis County wrote, "Some teachers cling with fondness to Lennie's *Grammar* and will probably continue the use of the book until the present supply is exhausted." The book was printed in Halifax as late as 1871 so the supply may well have been abundant. It also seems to have been one of the two most commonly used textbooks for English grammar in Prince Edward Island schools in 1843.

The use of Lennie's text in New Brunswick was approved by the Board of Education in 1852, and in 1861 it was listed as the text for English grammar in the Training and Model School in St. John. That same year it was listed by the chief superintendent as a grammar text observed in use on visits to grammar schools. It also found its way into the remoter classrooms; in the 1870s it was listed as an authorized textbook for grammar in the schools of British Columbia, and in the following decade it was approved for use in Catholic schools in the Northwest Territories.

In the 1860s and 1870s, as newer textbooks were introduced, school visitors' comments were beginning to be less positive about Lennie's book, and complaints were beginning to appear about the continued use of Lennie's text and methods. By 1870, Chief Superintendent Bennett was taking note of concerns about the need "for a new English Grammar to take the place of Lennie's which it must be admitted is behind the times." (p. xvi)

Its record of use in New Zealand and Australia is similar to that of Murray's *Grammar*; while not recorded as a text used in New Zealand, it was known in New South Wales. In the *New South Wales Education Gazette* in 1891, a question on the grammar examination for second-class pupil teachers was, "How many kinds of [...] are given in Lennie's Grammar? Give examples of each kind." (p. 21) In 1900, the same *Gazette* announced that Lennie's was no longer an approved textbook on grammar for purposes of teacher examinations.

4. An English Grammar for the Use of Schools

The fourth grammar textbook that supported memorization was *An English Grammar for the Use of Schools*, an Irish text introduced by many of the colonial administrations as part of the textbook package of over thirty titles produced by the Irish Board of National School Commissioners. The most attractive feature of this package was the Books of Lessons, or Readers, used as a framework for the organization of pupils into standards and, initially, as a de facto curriculum for the primary schools.

The origins of the ubiquitous Irish texts lay in the 1830s. In 1831, the British Government had appointed the Commissioners of National Education to provide day-school education at government expense for children of all religious denominations in Ireland. The Commissioners' task was to develop a system of teacher training, textbooks, and curriculum. In this early excursion by the state into school curriculum, the problem of textbooks was a particularly thorny one, because none could be found that was free of sectarian bias and therefore acceptable to all denominations. The Commissioners had to arrange to have their own texts compiled under the close scrutiny of their own clerical and lay members to ensure that no sectarian offence was included.

The success of the resulting texts, especially of the Readers, in achieving an appropriate tone of religiosity and morality with neutral doctrinal encouraged the British government in 1848 to offer them at a subsidized price to approved schools in England through the Committee of the Council on Education. Some reviewers claim that by 1859, because the discounted price and the volume needed to meet the needs of over two million day-school children prevented any other educational publisher from competing with the Irish texts, this series had captured 50 percent of the English school text market. So successful were the texts that the British government bowed to pressure from commercial publishers by requiring the Commissioners to stop publishing the texts themselves and put printing contracts out to private companies (Akenson, 1970).

Their sectarian neutrality made the Irish National Readers attractive to colonial administrators, whose educational policies were closely scrutinized by churchmen of the various denominations who were seeing their control of education pass to the secular authorities. In 1846 the Provincial Board of Education for Upper Canada accepted its assistant superintendent's recommendation that the Irish National textbooks be adopted as the framework for the province's first uniform curriculum for its common schools. The adoption was no doubt made easier by the Irish Commissioners' willingness to make the texts available at a cost lower than the retail price of the books in England and to permit Canadian publishers to reprint locally (Parvin, 1965).

Inspector Bowden of the Wellington Board in New Zealand found that the discount he was allowed on the texts offset the high cost of shipping them to the distant colony. The Readers, or "Books of Lessons" as they were called, were used to define six levels of instruction, called standards or classes, the first four of which Ryerson later reorganized into the familiar Canadian pattern of eight elementary school grades.

The series of over thirty Irish textbooks that Upper Canada and several other colonies adopted and authorized for use in their common schools included the grammar text, *An English Grammar for the Use of Schools*, and a separate *Key to the Grammar*. The chief author of these texts was Alexander McArthur. It was approved in 1836 by the Irish Commissioners and was still in use in the Irish National schools as late as 1870 (Akenson, 1970).

In 1846, Ryerson did not believe that this Irish *Grammar* had any intrinsic merit over and above some texts already in use in the colony, so schools were allowed to continue to use either Lennie's or Kirkham's[6] text as alternatives to the new grammar. For the sake of internal uniformity, schools were expected to select only one of the three. Many schools quickly adopted the Irish text, as shown by the statistics for the year 1847, only one year after the adoption. The Irish *Grammar* was in use in 220 schools in Upper Canada, compared to 717 for Lennie's, 649 for Kirkham's, and 321 for Murray's (Martyn, 1932).

In New Brunswick, the Irish National Readers were widely used until 1871, although there are very few references to the grammar text as such. Indirect evidence that the Irish *Grammar* was used in the province was contained in an 1867 report by William Crockett, principal of the Academy in Chatham. He described his program of teacher training for candidates in his normal school class, including preparation for the teaching of grammar. The work included "revision" of the "textbook by the Irish Board." (p. 47) The same activity was included in the 1869 report, but in the following year it had been dropped, probably in view of the book's imminent replacement. Inclusion of this work with the Irish *Grammar* in the teacher-training program suggests that the candidates were being trained to understand and use a text likely to be encountered in their subsequent teaching. However, while the Irish *Grammar* may have been important, it is unlikely that it was more widely used in New Brunswick than Lennie's.

There is no evidence in the Nova Scotia record that the Irish grammar text was ever used in that province, nor does it appear in the records for Prince Edward Island or Quebec. The use and influence of the Irish *Grammar* in New Zealand is impossible to assess. It was probably available by the 1860s, in the later years of the provincial period, at least in the province of Wellington, where Thomas Bowden introduced the Irish Readers.

In Australia, where the Irish National System of education was adopted by the colonies as a solution to intense sectarian opposition to state control of education, the Irish *Grammar* was definitely available to teachers in New South Wales and in its derivative colonies of Victoria and Queensland, as well as in Tasmania. In all four colonies, the Irish Readers were used as the foundation of the primary school program by the various National and Denominational Boards of Education from about 1850.

By the late 1860s and the 1870s, however, the popularity of the Irish textbooks

6   Kirkham, Samuel. *Kirkham's Grammar in Familiar Lectures* (1829). New York: Robert B. Collins.

was waning throughout the colonies, which were following the pattern in England. There the Revised Code of 1862 had brought in different prescriptions for each standard and introduced payment by results for teachers, based partly on examination of children on the new standards. The Irish texts, no longer aligned with the official specifications, were quickly replaced by commercial publications written with the new prescriptions in mind. By 1880, the Irish *Books of Lessons* were being replaced by *Australia Readers* in Queensland, and the Irish *Grammar* was no longer included in that state's list of authorized grammar textbooks.

By the time confederation had been achieved in Ontario in 1867, there was agitation against the general principle of using foreign textbooks to educate Ontario children. In 1868 a series of Canadian Readers and new grammar texts, all written and published within the province, were authorized.

The nationalist opposition to the Irish Readers is revealed by an anecdote reported by Inspector Morrison of New Brunswick in 1870 as part of his claim that the books had outlived their usefulness in his province. The report is also revealing about what classroom instruction could be like at that time. On a school visit in Northumberland County, Morrison had observed a lesson taught from the *Second Book of Lessons*. The inspector had then asked a group of eight- to twelve-year-olds to read a lesson that had been prepared just before his arrival. The preceding lesson had contained the words "The country where you, children, live is called Ireland," and this was followed in that lesson with "Both halves of the earth contains [sic] many countries. We live in the east half—in Europe, etc." Morrison then related what happened next.

> I asked the teacher to examine the class and to show me the method usually pursued in teaching. The lesson was read and the usual explanations were given, but all on the assumption that the children lived in Ireland. The teacher dismissed the class with the error uncorrected, and upon further examination I found that the children actually believed they lived in Ireland ... to teach young Bluenoses that they lived in Ireland is drawing too largely upon our good nature (Report on the Public Schools, 1870, p. 27).

Opposition like this on the grounds of both nationalism and pedagogy drew the twenty-year ascendancy of the Irish National textbooks in two Canadian provinces and four Australian states to a close. The grammar text, which had never enjoyed the exclusive use for its subject that the Readers had claimed for theirs, was replaced, together with Lennie's text, by Canadian grammar texts in Ontario and New Brunswick. In the Australian states, the approved lists tended to include a larger number of grammar textbooks from which teachers could select, and the Irish *Grammar* was simply deleted.

Textbooks and the role of memorization

All four texts were designed on the assumption that the learner would commit to memory at least parts of the material. Since the books first appeared at widely different dates between 1740 and 1836, there were variations in memorization's role. The oldest, Dilworth, assumed it was the only method of learning; the next two, Murray and Lennie, gave it a necessary but not sufficient role; while in the Irish *Grammar* memoriter work, although still important, did not constitute learning unless accompanied by comprehension of the material.

Dilworth

In the case of Dilworth, it was quite unnecessary to assert that the entire text of his "short but comprehensive Grammar of the English tongue" was to be committed to memory. The implicit message was clear enough in "the most familiar and instructive" question and answer format of the presentation, the first exchange of which was:

Q. What is grammar?

A. Grammar is the science of letters, or the art of writing and speaking properly and syntactically. (p. 74)

Under the heading "Analogy" came:

Q. What is analogy?

A. Analogy teacheth us how to know distinctly all the several Parts of Speech in the English Tongue.

Q. How many parts of speech are there?

A. Eight: viz, Noun, Pronoun, Verb, Participle, Adverb, Conjunction, Preposition, Interjection. (p. 83)

As pupils memorized their ways through the analogy section, they would come to the heading "Of Pronouns":

Q. What is a pronoun?

A. A Pronoun is a part of speech that supplieth the place of a Noun.

Q. How many things belong to a Pronoun?

A. There belong to a Pronoun, Number, Case, Gender, Person, and Declension.

Q. How many kinds of Pronouns are there?

A. Two: Substantives and Adjectives.

Q. Which are the Pronoun Substantives?

A. These; I, thou, or you; He, She, It; and their Plurals, we; ye or you; they. (p. 87)

With few examples and with a complete absence of exercises or any other applications, it is difficult to see how the textbook could have been used in any other way than as a compilation of material to be committed to memory. Certainly the question-and-answer format would have been convenient for the master during the recitation phase, saving him from formulating recitation questions, and in overcrowded "miscellaneous" (one-room) schools, helping pupils recite privately in a whisper (Woods, 1985). A schoolboy in America in 1765 later recalled, "I learned the English grammar in Dilworth by heart" (Lyman, 1922), and this would no doubt have also been the experience of young Nova Scotians schooled in Dilworth. Another implication of the absence of exercises and applications was that comprehension of the material memorized was neither ensured nor thought to be particularly important. "To say without book" was a key objective to be achieved by reading the part assigned, "over and over, forward and backward, until mechanically perfect" (Lyman, 1922).

Murray

Unlike Dilworth, Lindley Murray was explicit about memorization. He had selected and arranged the definitions and rules so that they could "be readily committed to memory and readily retained." To this end and to achieve harmony of expression, he had been "solicitous to select terms that are smooth and voluble." The more important rules, definitions, and observations, "the most proper to be committed to memory," appeared in large type, while corollaries, qualifications and examples, and footnote-type comments were shown in small print. This feature explains the title of the text; Murray had made it suitable for different levels of pupils. Younger ones could commit to memory the large print; older ones could wrestle with the fine print. Woods (1985) credits Murray with making English grammar teachable on account of this principle of differentiation of content. It was a principle that the Irish *Grammar* followed too.

The bulk of Murray's text consisted of the exposition of definitions, processing from general to specific categories. For example, in the large etymology section, substantives, or nouns, as one of the eight parts of speech were defined and then treated as either proper or common, each category of which was further defined. Then Murray moved to three characteristics of substantives—gender, number, and case—and proceeded to define each in terms of its subdivisions. The result was a deep hierarchy of definitions supported by short lists of examples. At least four pages of this exposition on substantives were in large type. The section on syntax consisted of the explication of twenty-two rules, together with examples of their violations, or false grammar. The large-print text for Rule 16, for example, was:

> Two negatives, in English, destroy one another, or are equivalent to an affirmative: as, "nor did they not perceive him"; that is, "they did perceive him." Or, "His language, though inelegant, is not ungrammatical"; that is, "it is grammatical." (p. 189)

Lennie

Lennie's *Grammar* (competing successfully with Murray's in the Canadian school market) indicated in intention a weakening of the belief in memorization as an adequate form of learning, although this intention was probably undermined, as far as its use was concerned, by the extraordinary difficulty of the text and its exercises. The emphasis that Lennie placed on application exercises in parsing and false grammar implies that his view of learning included the necessity of understanding the material being studied. Although the author saw the necessity of "getting by heart" lists of parts of speech (sixty-three prepositions, for example), their definitions, and the explanations associated with them, such memorizing was insufficient in itself. For example, after "getting all the pronouns very accurately by heart," pupils were to be exercised by having them point out the pronouns in sentences provided. (p. 53)

The need to achieve comprehension led to an expanded role for the teacher. Lennie claimed that with his *Key*, a separate publication, a grown-up person could teach himself using the *Grammar*. However, for younger pupils, the author assumed a teacher who taught rather than who was an overseer of learning. For example, Lennie pointed out that he had been content to provide an outline of the subject, leaving "much to be remarked by the teacher in the time of teaching." His justification, revealing clearly an apprehension of the difference between mere rote memorization and learning, was that:

> Children, when by themselves, labour more to have the words of their book imprinted on their memories, than to have the meaning fixed in their minds; but, on the contrary, when the teacher addresses them viva voce, they naturally strive rather to comprehend his meaning, than to remember his exact expressions. (p. 3)

Some of these exercises were preceded by instructions; others were not, so Lennie was probably thinking of oral teaching. Not only would the teacher hear recitations, but he would assign and explain the exercises, and, presumably, he could correct them. Lennie's view of teaching was clearly one that called for an active form of instruction. One implication of this view was that the teacher who used Lennie's text in the way the author expected was required to know English grammar. But from the many criticisms of teachers' work in grammar made by early inspectors of schools in the 1850s and 1860s when Lennie's book was widely used, it would appear that many teachers were incapable of its proper use and that many, like Mr. Scottinger in Victoria, employed it merely as a source of material to be memorized. Thus, by the 1860s Lennie was associated, perhaps not quite fairly, with the old-fashioned method of rote learning.

However, in fairness to the teachers, the *Principles of English Grammar* must have been exceedingly difficult as a textbook for primary-age children. For one thing the definitions and explanations were complex and abstract, general and technical: for example, "A relative pronoun is a word that relates to a noun or pronoun before it, called the antecedent; as, 'The master who taught us', etc." A footnote to the teacher pointed out the complication of relative pronouns whose antecedents were whole clauses. These technical abstractions, with no attempt to relate to children's own experience of life and language, must have been an enormous challenge to comprehension in early classrooms. Moreover, the exercises, consisting of sentences that were often turgid, literary, and moralistic, presented their own difficulties. Under "Exercises in Parsing, —No. f. The Nominative is often at a great distance from the verb," one example was:

> The man who retires to meditate mischief, and to exasperate his own rage; whose thoughts are employed only on means of distress, and contrivances of ruin; whose mind never pauses from the remembrance of his own sufferings, but to indulge some hope of enjoying the calamities of another; may justly be numbered among the most miserable of human beings; among those who are guilty without reward; who have neither the gladness of prosperity, nor the calm of innocence. (p. 63)

The intention of having comprehension achieved through the teacher's oral explanations and that true learning be obtained by means of application of definitions to parsing exercises was probably beyond the resources of teachers and children in mid-nineteenth-century common schools. In a regime of slates, with poorly trained and educated teachers and pupil teachers managing large classes in one-room schools, the intractability of the grammar to be learned from texts such as Lennie's must have led many teachers to resort in despair to rote memorization. Certainly the comments by school inspectors, employed to monitor the newly created state school systems in the second half of the century, indicated that memorization was well entrenched in the teaching of English grammar, as well as of other subjects in classrooms in Canada, New Zealand, and Australia.

The Irish Grammar

The Irish *Grammar*, only six inches by four inches, containing 176 pages of densely printed material, was explicit about the role of memorization. Following Murray's example, large type was used for the general principles and small print for the examples and exceptions. The Preface noted that, "The former [large type] are intended to be committed to memory" and children in "young classes" were expected to learn only those general principles. "In a second course, or with advanced classes, both rules and notes must be studied, and the exercises corrected and copied into a book for that purpose." However, comprehension was recommended. "[I]t is expected that in Grammar, as in every other branch of education, the pupils should be made to understand what they learn." (p. 3) In 1836, when the book was first published, obviously comprehension was not yet a commonplace of education that could be left unsaid.

Generally speaking, the material in the text was less taxing on comprehension than the ponderous style of Murray and Lennie. Examples of terms and concepts often consisted of sentences whose subject matter was closer to the experience of children. For example, the sentence used to illustrate the use of a pronoun was, "John was in the garden, he says that it is full of trees, which are covered with fruit." (p. 11) (Murray's equivalent sentence, containing the obligatory moral message, had been "The man is happy; he is benevolent; he is useful.") (p. 20) Although difficult material could be found in the large print—e.g., "When the affirmation is not limited to the subject, a complete proposition or sentence also contains an object" (p. 87)—the Irish *Grammar* gives the impression of having been written by men who had some sympathy for young learners. In this sense its recommendation on comprehension was not invalidated in the way that Lennie's was.

However, one feature of the text did not encourage or require comprehension. A new kind of exercise was interspersed throughout the exposition, consisting of questions on the section just completed. These were entirely in the form of prompts to the literal recall of material in the text: for example, "To what class do all names belong? What are used instead of nouns?" (p. 25) If teachers used these questions without checking for understanding on their own initiative, pupils would quickly see that any effort towards comprehension was not rewarded.

Michael (1987) maintained—without presenting any evidence—that teachers in this early period must have made sure that children understood the grammar they were learning. (pp. 337–338) However, there are multiple school inspectors' comments that many teachers not only did not take the step from rote memory to comprehension, but that some had not taken that step in their own study of English grammar. It seemed clear that an alternative method of tackling this difficult subject was necessary, and in the early years of the twentieth century, one did evolve: functional grammar.

CHAPTER 9
The New Education: Functional Grammar

SAB SB-7552

Children and school teachers in front of the original Victoria School, Saskatoon's very first school in Saskatoon, Saskatchewan. 1892 or 1893. Originally at the Corner of Broadway and 11th St, the "Little Stone Schoolhouse" was relocated to University of Saskatchewan grounds in 1911. Photo from Saskatchewan Archives Board.

Dominated by a mental discipline conception of aim and learning, the **Old Education** was concerned with methods of teaching compendia of subject matter, contained in textbooks viewed as authoritative sources, and separated into compartmentalized branches of knowledge, to children thought of as passive, generalized beings. Teaching methods to achieve mastery of abstract material that was strange and unknown favored memorization, recitation, and drills, leaving no room for original thought and expression. In contrast, the aim of the **New Education** was the full development of the individual. Using textbooks only when appropriate and only as teaching tools, it began with the known and the familiar, and, through varied and flexible programs that used interesting teaching techniques, attempted to draw energy from children's motivation to learn. It stressed correlation and integration of subject matter.

The intended removal of formal grammar study from the first four standards of primary school cleared the way for other significant developments in teaching grammar in those classes under the influence of the New Education. First, developmental theories of childhood emphasized the need to make grammar more accessible to the young mind by producing easier grammar textbooks for use in the primary grades. Second, a feature of these easier textbooks was the growing popularity of inductive teaching as a means of engaging pupils in more active learning of grammatical concepts. Third, the direct teaching of oral and written composition authorized by functionalist psychology led to the rise of composition as a school subject, dethroning grammar as the preeminent advanced branch of English studies. No longer justified as an autonomous subject by its contribution to mental discipline, primary school grammar was now relegated to the role of service subject to composition, and it began to appear in syllabi as a branch of that subject. And finally, the shift in rationale from grammar as a source of mental training to grammar as the "handmaid of composition" brought about reform in the content of primary school grammar, as it became evident that the old "word grammar" of the first colonial curses of instruction did not transfer to the skills of speaking, writing, and reading. This reform produced what was called *functional grammar*.

CHANGES IN ELEMENTARY SCHOOL GRAMMAR

> There is in progress at present throughout the British Empire and in still more active form in the United States, a complete change of attitude towards public education, both as regards the subject-matter of instruction and methods employed, and as regards the part which a completely organized education scheme should perform in national life (Phillips, 1985, p. 85).

With these words, Victoria's first director of education, Frank Tate, described the **New Education** to the State Parliament in 1904. Tate was the most prominent of a group of reforming educational leaders who were put in charge of departments of education in Australia and New Zealand at the turn of the century. Others were Peter Board of New South Wales, William Neale of Tasmania, and George Hogben of New Zealand. This new generation of officials, committed to "that confused and exciting set of ideas then disturbing overseas education systems" (Selleck, 1982, p. 93) called the New Education, set out to revitalize their school systems with a new sense of the purposes of education, a new curriculum, and new methods of teaching.

Three years after Tate's speech to the Victoria parliament, two New Zealand school inspectors gave their perception of the impact of the new thinking across the Tasman Sea. In their Annual Report, Inspectors Hendry and Wyllie from Southland quoted from an unnamed American author to draw a comparison between the old and the new.

> From the earliest times down to a generation ago education was a breathing-in-process that simply continued and expanded the original act of creation. Then there arose a new conception concerning the making of a man, and educational theory is slowly changing its form. Responding to influences from without, life is an unfolding process from within. This is the conception that is now shaping our methods of instruction. The old found satisfaction in the state of mind that was quietly receptive; the new sees hope in the turbulence of enquiry. (1907, p. 45)

The New Education arrived in Canada earlier and with less apparent fanfare. Perhaps as a result of closer proximity to American ideas of progressive education—for example, John Dewey and Colonel Parker visited Canada to address groups of teachers—the changes appear to have been more gradual, with a transitional phase between the Old Education and the New in the period after Canadian Confederation in 1867.

In spite of different timing and pace of change, educational reform in Canadian schooling was shaped by the same ideas in the same general way as in Australia and New Zealand. In all three countries there was a will to refurbish the old subject-centered, discipline-driven system of schooling, imported to "produce docile, law-abiding, and barely-literate citizens" (Selleck, 1982, p. 89). The talk was now of a more generous view of educational aims: to bring to children, in Matthew Arnold's words, "the best that has been known and thought in the world," and to foster in children the growth of their moral, artistic, and intellectual faculties towards a full personal culture. The talk was also of a richer, more unified, and more relevant curriculum to achieve these aims and of teaching methods designed to engage children's interests and active participation in learning.

In this new attitude to primary education, English grammar as a school subject found itself picked on as the epitome of what was worst about the old system of education. It was bookish, abstract, and often disagreeable to teacher and pupil and difficult to link to children's interests, experiences, and language. It encouraged learning that was merely passive; it seemed to bear little relationship to life beyond the classroom. As a school inspector in the Mallee area of northwest Victoria, the future director of education for the state, Frank Tate, had told an 1897 meeting of his teachers that grammar as taught under the old regime was a confusion of means and ends. The analogy he used was of the miser who gloats over his hoarded coin. The hoarder did not propose in the beginning to be satisfied with the beauty of the shining metal disks. He had wanted the money for what it would buy him, just as teachers had first valued grammar for its help in written expression. Yet as the miser came to love money for its own sake, so had teachers "gloated over their grammatical problems, their obscure uses of words, their far-fetched derivations" (Selleck, 1982, p. 91).

Thus, as the *bête noir* of the New Education, the teaching of grammar was one of the main targets of curriculum reform. By 1910 all educational jurisdictions in all three countries had attempted to reduce grammar's status as a school subject and to change both its rationale and the methods by which it was taught. In the official discourse of intention, as expressed by department of education publications, this reduction and these changes were radical. And although to some extent official intentions did manage to translate into changes in children's classroom experience of school grammar, the changes of the first two decades of the twentieth century were not universal, satisfactory, or successful in solving the problem of English grammar teaching in the primary schools. However, in spite of limited achievements in permanent reform of English grammar teaching, the New Education did inject new concepts and distinctions into the debate about the subject, so that the period from about 1900 to 1914 was highly significant in the curriculum history of English grammar.

INDUCTIVE GRAMMAR TEACHING IN ONTARIO, 1868–1887

The rigor of the old grammar course of the Irish *Grammar* or of Lennie's *Grammar* was gradually modified in later textbook adoptions. In 1868 the different needs of younger learners were recognized when two levels of grammar text were prescribed. Miller's *Analytical and Practical English Grammar* was for use in senior classes, while teachers of junior classes could choose either Davies' *English Grammar for Junior Classes* or Morris' *English Grammar (Primer)*. The Davies text further acknowledged younger readers by beginning with a twenty-two-page introductory section called "First Steps in Grammar," being a simple treatment of the parts of speech, "which, it is hoped, will render the study more congenial to the younger pupils, and enable them to take up the Introductory with more profit and pleasure." (unpaginated preface) The remainder of the text was a traditional, formal treatment of orthography, etymology, and syntax. The fourth topic of traditional grammar, prosody, was omitted, while punctuation and composition were left to the teacher, with the suggestion that they could be taught as part of dictation. In this introductory text, Davies had attempted to "alter the mode of expression" with a view to "rendering the subject more easily understood by the class of pupils for whom it is specially intended." In this respect the most notable difference was the use of illustrative sentences that spoke to children directly about their own experiences instead of remote literary and moralistic admonitions.

Following its predecessor, the *Irish National English Grammar for Schools*, the text assumed the guidance of a "judicious teacher." Questions were interposed in the exposition to help pupils test themselves on their study, and there was somewhat less emphasis on memorization. Parsing and analysis exercises were also provided. Thus the major attempt in this text to adjust the study of grammar to younger pupils was to simplify the presentation of the material. There were no other teaching innovations; *An English Grammar for Junior Classes* was simply a traditional deductive textbook that acknowledged the need for a more straightforward presentation for younger pupils.

In 1878 two alternative texts to the Davies' *Grammar* were added to the list of approved school books: both versions of William Swinton's *Language Lessons: An Elementary Grammar and Composition*. Both were published in Toronto, one by Miller (later taken over by W. J. Gage), and the other by James Campbell. In spite of the title, Swinton's text was designed to teach grammatical concepts. However, its pedagogy differed drastically from that of its predecessors. The preface claimed:

> This book is an attempt to bring the subject of language home to children at an age when knowledge is acquired in an objective way, by practice and habit, rather than by the study of rules and definitions. In pursuance of this plan, the traditional presentation of grammar in a bristling array of classifications, nomenclatures, and paradigms has been wholly discarded. The pupil is brought into contact with the living language itself: he is made to deal with speech, to turn it over in a variety of ways, to handle sentences; so that he is not kept back from the exercise–so profitable and interesting–of using language till he has mastered the anatomy of the grammarian. Whatever of technical grammar

is here given is evolved from work previously done by the scholar"
(Swinton, 1878, p.iii).

For children at and beyond the Third Reader level, Swinton therefore proposed a new grammar regime. The teaching method used a starting point that was inductive (often called *objective* at that time). For example, in order to teach the notional concept of a sentence as "a set of words making a complete statement," the teacher was instructed to dictate a short story from the text for the children to copy on their slates. Their attention was then drawn to two formal characteristics of each statement: the capital letters at the beginning and the period, or full stop, at the end. Then the definition was given, followed by positive and negative instances of the concept plus an exercise in sentence completion. It was suggested that teachers use material from the Reader to reinforce the concept.

The text did not go so far as to encourage children to produce their own language as a source of data from which grammatical concepts could be induced. The language data were all provided by the text, giving text and teacher firm control over all aspects of learning. In this sense, the encounter with the living language, claimed by Swinton in his preface to be a significant feature of the text, was limited to samples that flowed live from the teacher's pen or that were found in the Reader. However, as in the case of Davies' *Grammar,* the samples provided were contemporary, and they did represent the everyday life of the young learner.

Language Lessons was widely used throughout Canada. It was authorized in the 1880s in all provinces and territories with the exception of Nova Scotia, where the 1883 grammar text contained an introductory section of language lessons. The Nova Scotia text urged teachers to substitute "real teaching and learning" for the "memoriter recitation of definitions and rules." Instead of deductive teaching of "bald" statements of grammatical principles, it was recommended that those principles be "deduced by proper questioning from knowledge already possessed by the pupils."

In these suggestions for an oral, inductive approach to teaching grammar in the early grades, the new grammar text in Nova Scotia was following an approach that had been recommended as early as 1867 by an eminent Nova Scotia educator, Alexander Forrester. Forrester had been Nova Scotia's second superintendent of education (1853–1864) and principal of Nova Scotia's first normal school in Truro from 1855 to his death in 1869. In his book *The Teacher's Text-Book,* which was based on his normal school lectures, he argued against the premature memorization of rules, definitions, and formulas without their application or comprehension. The outcomes of such teaching, he claimed, were a distaste for the subject and the continuation of incorrect speech and writing that were unaffected by the instruction.

He maintained that in learning grammar, which was the scientific account of language, the child should be taken through the subject, much like the scientist who first analyzes and classifies the data from the senses and then turns to producing a systematic account of the phenomenon. In other words, Forrester recommended an inductive approach to teaching grammar, although he did not use that term. For Forrester, the conventional textbook was only the second stage of the language learning process. It is an interesting comment on the nature of change in schools that these ideas proposed by such an influential individual in Nova Scotia had to wait sixteen years before they were officially adopted by the Council of Public Instruction.

In 1890 an announcement in the *Nova Scotia Journal of Education* directed teachers on approved methods in grammar instruction. The method to be used was objective, or inductive, teaching. For example, children were to observe sentences and paragraphs and then to think out the rules that guided their structure. The announcement acknowledged that this method, being radically different from the traditional approach, was unpopular with the teaching profession because it increased the work of the "mechanical teacher." However, its introduction was "not at all a doubtful experiment" because it had been tested in the "most advanced educational centers of America."

Meanwhile, Ontario adopted a new grammar text for its public schools in 1887, using the same form of title as the textbooks for other subjects, *Public School Grammar*, and *Elements of Composition*. The *Language Lessons* text was discontinued in 1889, together with other optional grammar texts for the common school grades, leaving the *Public School Grammar* as the single authorized text for the subject. Part I of the text, covering the sentence and its parts, was intended for use with the junior division of the Third Reader Part II; classification of the parts of speech was designed for the senior division of the Third Book, while Parts III and IV, Inflection and Syntax, were to be used with Fourth Reader pupils.

The preface claimed that the language of the new text had been made simple and "semi-colloquial for easier understanding." The teaching approach was inductive, designed to "have pupils discover the principles of grammar through the observation of the facts of actual speech." The aim had been to encourage pupils and to make grammar "an exciting, rather than a boring or discouraging discovery for them."

By the end of the century, therefore, ideas from the New Education had succeeded in transforming grammar textbooks authorized for use in the elementary schools of two Canadian provinces. These textbooks showed two major advances over their mid-century predecessors; they were written with the intention that young children would be able to understand the content, and, through inductive methods, they were designed to encourage more active learning drawing on children's own experiences and language. Since other provinces, with the exception of Nova Scotia, tended to follow Ontario's leadership in curriculum development and textbook adoption, these textbook changes generally occurred across all Canadian jurisdictions.

The background to curriculum change

There are three aspects to the background of curriculum change: philosophical, psychological, and linguistic. The Scottish Common Sense School of Philosophy had provided the orthodox philosophical framework for education since 1800 in its conception of the knowing mind as an array of separate intellectual, moral, and emotional faculties, the balanced training of which (through education) was designed to equip the individual for the life-long task of reaching a morally disciplined understanding of a static and external reality ordered by God.

By 1875, this philosophical foundation for education had been undermined by a different science committed to nonstatic, unfolding visions of reality and a more developmental notion of the individual attempting to know that reality (McKillop, 1979). There was also a new interest in Hegelian idealism and the idea that a progressively unfolding universe could not be understood simply by empirical sense observation. Instead, experience of the world depended on the cooperation between observation and reflection, an idea that brought the knower into sharper focus in any consideration of what it meant to know and to learn.

Arising out of these epistemic changes in philosophy, new psychological accounts of learning took the place of orthodox faculty psychology. The theory of **associationism**[7] was influential in schooling by the 1860s, especially in the teaching of English; the central metaphor was the well-stocked mind, primed with verbal resources, efficiently defined and classified by the rules of

---

7   Developed by John Stuart Mill and Alexander Bain.

grammar and rhetoric. Ideas entered the mind via the senses, and thought was the process of manipulating these ideas, which were called up by the memory. Learning, the efficient acquisition and recording of ideas, was assisted by the laws of contiguity, similarity, and difference, which defined the relationships among ideas. According to this theory, learning was made easier by material that was restricted to a limited subject matter and that was presented in a step-by-step fashion, ordered from simple to complex and from small to larger units. Learning required drill, recitation, and frequent repetition to fix the associations that existed within a body of knowledge. Bain, the author of several textbooks on grammar and composition that were widely used in the colonies, advised against having children write their own compositions because it was too unfocused an activity.

Functionalist psychology, emerging in the 1890s, contrasted sharply with associationism. The metaphor was changed to growth and adaptation. Accepting the science of evolution, functionalism saw the mind's role as assisting the organism to adapt to the world it lived in. The emphasis moved from the idea that the mind had recorded, according to associationism, to the organism's adaptive response to the idea. This shift of focus had several implications for syllabus planning and instruction. First of all, the concept of response brought the role of interest to the fore; interest or self-interest helped to determine the response. Secondly, interest implied prior knowledge of the subject matter being learned and some creative synthesis between old and new information. Thirdly, the organism could no longer be regarded as having a merely passive role.

The popularity of functionalism led to the revival of an earlier concept from Herbart (1776–1841). **Apperception** enjoyed great vogue during the late nineteenth century. It referred to the active mental process of the mind seizing and merging with a new idea. A practical application of Herbart's ideas was the lesson plan of "five formal steps": recollection of what was already known, presentation of new information, comparison between old and new information, generalization of new principles, and application of them to new examples. This lesson planning formula was widely taught in Ontario normal schools, for example (Tompkins, 1986, p. 104).

In addition to changes in the philosophical and psychological foundations of educational practice, there was an epistemological shift in the theory of language knowledge. In the early 1800s, the principles of language had been assumed to be available only through reflection. They were not thought to be accessible by means of sense data based on observation of real language text, partly because that was not how language was learned and partly because of the assumed imperfection of ordinary language in comparison with the elevated form that was the target of instruction. By the end of that century the assumed gulf between ordinary language and the refined had been narrowed through the work of men, such as Henry Sweet and Otto Jespersen, in the new applied linguistic science of phonetics. By the 1880s, their claim that speech, not writing, was the primary form of language had given credibility to spoken language as an object of scientific study. This credibility allowed the fundamentally significant acknowledgment in education that the language experience of children was a permissible foundation on which to build instruction—not an entirely new idea, but one that had been previously submerged by orthodox theories.

Perhaps some educationists contemporary to the times could articulate these shifts in philosophy, psychology, and linguistics and could recognize their significance for school practice. What is more likely, however, is that for most school personnel those epistemic shifts were at an invisible level of discourse, in the Foucault (1970) conception of conscious knowledge and conviction at any time resting on an unconscious body of unarticulated assumptions and beliefs. As deep realignments of ideas were taking place, they gave a new authority to explicit beliefs and practices. Thus, as a set of such ideas and practices, affecting the aims, curriculum, and methods of schooling, the New Education represented the visible discourse of a new orthodoxy that rested on a novel but invisible worldview. Occupying a prominent and controversial role in the revised discourse of education, grammar as a school subject found itself subjected to a new kind of scrutiny, most of it critical.

CHAPTER 10
The "Handmaid of Composition"

First page of Calendar of Aberdeen High School and Grammar School of Westmorland County, Moncton, New Brunswick, 1899.

As the art of speaking and writing with propriety, grammar had always been regarded as an essential prerequisite for the proper use of language, but the transfer of its benefits had been assumed to take place without explicit attention to composition. As a result, in the Old Education, English grammar had been the senior partner of English studies. This seniority has an obvious example in the grammar textbook approved for use in Ontario schools in 1868, *An Analytical and Practical Grammar of the English Language*. In spite of its claim that grammar was taught as a means towards the achievement of skill in composition, the text devoted a mere seventeen-page appendix to the subject of composition.

Grammar's seniority was also reflected in the New Zealand syllabus policies of 1878; the approved textbook list from which local authorities could choose included sixteen grammars and only four composition texts. The New Zealand school inspectors reported that because grammar was such a difficult subject for both teachers and pupils, the pressure to prepare pupils to pass the promotion and graduation tests tended to overwhelm composition, to which it was linked in the standards of instruction.

As the authority of grammar waned through the last quarter of the nineteenth century, composition gained in status throughout the colonial school systems. The New Zealand syllabus revision of 1892 illustrated that shift in the relative prestige of these two English subjects. Grammar, separated from composition in the standards for primary school, lost its status as a pass subject in all classes except the Fourth, and in 1895 it lost it in that class too. Composition was made a pass subject in 1892 for classes Three through Six. In the years immediately following these changes, inspectors noted that there was a marked decline in grammar teaching, as teachers were free to put more emphasis on composition. For many of the inspectors, this decline was a cause for grave concern. In 1896, John Smith, inspector of schools for Marlborough District, reviewed what his New Zealand colleagues had said about the fate of grammar teaching under the subject's diminished status and concluded:

> In view of the remarkable concurrence of opinion shown ... it is impossible to resist the conclusion that 'one of the most truly educative subjects in the primary course of instruction' has ceased to be regarded as important in the majority of New Zealand schools, and that its removal from the pass to the class group has been the reverse of beneficial to the cause of true education through the colony. (p. 28)

His colleagues included several notes on the increased amount of time now being spent on composition. On the one hand, these comments show that composition was gaining recognition, while on the other the fact that the inspector thought it worthy of mention suggests that the teaching of composition was not yet commonplace in primary school education.

The promotion of composition over grammar in primary school programs can also be seen in the statistical summaries published by the Department of Education in New Brunswick. These summaries, available for the years 1861 to 1889, give the total number of pupils studying the different subjects in the province's public schools in each of the two terms that made up the school year. From 1861 to 1871 the English subjects were reading, grammar, and spelling—composition was not listed as a subject—but during that decade the percentage of pupils enrolled in the public schools who were studying grammar rose from 26 to 31. From 1873 to 1881 the statistical summaries included the subjects of reading, oral spelling, spelling book, dictation, English composition, and English grammar and analysis. English grammar and analysis was broken down into oral instruction and textbook lessons.

For this period total enrolments were not provided, but one can assume that the numbers given for reading were close to the total number of pupils attending school. The figures for this period show that pupils studying composition as a percentage of those taking reading shot up from 14 percent in 1873 to 57 percent in 1881. Also during this period, the equivalent percentages for grammar study fluctuated between 57 and 49 percent. Of pupils studying grammar as a whole, the percentage receiving oral instruction as opposed to textbook instruction remained fairly constant, between 30 and 39 percent.

Between 1883 and 1889 only total enrolments for three subjects in English were reported: reading, spelling, and recitation (as one subject); English composition; and grammar. As a percentage of pupils studying the first grouping, those taking composition continued the rising trend from the previous period, going from 86 percent in 1883 to 93 percent in 1889, the last year in which the statistical summaries were included in the annual reports. The equivalent percentages for grammar, having declined since the previous reporting period, were between 39 and 41 percent. These statistics permit the conclusion that between 1871 and 1889 the subject of composition, previously nonexistent in the syllabus of the common schools of New Brunswick, achieved status as a school subject and then rapidly became a required study for almost all pupils.

However, it is necessary to establish that changes in the *names* of school subjects did not mask continuity of content—in other words, what had previously been called grammar was now simply relabeled as composition. What constituted the burgeoning subject of composition in New Brunswick is revealed by the activities listed under composition in the provincial course of instruction for 1882. Consisting mainly of oral work for the first three standards and entirely of written work for the other levels, lessons in composition sought to provide direct instruction in the correct and conventional forms of expression. For the First through the Third Standards, three activities were listed.

1. correction of wrong forms of speech used by the pupil

2. repetition of the substance of reading lessons, and

3. written answers to questions on the reading lesson.

While there was little opportunity in the syllabus for children to express their own ideas and experience in language of their own choosing, as the New Education would recommend, these composition activities were by no means grammar masquerading under a new name. In fact, two articles by New Brunswick teachers published in the *Educational Review*, a journal that circulated in the Maritime provinces, suggest that some teachers found ways to extend composition toward the New Educational thinking, despite the prosaic nature of the syllabus specifications. The fact that these descriptions of innovative teaching were published in an officially approved magazine indicates that the educational authorities in the province were not opposed to them.

Clara Atkinson of Newcastle, New Brunswick, began by contrasting the old and the new assumptions about the young child as a learner:

> Some years ago it was taken for granted by many teachers that children knew nothing when they first entered the school-room, and had no power of acquiring facts, and that the first and for some time the only thing they should learn was to read. Now we regard these small folk as interesting possibilities, endowed with a complete mind (though in a rudimentary state), and know that they have already begun the storing up of facts and ideas to which it is our business to add, while constantly seeking to develop two things—thought and its expression. (1888, pp. 154–155)

She then went on to give several examples of lessons that encouraged children to talk about their experiences and then extended their vocabulary and expression. One technique was to ask the children to tell the names of familiar things, such as the different kinds of birds they knew. The teacher would write all the answers on the blackboard. The next morning the children would find the words and sentences neatly reprinted on the board to be copied down as "busywork" and later used in another oral lesson, when they would be asked to give each word in a sentence.

In the December 1891 *Education Review,* an unnamed Grade 3 teacher described how she taught composition to her class. Her account suggested her practice was in advance of the official syllabus insofar as the new ideas were concerned, and her method was in accordance with two of the three requirements of the syllabus as listed above. But she reported that she had found it difficult to manage the third requirement because "by the time the children have read the lesson several times they become so well acquainted with it that they adhere too closely to the words of the book instead of using their own language" (1891, p. 148).

Her solution was to encourage the children to write original stories or descriptions based on pictures the teacher provided or on their own experiences. Occasionally she would have the pupil write the story on the blackboard for others to read and discuss. The shift in this published article from paraphrase to original suggests the boundary between the old and the new in language teaching to younger children in the last decade of the nineteenth century. For younger children, the old assumptions about language as an external body of rules and categories that had to be mastered prior to proper use were being displaced at last.

For older pupils in Standards Four through Seven, the 1882 specifications for composition in New Brunswick all involved written work. The focus on expression of ideas gained from reading lessons continued, in Standard Four requiring narrative paraphrases and in Standard Seven abstracts of reading passages and "transposition of passages" from verse to prose form. What might be called creative writing in Standard Four consisted of letter-writing, including drawing an outline of the envelope, "correctly super scribed on the slates"; in Standards Five and Six a monthly "exercise in simple narrative on familiar occurrences" (p. 4); and historical narrative in Standard Seven.

The 1898 revised course of instruction placed more emphasis on the expression of personal experiences for younger pupils, who were to orally describe familiar objects and experiences, as well as reproduce Reader stories. Written composition in Grades 4, 5, and 6 included short narrative and descriptive essays. In Grade 7, composition was to be studied using the appendix of Meiklejohn's *Short Grammar* (1891). In Grade 8, the subject included properties of style, unity, clearness, strength, and harmony, plus the structure of paragraphs.

Meiklejohn's text was widely used in Canada, and its appendix on composition gives some insight into the nature of the subject as taught to older pupils. In New Brunswick, Grade 7 pupils were studying formal composition from the Appendix concurrently with their second year of grammar work from the same text. The emphasis was on mastering the forms of description and narration. Pupils copied models, corrected sentences, rearranged sentences in paragraphs, and wrote descriptions, following strict topical outlines. A description of a dog, for example, was to follow one of three topical outlines, one of which was "form, size, color and covering, parts, uses, and habits" (p. xiii). Pupils also reproduced material as abstracts, or summaries, paraphrases, and amplifications. In other words, composition involved recomposing given information or casting new information into strictly defined patterns.

Based on this New Brunswick evidence, one can presume that although the emerging subject, composition, was hardly revolutionary in its application of New Education principles, it was definitely not grammar under another name. The expression of ideas, orally and in written form, was taught directly; it was no longer assumed that mastery of grammar, the theory of language, would transfer automatically to effective language use. Direct teaching of the expression of ideas had overtaken the teaching of grammar. Grammar's role, still necessary in providing knowledge of the structure of language, was now subservient to that of composition. Skill at composing in speech and writing was now the most important objective of language study in the elementary school. Knowledge of grammar was only useful to the extent that it supported effective composition at that level.

The linking of grammar and composition was encouraged by the popularity in the late nineteenth century of the Herbartian idea of correlation among school subjects to achieve a unity in the school program that would be consistent with the unity of the child's mind. In fact the concept of correlation encouraged the drawing together of all the subjects concerned with learning the mother tongue under the heading of English. In the revised course of study brought out in Queensland in 1904, for example, correlation of subjects was stressed, with "English" now used for the first time as a heading, "correlating" correct speech, reading, writing, spelling, composition, recitation, and grammar. The Queensland Department of Education attempted to give force to its conception of grammar taught in relationship with composition through instructions to its corps of inspectors. A circular sent out to district inspectors explaining the new course of studies contained a request that they reorient their tests in English away from grammar towards language performance.

Useful as parsing and analysis are for gaining a knowledge of the language or testing that knowledge, and of sharpening the intellect and reasoning faculties of the pupils, the tendency has been to make of these exercises an end instead of a means. In their examinations, inspectors are requested to keep that end in view, and to prove the value of instruction in grammar by sufficient tests both in oral and written composition. (1904)

THE GROWTH OF FUNCTIONAL GRAMMAR

Grammar's new service function for composition was impossible, given the nature of traditional grammar (for purposes of mental discipline rather than transfer of learning). The grammar of the word involved classification of individual words according to a mix of notional definitions and inflected forms. Mastery of that classification system, as proved by parsing exercises, bore no relationship to composing, and it is difficult to see how it could have brought any benefit to reading comprehension, since the analysis of sentences into individual words is not a recognized way of accessing meaning. As Halliday (1985, p. 159) observed, describing a sentence as a construction of words is rather like describing a house as a construction of bricks, without recognizing the walls and the rooms as intermediate structural units.

This mismatch between "word grammar" and the demand for transfer to composition was resolved, gradually, with the emergence of functional grammar. This can be seen in the detailed annual reports of the New Zealand school inspectors for the twenty-six-year period between the introduction of the first New Zealand national syllabus in 1878 and in the major revision of that syllabus in 1904. In the first syllabus, grammar was the grammar of the word, requiring two years of word study and parsing before sentence analysis was introduced in Standards V and VI. Inspectors used their annual reports to campaign for a reorientation of the grammar syllabus to functional grammar, and the 1904 revision followed their recommendations; grammar instruction, beginning with the sentence as the primary unit, was now based on the functional grammar of the New Education.

However, the change did not come quickly or easily, even for the inspectors themselves. The incongruence between the 1878 grammar syllabus and what the New Zealand inspectors wanted it to achieve was at first invisible to the inspectors. In their earlier annual reports they recorded the difficulty that teachers and pupils were experiencing. The inspector for Grey pointed out in 1888 that "the most difficult problem seems to be, how to make the study of formal grammar bear fruit in connection with composition." The Otago report of 1888 regretted that "we cannot report any general improvement in composition." For Southland in the same year, the inspector reported that, "the practical object of grammar teaching—viz., composition—seems to be lost sight of by many teachers."

As the inspectors supervised their schools and tested their pupils for promotion and graduation under the new national regulations of 1878, they blamed the teachers for the lack of success they observed in grammar instruction. It was the worst-taught subject in the program, and the results were discouragingly low, bearing no relationship to the amount of effort that teachers and pupils expended. Children seemed unable to learn how to parse; there seemed to be no transfer to speaking and writing; composition results were deplorable; teachers put too much emphasis on rote methods of learning grammar and failed to emphasize the need for children to understand what they were learning. In some cases teachers were blamed because they themselves had a poor grasp on the grammatical concepts they were trying to teach.

Philip Goyen, for example, who maintained a special interest in grammar and composition throughout his long and distinguished career as an inspector, suggested in his 1881 report for Southland that the solution to the parsing problem lay in the hands of the teacher. He recommended that they make sure that children understood the meanings of the words they were required to work with. He suggested a method of teaching the parts of speech to a Standard Three class using the sentence, "Bees gather honey all the day." The method would be:

> Question: What is the word 'bees' used for?
>
> Answer: To name the little animals that gather honey from the flowers.
>
> Question: What are the words called that are used to name?
>
> Answer: Nouns.
>
> Question: What follows then?
>
> Answer: That the word 'bees' is a noun.
>
> Question: What is the word 'gather' used for?
>
> Answer: To tell what bees do.

Question: What are those words that tell what things do?

Answer: Verbs.

Question: What follows then?

Answer: That the word 'gather' is a verb. (1881, p. 38)

In this 1881 report, Goyen affirmed his belief in the value of parsing; yet in his suggestion on how teachers could better approach the syllabus can be seen the beginnings of a different grammar. Although his aim was to teach children to recognize the parts of speech in a sentence, he was teaching them to do this on the basis of what words *do* in sentences, not on the basis of notional definitions on the parts of speech. His own remarks later in 1883 follow up this point: "The function of a word or phrase depends upon its meaning in the sentence in which it is employed … if the sentence is not understood the function of the word, etc., cannot be determined." (p. 43) He continued to argue for the importance of comprehension and the need for a focus on the functions of grammatical units in his reports for subsequent years.

Then, in 1896, he and his colleagues in Otago seemed to realize that the problem was deeper than the way teachers taught the syllabus in grammar; the syllabus itself was at fault.

> The course of grammar prescribed by the department appears to us to be faulty. Instead of beginning with the classification of the ultimate parts (single words) of the sentence, the course should undoubtedly begin with the study of the main parts of the sentence—in technical phraseology, the logical subject and the logical predicate … a scheme of grammar teaching that does not rise above mere classification ought not to be regarded as satisfactory one; and classification is all our syllabus provides for in the two highest standards. (p. 45)

In 1898, Goyen and his colleagues from Otago again called for reform in the grammar syllabus: " … the grammar syllabus should be recast and the work prescribed made to bear, from beginning to end, on the practical requirements of composition." (p. 51)

By now other inspectors were reporting the same insight. In 1898, Petrie of Auckland criticized the grammar syllabus on the same grounds, but he also laid blame for the "numerous and grave" difficulties preventing the intelligent teaching of grammar on the way grammar textbooks presented and defined grammatical concepts.

> They almost ignore sentence-structure and the linking and subordination of clauses except as exercises in abstract analysis; and they do not show clearly that certain pronouns and adverbs, which children use every day with perfect correctness and ease, do connect clauses … Such clear and decisive descriptions as "adjective phrase" or "adjective clause" to so-and-so, or "adverb phrase" or "adverb clause" to so-and-so, are for beginners infinitely preferable to such vague terms as "enlargement," "extension," etc., that usually convey little or no meaning to their minds, and tend to obscure the processes of thought necessarily involved. (p. 5)

In 1899, the inspectors from Wanganui took up these criticisms of the syllabus and of grammar textbooks; the former failed to indicate that the teaching of grammar in the elementary schools should be based upon its benefits to composition; the latter failed to treat grammatical concepts functionally.

> The more modern books certainly have improved in this respect, but they're too loose in their treatment. For instance, the child is told in one lie that 'The verb is a telling word,' in the next that 'The adjective tells what sort, etc.,' and in the next that 'The adverb tells how, when or where.'
>
> Now why should not the adjective and the adverb have their own exclusive technical terms–viz., 'limiting, describing, or modifying'? Then we would have generally:
>
> (1) The naming word,
>
> (2) The telling or stating word,
>
> (3) The limiting word of (1),
>
> (4) The limiting word of (2),
>
> (5) The connecting word of sentences,
>
> (6) The connecting and governing word of words. (p. 15)

In 1900, Goyen and his fellow Otago inspectors returned to their strong attack on the grammar syllabus, claiming that the separation of grammar and composition, the solution of 1892, had been a mistake.

The problem was that the grammar syllabus, though in perfect accord with the ideas that prevailed when it was devised, about twenty years ago, is utterly at variance with present-day conceptions ... The complex sentence, the typical sentence of English speech, finds no place in grammar below Standard VI. This means that, if the syllabus is adhered to, only those children who remain in school after passing Standard V ever enter upon the study of a type of sentence they have for years been using in their spoken and written speech. The most useful as well as the most educative side of grammar is its constructive side; yet this department of work is entirely ignored in the prescribed grammar course. No wonder that teachers complain that the grammar prescribed for the classes is useless for the purposes of composition. (pp. 39–40)

In 1902, Inspector Spencer of Taranaki reported that he had instructed teachers to begin the study of grammar in Standard III with the easy sentence and its component parts before proceeding with the official syllabus requirements. Inspectors Gray and Milne of Wanganui, referring in 1903 to grammar as "perhaps the most ill-used and most misunderstood subject in the syllabus," offered some suggestions for a proper focus in grammar teaching:

We feel bound to say that a great deal of what has long been regarded as an essential point in the teaching of grammar—i.e., detailed parsing—is worth very little from the point of view of primary-school education. The points upon which stress should be laid are these: (a) Functions of words phrases, and clauses; (b) analysis and synthesis of sentences; (c) position of words, phrases, and clauses in a sentence; (d) active and passive constructions; (e) chief syntactical relations. (p. 13)

Then in 1904, the new inspector-general of education, George Hogben, brought in the revised course of study, which gave official sanction to functional grammar as a component of composition starting in Standard III. The sentence was now the primary unit of study. Instead of starting with the parts of speech, as the old syllabus had done, Standard III pupils were now to start with "analysis of easy simple sentences into subject and predicate," and, adding a constructive dimension to language work, analysis was to be complemented by activities in synthesis whereby pupils learned to use subjects and predicates to build their own sentences. This work was continued in Standard IV, where variation in the form of very easy sentences was added to analysis and synthesis. In Standard V, pupils were required to demonstrate knowledge of "the function of" different kinds of phrases and clauses.

> Complete analysis is not to be expected, nor are the children to be required to pick out adjective phrases and clauses except in answer to such questions as 'What kind of?', 'Which?', 'What?', 'When?', 'Where?', 'How?' They need not even know the terms 'adjective phrase', 'adjective clause', etc. (pp. 276–7)

The functional grammar program was brought to a conclusion in Standard VI, where it was to consist of a review of the work of the previous standards.

> Treated in such a way as to give average children of twelve to thirteen years of age a reasonable knowledge of the structure of easy sentences, the exercises in analysis and synthesis being directed always to the practical end of securing clearness, accuracy, brevity, fluency, and force in the use of language. (p. 277)

Parsing was not mentioned anywhere in the prescriptions. The parts of speech received attention only in Standard IV, and their study was given a strong functional emphasis in the prescription:

> The recognition of nouns, pronouns, adjectives, verbs, adverbs by their functions in easy sentences; distinction between singular and plural, between past and present, present and future; correction of common errors of the spoken and written language corresponding to this stage. (p. 276)

Based on the suggestions put forward by the New Zealand inspectors and the wording of the 1904 prescriptions for grammar, it is possible to summarize the essential features of functional grammar. To achieve its practical ends of more effective expression, functional grammar teaching should start with the sentence as the primary unit of language. It should go beyond the mere classification of grammatical concepts—the focus of parsing and sentence analysis—to the application of these concepts in sentence construction. In other words, instead of using given language samples as sources of grammatical concepts, the concepts should be used to generate language. Constructive activities, such as synthesis of elements into sentences and the variation and order of elements, should follow or replace activities in analysis. Grammatical labels should be clear and should reveal the function of the element in a sentence.

FUNCTIONAL GRAMMAR IN TEXTBOOKS

It was one thing to proclaim functional grammar in departmental courses of instruction, but *how* such grammar could be taught was a matter for teachers and textbook writers. As far as grammar textbooks were concerned, they did change under the influence of the functional approach. This change can be illustrated by a comparison among three textbooks in their treatment of grammatical concepts. The three treatments of just one grammatical element, the adjective, as representative of their overall approaches to instruction are summarized here.

The first book is the Nova Scotia text, *An English Grammar for the Use of Schools* by J. A. MacCabe, published in 1873 and authorized for a ten-year period from that date. This is an example of a traditional grammar text and would have been used in Third Reader classes and upwards.

The second is David Goggin's *New Elementary Grammar*, first published in 1899 and widely used throughout Canada before the First World War. A functional treatment could be expected from Goggin's Fourth Reader-level text; in his preface he noted that lessons in grammar for elementary pupils should be "simple, should deal with essentials, and should be turned to use in reading and composition." (p. i)

The third, *Lessons in English, Standard IV*, written by T. Cheyne Farnie (although his authorship was not acknowledged in the texts) was part of a five-volume series that was widely used in New Zealand primary schools between 1915 and the early 1930s. Following the practice of Whitcombe and Tombs[8], its published *Lessons in English* was written to follow the revised composition syllabus brought in by Hogben in 1904.

An example of the difference between traditional grammar and the functional approach is the kind of identity that the adjective is given as a grammatical element. In MacCabe's text (a grammar of the word), the adjective is presented in the section on etymology as one of the eight parts of speech. The pupil's task is to learn to distinguish it from its fellow parts of speech in learning activities that are restricted to analysis, classification, and parsing.

In Goggin's book, the classification as a part of speech survives, but the adjective is placed in another category as well when it is linked explicitly and in sequence with other modifiers of nouns and pronouns—adjective phrases and clauses. The basis of this second classification is function.

---

8   New Zealand publishing company that held the market for several decades, publishing many school texts, as well as story books.

In the third text, *Lessons in English*, the adjective's identity as part of speech has almost disappeared, and its functional identity as a modifier is highlighted by its explicit association with adjective phrases. The transformation exercise is a learning activity that arises from this functional orientation, in which pupils are asked to substitute adjectives and adjective phrases for each other in sentence contexts. In other words, a functional approach to teaching grammar has implications for the categorization and ordering of grammatical content, as well as for the kinds of learning activities that are authorized.

The fact that the adjective phrase was taught as a functional alternative to the adjective is a further indication of the functional approach. Exercises to reinforce the teaching of the adjective and adjective phrase included synthesis activities, such as filling in blanks in sentences or using given adjectives in the pupils' own sentences. Some transformation exercises were included, calling for pupils to change single adjectives into phrases and vice versa.

Recognition exercises survived, not surprisingly given the syllabus of 1904 for Standard IV, which included "the recognition of nouns, pronouns, adjectives, verbs, adverbs by their function in easy sentences" (1904, p. 376). Recognition was taught using functional criteria; nevertheless, the exercises requiring pupils to pick out adjectives or certain kinds of adjectives from sentences was, as an activity, nonfunctional in the sense that they did not relate directly to the expression of ideas. The survival of *analysis* together with the more functional *synthesis* and *variation* in the Standard IV syllabus was perhaps a nonfunctional residue of parsing.

In some ways Goggin's book appears to be a transitional text between traditional and functional grammar. He starts with the sentence; in the introductory section of the text, the adjective (with the other parts of speech) is treated functionally as a modifier that can appear within either the subject or the predicate parts of the sentence. However, in the rest of the text he reverts to a more traditional word-grammar presentation in which the adjective is located in its class as a part of speech and in which its subcategories—attributive, predicative, and pronominal adjectives—are fully defined and classified. A consequence of this arrangement is the perpetuation of parsing, a totally nonfunctional learning activity. The adjective clause is not presented until much later in the text, when it is discussed as part of sentence analysis without any linkage to adjectives being made explicit.

With regard to application of grammar to language use, a necessary feature of any grammar text with claims to be functional, MacCabe demonstrates the traditional approach's lack of concern for the need to teach explicit links between adjectival concepts and reading or composition; his grammar is a self-contained body of propositions about language structure. Goggin, on the other hand, recognizes the need for the teaching of transfer. First of all, there are specific regular exercises in which pupils practice writing sentences containing adjectives on given topics. Secondly, Goggin demonstrated for teachers a general, but rather forced, two-step procedure for making grammar applicable to "oral reading with intelligence." He showed how a stanza of poetry could be subjected to a "grammar study," an analysis of the classification and function of each grammatical unit. This led to a "thought study," in which each line was interrogated as to its purpose—e.g. "What is the purpose of line one? To state the action, its place, and the time." (p. 42) After these analyses, the pupil was ready to render an intelligent oral reading of the stanza. As far as general composition was concerned, Goggin relied on exhortation: "What has been learned so far should be put to use in ... composition." (p. 42)

The five-volume *Lessons in English* provided for transfer to composition by a wider range of specific composing exercises, including synthesis activities, such as placing appropriate adjectives in blank slots in sentences and having children write their own sentence examples. There was no explicit linkage to general composition. The fact that grammar lessons alternated with other language lessons, including frequent composition lessons, no doubt made it much likelier that teachers themselves would remind children to use adjectives when they wrote their stories and descriptions.

In fact, it is hard to see how any textbook that presents grammar in any organized way could do more than provide structured local exercises to teach transfer from grammar to composition. The only solution would be to teach the grammar incidentally as the need for explanation of particular elements arises out of composition lessons. Whereas some inspectors had suggested that this kind of incidental teaching of grammar should occur in reading and composition lessons, such a proposal was still too radical for the period and would have been too idealistic given the prevailing low level of teacher education and training.

PURE GRAMMAR: THE NEWBOLT REPORT 1921

Grammar teaching received some stimulus from the concept of pure grammar. The *Western School Journal* of 1915 carried the statement, "There is an absolute necessity for the teaching of pure grammar, and not of aiming at the deduction of rules from reading." (p. 173) The implication was that the study must be systematic and not merely incidental, as the functional approach in its ideal sense had advocated.

What was this *pure grammar*? The answer emerged in England from the influential Newbolt Committee Report (1921).

> There is a grammar which can be taught through the medium of the English language. But this grammar is not 'English' grammar, it is pure grammar: it is concerned with the essential modes of thought of all people … it is a true introduction to linguistic study, whatever foreign language may be taken up later. Indeed, even elementary school children, for the majority of whom the chances of learning a foreign language are remote, would assuredly benefit from some consideration of these fundamental laws which govern the expression of their thought. (pp. 290–291)

According to the report, pure grammar was the grammar of function, not form, and it reflected the new emphasis in linguistics, namely of focus on the spoken language as the primary form, with writing as a secondary representation, as argued by Jespersen[9] and others. The Committee's recommendation stopped short of the mental discipline argument for elementary pupils.

> The proper grammar to study in school is not English grammar, but pure or functional grammar, including the elements of phonetics, analysis and a little parsing. This should be taught to all who are to learn foreign languages, while there seems no reason why it should not be introduced in the higher classes of the elementary school, provided those who teach it understand exactly what it is they are dealing with and above all keep it simple. (pp. 292–293).

The Committee's argument for introducing grammar into the elementary school when its major purpose was to prepare children for the study of foreign languages was neither strong nor visible. However, it was probably related to the demand of secondary teachers that pupils receive a grounding in grammar before they reached that level of schooling.

Pure grammar *seems* to be linked with functional grammar, but with a very different aim—no longer learned for its benefits to composition and

---

9   Otto Jespersen (1860–1943) was a Danish linguist who specialized in the grammar of the English language. Along with Paul Passy, he was a founder of the International Phonetic Association.

reading in the native language. Presumably theories of imitative learning had undermined the argument. It was as though the grammar lobby could always retreat to some other grounds from which to defend the subject.

Alberta's first real reform of grammar teaching in the elementary school in 1922 made reference to pure grammar. It was to start in Grade 7, when minds were able to handle abstract thinking—a delay to age thirteen had been recommended by an 1892 Committee on the matter—and it was to be descriptive, not legislative. There was an unacknowledged quotation from the Newbolt Report: "Grammar is not a body of doctrine upon correct speech, but a scientific description of the facts of language." (It was in quotation marks but not referenced—page 292.) In fact, the section on grammar followed Newbolt closely, except that it emphasized the difference between English and other languages, leading to the recommendation that the amount of time spent on it be curtailed.

That does not seem to be quite the emphasis of the Newbolt Report, which focused on the underlying commonalities of languages. Less time should be spent on it, and it should be confined to the fundamental rules of pure grammar. English has evolved beyond other languages; therefore language is more effectively learned by good models, correction, reading good literature, and practice of oral and written composition. Aims of grammar study were to make knowledge of grammar conscious and explicit; to provide a terminology with which to talk about language; to prepare students for the advanced study of English and other languages; to facilitate comprehension; and to discipline the mind.

At the official level of approved syllabi and prescribed textbooks, the New Education had wrought substantial changes in the teaching of English grammar by the first decade of the twentieth century. Formal grammar, with its humanist rationale in intellectual training, had been pushed out of approximately the first seven years of public schooling and was not to start until Grade 8 (or the Fourth Reader, or the Seventh Class), when children were assumed to have the mental capacity to deal with abstract linguistic ideas. Under a revised order of priorities in the elementary school, grammar (correlated with its superior in English studies, composition) was changed in both substance and teaching method. In substance it became functional grammar in order to achieve the required transfer to composition, and in method it adopted inductive teaching as a way of building on what children already knew about language and as a way of engaging them more actively in learning the subject.

CHAPTER 11
Reform in New Zealand & Australia

Rangaiawhia School, Whatuwhiwhi, New Zealand. 1910. (Northwood Collection, Alexander Turnbull Library, Reference Number: 1/1-010685-G.)

SUCCESS OF NEW EDUCATION REFORMS:
THE CASE OF NEW ZEALAND

Hogben's 1904 syllabus revision had mounted a more fundamental attack on formal grammar than any jurisdiction in Canada or Australia. For several reasons, New Zealand's was the one syllabus reform that had the best chance of affecting what teachers did with the subject of grammar in their classrooms. Its guidelines for teaching functional grammar were spelled out more clearly and unambiguously than other contemporary reform syllabi; it made consistent use of the language of functional grammar in the prescriptions; it was explicit about the teaching activities that were not to be used; and it provided numerous examples of the new methods to illustrate to teachers what they were being asked to do.

In addition, and most helpfully, by 1915 teachers had a new series of textbooks available for composition, which, written according to the requirements of the 1904 syllabus, treated grammar according to official policy. Moreover, with the transfer of authority over the influential school inspectorate from local education boards to central departmental control in 1914, the Department of Education had the means to exercise greater influence on teachers' interpretation of the official syllabus.

In spite of these favorable conditions, twenty-five years after Hogben's reform syllabus was gazetted, a new syllabus still found it necessary to launch a strenuous attack on grammar teaching in the primary school. The language of the attack made it clear that the target was that old demon, formal grammar. The syllabus for Standards I through VII (1929), called the "Red Book" from the distinctive covers that enclosed the 223-page document, criticized the "excessive formalism" of the past, in which grammar was "an isolated subject" and a "series of abstractions" based on an outmoded belief in its value as mental training. Grammar teaching, the new syllabus said, had been one of the "many meaningless and profitless occupations which have been the bane of English teaching in the past." This antiquated approach to English grammar, the Red Book asserted, was no longer acceptable.

Presumably the 1929 syllabus was not attacking a form of grammar teaching that was no longer current. The formal teaching of English grammar must have either survived Hogben's syllabus reform of 1904 or had been revived at some point in the intervening quarter century. Whether it was a matter of survival or revival can be determined from the comments by observers of classroom practice, mostly school inspectors, in the period after the reform syllabus was gazetted.

The effect on grammar teaching

The reports of school inspectors between 1904 and 1908 made frequent reference to the teaching of grammar under the new syllabus. Their comments, whether approving or disapproving, give the impression that the new official sanction for functional grammar had substantial effects on how the subject was taught in New Zealand classrooms. If formal grammar survived in

New Zealand primary schools, it was not because teachers refused or failed to change their methods of teaching. The Taranaki inspectors observed in 1904 that formal grammar had disappeared from the first six standards, although they went on to note that in this respect the revision of the syllabus had merely brought it into line with much current classroom practice. The Nelson inspectorate agreed with their colleagues in Taranaki; grammar had been relegated to Standard VII. In 1905 to 1906, the Wellington inspectors reported that formal or technical grammar had practically disappeared from the syllabus, while other inspectors, like Petrie of Auckland, thought that the effect had been to reduce the amount of formal grammar, not to eliminate it entirely.

Some inspectors, like Hendry and Braik of Southland, approved of the changes that the revision brought about. Inspector Hill of Hawkes Bay, never an advocate of grammar teaching, reported in 1906 that he found greater freedom and less formalism in children's writing as a result of the changes in the composition requirements. (p. 21) The Nelson inspectors Harkness and Strachan were optimistic about the changes. Their 1904 report said, "In future the grammar of function will be treated broadly and formal grammar only in more restricted instances." (p. 27) The North Canterbury inspectors reported good results in composition in 1907 and expressed their confidence that grammar was not appropriately treated in the official syllabus.

Others, however, expressed strong reservations about what they saw happening in the schools. Inspector Smith of Grey, for example, complained in 1906, "There is an idea in the minds of some teachers that grammar need not be taught." (p. 44) The 1908 Taranaki inspectors Ballantyne and Whetter wrote in their comments about the teaching of composition:

> ... [T]he absence of a sound training in those portions of formal grammar that bear directly on composition is bringing in its train many defects in written essays ... We do not advocate returning to the drudgery of former years, but now so little grammar is taught that it is not uncommon to find pupils, even in the higher standards, unable to recognize the subject and predicate of an easy sentence. (p. 9)

The Wanganui inspectorate reported in 1908 that whereas they had found written composition in their district to be uniformly good, they regretted "an indisposition to tackle with serious intent the subject of the formal study of composition." They went on to explain the effect of the new syllabus in this respect:

> The simplicity of the subject (of composition) as set out in the syllabus has proved a snare to the unwary. It has been assumed by such that the study of formal grammar may be entirely overlooked, whereas it is the experience of thoughtful teachers that the extent to which grammar is neglected, the foundations of composition in all its forms are sapped. (p. 13)

The Otago inspectors, including the venerable Goyen, did not like the reduced role of grammar in the syllabus. They identified three requirements for composition: substance, or having something to say; language, or having the words to express that substance; and grammar of form, the ability to shape those words effectively. The last, they said, "Is nearly what the Department intended it to become in the schools, namely as dead as a doornail. Children resolve problems of form by feeling or guessing, not by reasoning … To us it is an ugly fact that the children leave our schools deplorably ignorant of the grammar of their mother tongue." (p. 48)

The Cohen Commission 1912

Some secondary teachers criticised children's ignorance of grammar upon graduation from primary, as seen in testimony given before the Cohen Commission in 1912. The New Zealand government had set up the commission to inquire into the educational system, including the program of instruction. For example, an English teacher from Auckland Grammar School, Mr. Mahon, appearing as a witness before the commission, was asked about the standards of English in children graduating from primary school, and whether he thought that the "doing away with the teaching of formal grammar in the primary schools" had anything to do with a falling-off in the quality of English." In reply, Mr. Mahon said that children tended to be unable to express themselves simply, striving instead after effect in their compositions. However, he agreed with the exclusion of formal grammar teaching from the primary schools. (p. 97)

Another witness, Flora Allen, principal of the Otago Girls' High School, said that in the primary school, "Grammar was not taught on the same lines as formerly," and that many pupils beginning the study of a foreign language found that branch of work very difficult. Another girls' school principal, Nancy Jobson from Invercargill, was asked to give her opinion of the abilities in English of the girls who came to her school from primary. She replied that she thought their absolute ignorance of grammar was a serious drawback to their building up more advanced English. (p. 317)

Yet another witness, T. D. Pearce, rector of the Southland Boys' High School, spoke strongly about the grammar issue.

> In grammar, or the absence of it, I find in the secondary school the greatest handicap. The syllabus lays down that the functions of words should be known, but discourages the use of technical names. From my talks with primary teachers, I find that they themselves experience the greatest difficulty with this subject. I further find by inquiry from pupils that in many schools no grammar textbook is used. That, I think, is where the mistake lies. The function of words is not taught fully enough. The consequence is that on their arrival at the high school there is great difficulty in learning a foreign language such as French or Latin. It is some considerable time before the grammatical sense so necessary for composition is developed. I should advocate more attention to the elements of formal grammar, with the use of grammatical terms, in the Fifth and Sixth Standards. (p. 319)

A teacher of English at a technical day school, Oliver Duff, spoke vigorously to the commission about the poor level of English skill of his students, aged between fifteen and twenty, all of whom had completed the Sixth Standard. "Of grammatical accuracy not two in ten would know anything." (p. 331) Mr. Duff's teaching experience of eight years coincided with the period of time following the introduction of the new syllabus in 1904.

The comments by school inspectors and teachers under the functional regime of the revised syllabus indicate that traditional or formal grammar teaching in the primary classroom was at least badly scathed by the change of policy. Whether the commentators thought that formal grammar had disappeared from the primary school or merely been reduced, and whether they spoke with approval or disapproval, their comments leave little doubt that the official policy changes of 1904 did have a major impact on what teachers did with English grammar in New Zealand classrooms, at least in the first dozen or so years of operation of the new syllabus. This suggests that if formal grammar was prevalent in New Zealand primary schools in the 1920s, as implied by the 1929 syllabus revision, its presence was the result of *revival* rather than of *survival*.

That is not to claim that the change from formal to functional grammar teaching would have been universal. Not all New Zealand teachers would have been able or willing to switch from one approach to a radically different one in a matter of a few years. However, contemporary comments suggest that the overall character of grammar teaching in New Zealand primary schools did manifest a perceptible shift from formal to functional as a result of the New Education reform of 1904.

REFORM IN AUSTRALIA

New South Wales

One year after Hogben's syllabus revision in New Zealand, New South Wales followed suit. In a 1980 assessment of that revision, an official history of education in New South Wales declared that its effects "were profound." The assessment continued:

> Initially it unhinged the work (and perhaps the teachers) of many schools, caused uncertainty among teachers and was misunderstood by many parents who could not fathom why little Johnny would want to take live "santapedes" to school. The teachers most confused were the older teachers and the untrained teachers in small schools, who formed the majority at that time. This confusion lasted only a few years: by 1910 the New Syllabus had been accepted. (p. 139)

This assessment of the overall syllabus provides a background against which to consider the effects of the changes in grammar teaching that the 1905 syllabus brought about. In general, the intent of the changes had been to reserve formal grammar to the higher primary course, Classes 6 and 7, and to adopt a functional approach to the subject in the lower classes so that grammar was taught only "so far as it assists in intelligent understanding of the structure of sentences in composition." The recommended method of instruction was inductive.

The annual reports of New South Wales school inspectors in the years immediately following the new syllabus revision indicate the extent to which the syllabus changed the way grammar was taught. The reports of this period made little reference to teachers failing to make the change from formal to functional teaching of the subject; for the year 1905, most reports agreed that change was taking place and that English (a term now in use) was better taught as a result. For 1907, Inspector McKenzie of the Wollongong District noted that the "teaching of English is in a transition stage at present. The old formal teaching is giving way to broader ideas and more natural methods."

On the other hand, the transition from the old to the new was not always a smooth one. There was reference in 1905 to pro-grammar prejudices that were dying hard, and there was the problem of vulgar errors from the home, which caused some to point to the need to retain a place for formal grammar in the program. Inspector Walker of Braidwood District thought that the change had been too extreme in some classrooms. In his report for 1907 he wrote,

> There is a disposition very marked, in some schools, to neglect formal grammar. In the desire to get away from the 'Parsing' incubus of the past, they have gone to the other extreme, and have almost totally neglected this feature of instruction. It is not uncommon to find fairly advanced pupils unacquainted with the 'case' of nouns and the agreement between the verb and its subject. So much of grammar as is necessary to enable pupils to understand the reasons for various forms of speech should be taught; where it is not done teachers are failing in their duty. (1908, p. 291)

South Australia

As the other Australian states were proceeding towards grammar reform, beginning in 1901 South Australia engaged in a conservative reaction. The evidence from inspectors' reports in that year suggests that the Department of Education in South Australia had taken an early lead in the reform of grammar teaching. In their reports for that year, several contrasted prevailing practice, which tended to be superficial, leading to poor results, with more impressive achievements in former years. Inspector Whillas (1901) noted:

> Grammar is the most disappointing subject of all. Twenty years ago our pupils could parse and analyze very fairly. The subject was recognized as an all-important one. Now we find that, except in a few of our very best schools, it is very badly taught. (p. 23)

Inspector Clark agreed that in comparison with an earlier period when "grammar ... enabled children to analyze difficult sentences and to elaborately parse equally difficult words," present teaching was superficial. He was less certain, however, that the change was a cause for concern. He was convinced that conversation and composition were much better than they had been and that this again was to be attributed to the "practical trend given to language to the neglect of the grammar book." (p. 16) Inspector Smyth estimated that the reintroduction of grammar was occurring after a ten-year period of what he saw as neglect. (p. 18) Inspector Neale, who was to go on to become director of education for Tasmania, noted that very little grammar was expected by the syllabus and that "for some years preceding this practically none has been taught in the majority of schools." (p. 113) It was clear from the inspector's comments that an official restoration of grammar teaching had been instituted in 1901 by a stiffening of the examination requirements for composition to reintroduce a mandatory written test for grammar.

By 1903, Inspectors Burgan and Smyth both commented on an improvement in grammar teaching under the new provisions, but both felt that the situation left considerable room for improvement if the former standards were to be restored. (pp. 121, 129)

CHAPTER 12
The Revival of Formal Grammar Teaching

"New Zealand School Photographs, 1950 and 1964 [Photographs]," in
Children and Youth in History, Item #88, http://chnm.gmu.edu/cyh/primary-
sources/88 (accessed October 5, 2011). Annotated by Jeanine Graham.

New Zealand

The attack on formal grammar in the 1929 Red Book suggests that the reform movement had lost its momentum by the 1920s and that some reaction had set in to revive the old formal teaching of grammar. This reversal can be traced in the syllabus policies of the New Zealand Department of Education between 1913 and 1919.

As early as 1907, the Wellington inspectors hinted in their annual report that the Department was considering some modification of the syllabus statements regarding grammar.

> Though the teaching of the technical complexities of grammar as a necessary part of composition is still discouraged by the regulations, the proposed rearrangement of the subject matter of the syllabus will indicate more clearly the requirements in grammar as a branch of composition. (p. 14)

In their 1908 report, the same inspectors returned to this issue with some quite ominous overtones of formal grammar in their comment.

> Though we maintain that [grammar] has little or no bearing on the teaching of composition as an art, we are by no means insensible of its value both as a mental exercise and as an aid to the analytical and critical study of language; as such we welcome its reappearance in the syllabus in the modified form proposed by the Department. (p. 17)

This change does not appear to have been implemented by the Department, perhaps as a result of the growing spirit of acceptance that the new syllabus was beginning to enjoy by the end of the first decade of the century. In spite of this acceptance, Phillip Goyen, just before he retired in 1910, was able to gain the majority support of his inspectorial colleagues at their conference for his motion that the requirement for Standard IV pupils should include recognition of all the parts of speech (Ewing, 1960, p. 121). Again there is no evidence that the Department followed through on this recommendation to restore some formal grammar to the syllabus.

Indeed, the major syllabus revision of 1913 left the composition requirements unchanged as far as grammar was concerned. A new emphasis on purity of speech arose from a recommendation of the Cohen Commission. However, the Commission had refrained from using this issue to urge a return to formal grammar, acknowledging the prevailing wisdom that pure speech was a matter of imitative learning from teachers who presented themselves as good models.

The next major revision, however, was a different matter. In 1919, with Hogben retired, new regulations restored grammar to the school program as a separate examinable subject in Standards IV to VI. Its value was set at one-sixth of the mark for English as a whole. There was a stiffening of the prescription for Standard VI by the inclusion of cases of nouns and pronouns and the infinitive. Hogben's cautionary statements that definitions and abstract rules of grammar were not required, which had been retained in the 1913 revision, were now significantly dropped from the syllabus. These changes seem to have been a response, not so much to a conscious retreat from the principles of functional grammar but to the exigencies of an examination system that demanded greater precision in the syllabus prescriptions than had been desirable under a more child-centered regime. The changes in the grammar component were also aimed at better preparing primary-age children for English and other language studies at the secondary level, a level of education to which many more pupils were by then aspiring (Ewing, 1960, p. 163).

Australia after 1910

The Australian experience of grammar teaching in the primary schools of the five most eastern states recapitulated the general pattern of New Zealand, with some variation among the state jurisdictions. There is evidence that some retreat from the enthusiasm of the New Education occurred in Australia after 1910. This erosion was particularly evident in Queensland, where the primary school syllabus was revised once again in 1914. In spite of the reaffirmation of New Education principles, such as correlation, self-activity, and links between schoolwork and the outside world, there were several cautionary statements. The introduction to the new course of study implied that the 1905 revision had been too drastic and that there were dangers in a program that over-emphasized activity learning; the result could be "superficial, inaccurate, unmethodical work." The document went on:

> Every branch of knowledge has its fundamental facts and principles that form, as it were, the backbone around which the complete body assumes its shape. These must be recapitulated and committed accurately to memory when once the pupils have become familiarized with them in a rational manner. (p. 8)

With this conservative principle in place, it was inevitable that grammar should be identified as one branch of knowledge that possessed a set of essential facts and principles to be learned, and in this respect rote learning was authorized, with the claim that "children learn easily by rote, and the feeling which is derived from committal to memory is still an essential part of education." These statements sound very much like a manifesto.

Any dissonance that Queensland teachers might have detected between the conservative spirit of the general principles and the progressive nature of the specific principles related in grammar teaching would have been resolved by an examination of the English course prescriptions. In the 1914 syllabus revision, grammar content did not appear under that heading, but grammatical concepts were included from the Third Class with a significant change of wording from the 1905 syllabus. Classes Three and Four were now to learn not the functions of parts of speech but "to define and recognize" them—a reversion to the language of formal study. In Class Five, the same direction of change was evident in the replacement of a 1905 reference to constructing sentences containing qualifying clauses with the wording, "separation and classification of the clauses of a sentence." It also stated that "detailed analysis of compound and complex sentences was not required." (p. 57) Thus, in these small wording changes there was considerable loss of a functional approach to grammar and a strong reassertion of the subject as a body of definitions and propositions to be learned as the basis for classification of language elements.

Tasmania

Tasmania's primary syllabus of 1910 was revised again in 1915. While the flawed prescriptions with their formal grammar wording were retained, a new set of notes for teachers were included in the syllabus. These notes, perhaps trying to reconcile two fundamentally opposed approaches to grammar teaching, urged a functional emphasis for grammar study in Classes Three and Four.

> All instruction in formal grammar has for its object correct speech and a graceful style. All unnecessary technicalities must therefore be excluded from the curriculum; in other words grammar must be considered the handmaiden of composition. Analysis is given only because the pupils learn from the exercise the structure of a good sentence; it is useless unless it follows, and is followed by, synthesis. Parsing is valuable only when the pupils learn how words are related in a sentence. If properly taught, the grammar of the primary school may be made a most interesting and practical study. (1915, p. 34)

The wording of the class prescriptions was scarcely changed. The only sign of retrenchment of grammar teaching was that the subject now began in Class Two instead of one year later, as in the earlier version. The prescriptions for Classes Five and Six retained their formal grammar characteristics.

By the 1920s another change of attitude was apparent in Tasmania. In 1929 the revised course of instruction, which may have been little changed from a major revision in 1921, made some strong statements about grammar in the introductory section. The official opinion seemed to be that the attempt to remove formal grammar from the schools had led to the neglect of all grammar. Restoration of functional grammar was an urgent priority.

> In recent years nothing but disaster has followed from the neglect of the simple grammar necessary to teach and understand good prose. The new syllabus places great importance on the teaching of the grammar necessary for a working basis for the written composition. Take, for example, the use of link words. How can a sentence be taught without a knowledge of the function of conjunctions? It is not necessary for the primary pupil to distinguish between coordinating and subordinating conjunctions; the emphasis in such teaching is placed on the wrong thing. Again, it is quite unnecessary that our children should be taught to parse relative pronouns, or to enter into all the intricacies of phrase relative pronouns, or to enter into all the intricacies of case in nouns, but it is valuable to know the double function of the relative as a pronoun and a conjunction. In cases of nouns there is only the possessive that needs attention, and in pronouns the simple distinction between the use of 'I' and 'me,' 'my' and 'mine,' 'he,' 'his,' and 'him,' 'who,' 'whose,' and 'whom' … The kind of grammar that was taught presupposed a language or precise form to be exactly learnt; the kind of grammar that English children need is part of their lessons in language. (1929, p. 18)

A rare glimpse of a Tasmanian teacher's plans for grammar teaching within a perception of official policies is provided by a surviving record of a "Programme of Lessons for Classes VI to Preparatory" from 1925. The plans were written out on printed forms provided by the Education Department. One column on this form was for Sentence Structure and Grammar (an arrangement that did not seem to encourage the official integration of grammar with composition). For the most part, the handwritten plans indicated a formal approach to grammar. For October they indicated the intention to have Class VI revise the adjective phrase and clause; study the grammar of noun, pronoun, and adjective; and learn the noun clause in full. For November, the teacher intended the Sixth Class to revise the adverb phrase and clause and study the grammar of adverbs and verbs and participle phrases. The December plan included one (possibly) functional activity: to revise the use of linking words to form simple sentences into compound sentences. The other topic for that month, study of the absolute phrase, was a more formal one. In accordance with the syllabus, grammar work was planned for all classes except the Preparatory and Class I.

In New South Wales, a reaction had set by the mid-1920s against the "soft" approach of the New Education. After Peter Board retired as director in 1922, there were accusations that standards in the basic skills had dropped. The 1905 syllabus had given teachers the right to draw up their own programs of instruction, provided they followed the guidelines and principles declared in the syllabus. By 1925, this freedom was being reduced, and the syllabus was becoming more prescriptive and centralized. The concern over standards was shown in a 1924 statement by Director of Education S. H. Smith. He had set up a committee of inspectors to inquire into the teaching of English composition in the primary school. where standards in the subject were thought to be low. The committee attributed the poor standard of work to unsystematic teaching. It was acknowledged that the syllabus emphasis on the free choice of topics for pupils' compositions had produced a great improvement in the independence and naturalness of speech and writing.

However, in many cases that freedom had been gained at the expense of correctness. "There was a danger," Smith said, "that ungraded and unsystematic teaching will fail to train the pupils in correct English." He wanted teachers to use a definite, orderly approach to teaching composition. While he admitted, "Experience has shown that a purely grammatical treatment of the formal side of English does not necessarily help expression," he was willing to allow teachers for whom grammar provided a suitable structure for teaching composition "to use a grammatical technique in dealing with language difficulties if he believes such a technique to be the best to give the pupils power to cope with their difficulties" (*New South Wales Gazette*, 1924).

No doubt many teachers would have interpreted Smith's permission to use a "grammatical" approach as encouragement to do so. While the syllabus for 1925 maintained New South Wales' formal allegiance to a functional approach to grammar in the primary school, it also reflected the great preoccupation with the issue of correct form that Director Smith had shown in his advice to teachers the year before. In 1905, the stance of the syllabus to grammar had been professed in negative terms; in 1925, there was a sense that grammar was enjoying a rehabilitation in the primary school program, even though great pains were taken to distance the recommended teaching from traditional formal methods. The syllabus seemed to base its recommendations for grammar teaching on the assumption that correct language, which was a matter of habit formation, could be reinforced by the conscious control over language habits that the study of language structure and rules could provide.

In this respect, grammar was said to have an important role in the larger campaign to replace children's inferior speech patterns, picked up in the community, with proper English. While this campaign depended primarily on the child's exposure to best use of language through the teacher's example, knowledge of grammar would put children on their guard against inferior speech through a trained understanding of the correct forms through "the possession of a number of general ideas which will be serviceable to them for self-correction in their post-school days." Teachers were urged to adopt such measures as they could most effectively handle. The syllabus suggestions included the prompt correction of errors as they occurred and the grouping of errors under generalizations and rules governing practice. In any case, the eradication of impurities in the pronunciation and grammatical forms "should be a thorough and insistent effort on the part of teachers." (pp. 41–42)

While affirming the need for instruction in grammar, the syllabus did not envisage a return to the subject in the narrow sense of grammar that began with picking out nouns and verbs and ended with parsing and analysis of a complex sentence. "Grammatical instruction which deals simply and clearly with the functions of words and their relation to one another will be found serviceable." (p. 42)

The past participle was one example of the syllabus's concern: the misuse of it was said to be one of the "gravest defects in the speech of our people." After early attempts at correction, the term could be introduced later in the course without definition. "A past participle campaign might from time to time be instituted and vigilance committees appointed." The aim was the elimination of forms such as "I done it"; "I seen it"; "I had went there"; "I laid down to sleep."

The syllabus suggested that the method used in nature study would serve language well. Children could be encouraged to collect language "specimens." Curiosity would be aroused and power in using the insight successfully would result.

The efforts of the Director of Education to restore formal grammar to the primary course of study seem to have been successful. In his 1926 speech to the Teachers' Federation Conference, he said, "Formal grammar during the past has been receiving more close and careful attention, and the result has been gratifying to the Department" (Address by the Director, 1927).

South Australia

The South Australia record for the 1920s also indicates that there was some revival of interest in grammar teaching in that decade. In 1921, the Superintendent of Primary Education noted in his annual report:

> The new Course of Instruction reintroduces the subject of formal grammar. Commencing in grade four with the recognition of the parts of the simple sentence and the functions of the elementary parts of speech, the work is carefully arranged so that in grade 7 the pupil is able to deal with full parsing, the analysis and synthesis of complex sentences, the ordinary rules of syntax, and simple figures of speech. Now, since the ultimate purpose of grammar is to produce correct speech and graceful style in speaking and writing, the value of this subject is to be assessed by the extent to which it is linked up with oral and written language and employed therein. (p. 29)

Victoria

Frank Tate brought out another revision of the primary syllabus in 1911 that was directed at the eight grades of what was called elementary schooling. In the introduction, Tate said that he hoped the spirit of the "New Programme" of 1903 would be maintained. The prescriptions for grammar were more detailed than those from 1904, but the increased specificity seemed to have been designed to make the functional approach clearer for teachers and to bring the expression of the grammar content more in line with the intentions of the reforms: for example, more emphasis on the use of grammatical concepts and on constructive activities at the expense of recognition and analysis.

Under "Notes on English," the 1911 syllabus noted that correctness in the expression of thought depends partly on instruction in formal grammar, partly on correction as errors occur. Formal grammar should be strictly limited to giving pupils correct ideas about functions and relations; less time should be allocated to it; properly taught, it should react upon the pupil's speech and writing.

In 1914, the principles of functional grammar were still in operation, according to the Report of the Minister of Education.

> The amount of formal grammar taught is limited to what is required to enable pupils to express their thoughts orally and in

writing in a clear and grammatical manner. Hence grammar and composition are associated in the instruction. (p. 17)

However, there was an indication that the tide might be about to turn in a call for greater attention to grammar teaching. This was a reaction, not against functional grammar but against a failure to teach any grammar. The report referred to an unfortunate neglect of grammar:

> A tendency to put instruction in formal grammar too much in the background has called for correction. The functions of words, of phrases, and of clauses must be taught. Constructive exercises to furnish a training in the power to write well-balanced sentences free from ambiguity should occupy a large place in the teaching of grammar and composition. (p. 19)

FACTORS CONTRIBUTING TO THE RESTORATION OF FORMAL GRAMMAR

All three countries failed to establish the functional teaching of grammar as a commonplace of primary schooling. In all three, the enthusiasm for the reform of grammar teaching that had marked the opening years of the century seemed to have abated by the 1920s. Whereas grammar had been the object of much negative comment in the reforming syllabi, it was a more reputable topic.

Several factors were implicated in this trend towards a more conservative attitude to the subject. First of all, with the exception of New Zealand, departments of education failed to distinguish the differences between the new functional grammar and the old formal grammar of ingrained traditional practice clearly enough for their teachers. Many teachers found it difficult, and some found it impossible, to translate the new principles into tangible, definable classroom programs. The problems of interpretation and implementation allowed conservative teachers and inspectors to continue with the old methods, and not enough help was provided to retrain teachers in the new methods.

Since the syllabus prescriptions themselves were often unclear and even contradictory, many teachers, poorly trained and facing large classes and inadequate resources, simply did not understand the new functional grammar and had to continue in the only way they could, teaching parsing and analysis as a separate body of knowledge and skill. Such teachers were particularly vulnerable, and perhaps sympathetic, to criticisms that the demise of formal grammar had led to the disappearance of systematic programs of instruction in English. The absence of structure was blamed for an assumed lowering of educational standards. The argument was that functional grammar was proving to be inadequate as a foundation for the coherent teaching of composition.

The second and perhaps most powerful cause of the survival of formal grammar was the failure of departments of education to bring their examination practices into line with their curriculum policies on English as a school subject. Examinations at the end of primary education, providing both school-leaving credentials for pupils entering the workforce or entrance qualifications for those going on to post-primary schooling, continued to include either separate examinations in English grammar or questions on grammar in English papers. The social and educational significance that was attached to success in these examinations by teachers, pupils, parents, and employers inevitably meant that teachers were under great pressure to teach to the examinations, and if the examinations demanded parsing and analysis, that was the grammar that teachers taught.

A third factor, intertwined among the other sources of grammar's rehabilitation after 1910, was a growing preoccupation with pure speech. The need to defend spoken English against the deleterious effects of so-called colonial usage led to a concern about the formal properties of language at the expense of New Education's priority on content and meaning. The teaching of grammar was promoted as part of the campaign against impure speech.

Finally, a fourth factor that fostered the status of grammar as an important school subject was a reconceptualization of its rationale under the new term *pure grammar*. This was a further transformation of the old humanist belief in the value of grammar as general intellectual discipline for the mind. The idea that the study of grammar was the study of thinking re-emerged as pure grammar, which referred to universal aspects of language structure and thought. These aspects, independent from the grammar of any particular language such as English, were principles that underlay all languages. It was thought to be essential that any pupil going on to the study of a second language should have studied these principles. For those whose education would end at the conclusion of the primary course, it was thought that the mental training obtained from such a study of pure grammar would give them thinking tools that would be valuable as part of a general education.

THE FAILURE OF DEPARTMENTS OF EDUCATION

The shift from formal to functional grammar was a complex, and in many ways, ambiguous change. In general, the reform syllabi probably underestimated the difficulties of implementing syllabus change in classrooms. The radical syllabus revisions were introduced before departments had begun to publish detailed manuals of instruction for their teachers to guide them in the translation of official policies and curriculum into classroom instruction. The reform syllabi of the first decade of the century were, for the most part, little more than statements of topics to be covered at each level, accompanied by briefly stated rationales and some explanatory notes. Except in New Zealand, teachers had to do the best they could with rather laconic statements of the new grammar.

Not only were the statements terse, but in some cases the actual prescriptions for the different classes of pupils were inconsistent with the principles of functional grammar. Much of the wording of the specifications for grammar failed to pass beyond the formal study of language structures to a genuine functional approach. In Victoria's case, for example, grammar work was predominantly defined in the old vocabulary of propositional knowledge, using such specifications as "to have an intelligent knowledge of"; "to distinguish"; "to know"; and "to analyze." Less prominent was the vocabulary of functional grammar: "to be able to use"; "to arrange in the most effective manner"; and "to construct." Queensland's revision of the 1905 syllabus used functional terms such as "combination of subjects and predicates to form simple sentences" and "functions of all words in a sentence." However, these were mixed with the language of analysis ("dividing sentences into subject and predicate") and parsing ("accidence of noun and pronoun," "classify the clauses of a sentence").

In some cases, the language of the prescriptions left the intentions quite vague. In Tasmania, for example, the 1910 syllabus failed to indicate any method direction to teachers with statements that merely identified topics without any indication of the objectives involved. Examples were topics expressed as "The verb, kind, mood, voice, tense; full parsing of the noun." Canadian syllabi also failed to find a consistently functional form for the grammar prescriptions. In 1912, for example, Nova Scotia's course of study included directionless injunctions, such as "teach noun, pronoun, and verb." In several cases, *parsing* (a term incompatible with functional grammar) was retained.

The stronger survival of formal tendencies in grammar teaching in the syllabus prescriptions than was intended must have encouraged a conservative tendency to retain the older practices of the subject by teachers who were out of sympathy with the reforms or who found the new ideas difficult to understand and put into practice. If you were at all unsure of what a functional approach to teaching grammar actually meant, in the concrete sense of what as a teacher you had to do on Monday mornings, these syllabus statements probably permitted a very conservative interpretation.

THE EFFECT OF FAILURE

These deficiencies in the syllabus statements about grammar as clear guides to teachers allowed scope for error in the discrimination of the instructional differences between formal and functional grammar. In spite of the exemplary clarity of Hogben's syllabus revision, there was some confusion among New Zealand teachers about the new grammar teaching. The Marlborough inspector, for example, referred in 1908 to the problem of grammatical terminology such as *subject* and *predicate*, whose use the new syllabus discouraged. Inspector Strachan thought that teachers were missing an important distinction.

> The trouble that used to present itself to the teacher was not so much in the use of these names as in the request for the definition of them. A precise definition sometimes calls for a faculty of abstraction with which the child is ill-equipped. The use of a roundabout phraseology for subject and predicate simply presents this difficulty in a new form. (p. 26)

In this comment can be seen some of the struggle that teachers were engaged in as they grappled with the meaning of the new dispensations for their day-to-day teaching, often with very large classes of over sixty pupils (Ewing, 1960, pp. 109–110). The Department did not have the resources to mount a retraining program; not until 1914 did it gain control of the inspectors who, as local board appointees, were the only means by which syllabus policies could be monitored and enforced.

There is no doubt that the new syllabus, with its radical change of emphasis towards grammar among other aspects of education, as well as its suggestive rather than tightly prescriptive character, was a challenge to many teachers, who found that they were expected to draw up their own programs for teaching based on the principles explained in the syllabus. The syllabus was reported to be hard for teachers to understand, and many, including Frank Tate of Victoria, thought that it was overloaded (Ewing, 1960, p. 115).

Speaking of grammar, the Wellington inspectors noted in 1906 that the "perplexing old" had been replaced with a "saner and more rational system." In spite of that improvement, they went on to say, "Some teachers appear to be in a fog as to what the new requirements with regard to grammar are." These Wellington inspectors believed that the syllabus was permissive with respect to grammar. For example, according to the regulations it was sufficient, they said, if children could explain the function of the first phrase in the sentence, "Amidst thy bowers the tyrant's hand is seen," with the answer that it told where the hand is seen. However, they continued:

> If a teacher feels he can convey to the pupil a clearer and more intelligent comprehension of these functions and relations by making use of the term 'adverbial adjunct of the predicate,' so far as we read the syllabus, there is nothing to prevent his doing so. (p. 25)

While this interpretation may have been within the letter of the syllabus, it is hard to see how a teacher might have taught the particular grammatical concept without offending its spirit. The point is, however, that the syllabus may have permitted a range of interpretations by both inspectors and teachers, allowing the perpetuation of more formal grammar than Hogben had intended in some districts and classrooms. Variable interpretation and conservative opposition to the new methods and content would have been encouraged by the forthright criticism that influential inspectors, such as Philip Goyen, made of the new provisions for grammar teaching. The 1907 Inspectors' Report for Otago, where Goyen was concluding a distinguished career, carried an uncompromising claim.

> Grammar is the bedrock of correct form in speech, and the time will never come when we can afford to neglect it. This, we regret to say, appears not to be the view of the Education Department. (p. 44)

Goyen and Hogben had earlier exchanged sharp words on the grammar issue at a 1904 meeting of school inspectors; Hogben replied to Goyen's criticism of the reduction in grammar content by saying, "It is no more necessary to teach composition by grammatical terms, than to teach billiards by a compulsory knowledge of the coefficient of restitution." In fact, for about the first six years of its operation, the new syllabus was the subject of much controversy, the question of its treatment of grammar often emerging as a favorite subject of debate (Ewing, 1960, pp. 111–112).

In that atmosphere of controversy, the North Canterbury inspectors made no bones in their 1905 report about their intentions to protect grammar teaching, that "much maligned element of English education." They gave clear notice that "It is not our intention to call the composition satisfactory in the school which does not disclose fairly efficient treatment of that branch which has hitherto gone under a separate name." (p. 39)

It therefore hardly seems likely that some amount of confusion and surviving intransigence on the part of elderly inspectors and some teachers could have accounted for the apparent failure of the new syllabus to establish functional grammar teaching as a commonplace of schooling.

However, in spite of this sign of a change, the new syllabus of 1920 maintained the functional approach held in 1905 and reaffirmed in 1911. The 1920 syllabus repeated the principle that formal work in grammar should occupy a subordinate place in the teaching of English. The grammar requirements remained unchanged in the 1923 version of the syllabus, except for one small but significant omission: the principle that grammar's position in English studies was a subordinate one, explicitly stated since 1905, was dropped.

CHAPTER 13
The New Thinking about Grammar

Shanks Lake Schoolhouse, near Del Bonita, Alberta.
(Courtesy Galt Museum & Archives, UID 19841071039.)

The nature of the criticism of school grammar leveled at it by the new educational thinking is captured in the record of a 1904 conference in Queensland. The Department of Education called a meeting of leading state educationists to consider an overhaul of the state's public education system, including the course of study that had been in place with only minor changes since 1876. A three-man subcommittee was established during the conference to recommend revisions to the grammar component of the primary school course of study. This subcommittee brought forward three recommendations for changes in the grammar syllabus.

1. That analysis and parsing not be taught in classes three and four and that easy composition take their place;

2. That the requirements in grammar for class five be accidence,

148

syntax, easy parsing, the analysis of simple sentences, and composition; and

3. That the requirements for Class Six grammar be those currently prescribed for Class Five.

In 1904 those were radical proposals, calling for a major reduction in the amount of grammar to be taught. Comparatively, in the 1892 version (in which there were only five classes, not six) grammar for Classes Three and Four each consisted of one and a half year's work. Pupils at the end of the Third Class, who would have been approximately ten years of age, were to be able to define all the parts of speech and distinguish them in a sentence, and they were to be able to divide an easy sentence into its subject and predicate. The standard for the Fourth Class included full parsing of the noun, adjective, and adverb and analysis of simple sentences. The heavy program in grammar for the Fifth Class, now recommended as Class Six grammar study, included full parsing of the noun, pronoun, adjective, and adverb; accidence of the verb; and analysis of compound and complex sentences.

In justifying its recommendations, which meant that pupils would not begin the formal study of grammar until the age of eleven and a half, the subcommittee used arguments that reflected the changing ideas about children, language, and learning embodied in the New Education. The postponement of formal grammar until the Fifth Class was advocated on the grounds that "Children aged 8-1/2 to 11-1/2 do not have the mental development to learn about abstract subjects." The justification continued. "Far too much time is spent on, and too much importance is attached to, the teaching of formal grammar," with the result that English composition was neglected. The traditional definition of grammar was noted as the "Art of speaking and writing the English language with propriety," to which was added that grammar was also the "Science of words ... As an art it is learned by practice; as a science it affords a form of mental culture not to be obtained from any other study." However, the recommendations added:

> We contend that the scientific treatment of the subject should
> be deferred until the pupils reach the Fifth Class, and that the
> teaching of the subject prior to that period should be confined
> to actual practice in the correct use of words, in the enlargement
> of the pupils' vocabulary, and in training them to express their
> ideas tersely and suitably, both orally and in written form. This
> objective can be attained without any reference whatever to the
> technical terms used in teaching grammar. Technical terms

should follow, and not precede, practical work in the expression of ideas in sentences. (Papers relating to the new syllabus on instruction, 1904)

This rationale, drawn up by three Queensland educators in what was no doubt the heady atmosphere of an educational conference, reflected the basic change that had taken place by the end of the century in the prevailing conception of grammar as a school subject. This basic change was that a monolithic notion of school grammar was divided into two grammars. On the one hand, there was **formal grammar**, associated with the humanists' belief in the subject's value as mental training and now suitable only for older pupils. In contrast, **functional grammar** was a more practical study of language in closer relationship to composition, and suitable for younger children. This distinction, as it settled into educational thinking during the last quarter of the nineteenth century, had great significance for the rationale for grammar teaching, its content and its method.

FORMAL GRAMMAR AND LANGUAGE LESSONS

The deconstruction of school grammar into a formal subject for older pupils, sometimes referred to as "textbook grammar" or "technical grammar," and a more functional study for younger ones arose from the confluence of two lines of thought: one from an essentially conservative humanist view of language learning and the other from a developmental view of childhood that was unreservedly progressive. The division was derived from the older distinction between grammar as the science of language and grammar as the art of language.

Grammar as the art of speaking and writing with propriety had been the old conception of the subject as the reflective, non-empirical study of the norms of correct usage. Then educationists began to refer to grammar as the empirical science of language, whereby following the methods of science, language data could be observed and ordered to reveal the laws and principles of language. Humanists regarded the scientific study of grammar as a major contribution to their view of educational aims, namely intellectual development.

However, the new interest in child development had moved the starting point in curriculum planning from the subject matter to the pupil as learner. It was then possible to consider that some material was unsuitable for younger children because it was too complex or too abstract for their level of thinking. This developmental perspective argued for the postponement of the scientific study of grammar until pupils had reached the level of intellectual maturity at which they could profit from formal study.

The nature of these humanist and developmental lines of thought was well illustrated by two articles that appeared in 1894 in the *Annual Report and Proceedings* of the Ontario Education Association. Although the authors lived thousands of miles away from Brisbane, their thinking about grammar had a lot in common with the arguments presented to the Queensland conference.

J. Jeffries of Peterborough, Ontario, wrote an article entitled "Aims and Methods in the Teaching of English Grammar," in which he developed the humanist case for teaching formal grammar as the science of language. The inductive observation and analysis of the facts of language as found in speech and literature, followed by the deductive application of the laws and principles induced, gave "exercise and imparted accuracy to the thinking processes." This study made demands on the faculties of "observation, reproduction, abstraction, assimilation, discrimination, and judgement [sic]." For older pupils, grammar study "may be made a severe test of the powers of concentration and mental acuteness" (1894, pp. 218–219).

The method of teaching, according to Jeffries, had to consist of observation of "the facts of language as found," which should be analyzed to produce an understanding of the underlying principles. Any other method would constitute "a palpable psychological error." Although he listed performance benefits that arose from the study of grammar, such as enhanced ability in composition, avoidance of improprieties, and an increased range of language, Jeffries was adamant that the intellectual gains were far more important than these mere utilitarian ends.

Although Jeffries claimed that for younger pupils, grammar could be taught to obtain "gentle" exercise, this proposition would have been rejected by the author of the second article, C. B. Edwards of London, Ontario. In "What Should be Taught in the Canadian Public Schools?" Edwards maintained that the required level of mental development for the study of grammar as a science was not reached until the age of fourteen; consequently grammar in that form should be postponed until the secondary level of schooling. Writing from what Kliebard (1986) called the *social efficiency* perspective, which saw the function of education to be the preparation of young people to serve the society in which they would live, Edwards argued that English grammar should be removed from the elementary school curriculum to allow more time to be devoted to nature study and science. These were of more value than grammar for pupils who would leave school at the end of primary.

According to Edwards, the public school years from age seven to fourteen represented the period in a child's life when the observing faculties were at their best. It was a serious error, he argued, to neglect these faculties by putting too much emphasis on the reasoning faculties that grammar required. Public school children ought to be engaged in the study of real things found in nature and the sciences rather than of formal grammar, which is "mentally unsuitable to the age of the child to whom it is attempted to be taught." A practical training in the use of the vernacular language could be provided more effectively through the study of composition (Edwards, 1894, p. 165).

Related to this developmental insight, as the Queensland committee pointed out, was the argument that the art of grammar—propriety in speaking and writing—was more appropriately taught to younger children in the form of oral language lessons. The advantages of this pedagogy were that it allowed the use of familiar language arising from the pupils' own experience; the emphasis could more readily be placed on the meaning rather than on the form of the language. Both these claims to advantage derived from concepts in functionalist psychology: namely, the role of interest in learning, prior experience as a base for new learning, and the pupil as an active participant in the learning process.

By 1910, official policies in all three countries reflected the distinction between formal grammar for older pupils and language lessons for younger ones. Approved courses of studies and textbook authorizations directed and urged teachers not to teach technical terms too early and not to use textbooks with younger pupils but, instead, to emphasize oral teaching and to relate grammar instruction to work in composition and reading.

Postponement of formal grammar teaching: Canada

Canadian jurisdictions, unlike their counterparts in Australia and New Zealand, often specified their grammar courses in terms of particular textbooks, usually indicating the level of classes at which use of the text was permitted and sometimes indicating precisely which pages were to be studied at particular levels. In regard to grammar textbook policies, Ontario's adoptions often influenced the decisions made by other provincial departments of education from Victoria to Charlottetown. At his retirement in 1876, Ryerson had left three grammar texts in place. Senior classes used Miller's *Analytical and Practical English Grammar*, while either Davies' *English*

Grammar for Junior Classes or Morris' *English Grammar (Primer)* was available for use with younger pupils (Parvin, 1965). Under the previous Irish National course of study, grammar had established its starting point in the junior textbooks before the Third Book Class.

The practice of starting textbook study of grammar in the Third Class was formalized in the provincial courses of study that were issued from 1877, with the short-lived exception of the 1880 course, which had grammar beginning in Second Reader classes. In 1910, the formal study of textbook grammar was further deferred to Fourth Class, and a new textbook provided a fuller treatment of the subject. At the same time, a new and separate composition textbook was adopted to begin in the Third Class, which included an informal treatment of the elements of English grammar and served to prepare the pupil for the formal study of the subject in the Fourth Class.

Nova Scotia recognized the unsuitability of the formal study of English grammar for younger children in 1883, when a new common school grammar textbook was authorized to end the ten-year mandate of MacCabe's text. Published by A. & W. MacKinlay in Halifax, the first sentence of the page of suggestions to teachers said, "It is proposed that the textbook shall not be placed in the hands of pupils until they are prepared to enter upon the studies of the sixth grade of the Common School Course" (*An English Grammar for Schools*, 1883).

In 1890, the Council of Public Instruction issued a further directive on the use of the grammar text that somewhat amplified the statement in the preface to the textbook. It was to be used as a guide to the teacher until the end of Grade 8. In the lower grades, teachers were to select for instruction portions of the content "suitable to the age and ability of their pupils." Study of the text was to be completed by the end of Grade 8.

A much more stern regulation was issued by the Council in 1898. "The textbook has been abused to such an extent in English grammar, that after the present school year it is not authorized to be used in the hand of the common school grades." Common school teachers were to use a reference book for lessons on English (Kennedy and Marshall's *Lessons in English*), and the grammar text was reserved for the high school. In a critical statement about its own past policies, the Council justified its decision to drop the grammar text from the elementary grades by pointing out that there would be a financial saving for those parents whose children did not go on to high school and who would thus not need the text, "the study of which they would never complete and the memorization of which in many schools was more a torment than a benefit to them" (*Journal of Education*, 1898, p. 161).

The 1880, the New Brunswick course of instruction prescribed grammar as a textbook study for Grades 6 through 8. Sections of the textbook Robertson's *English Grammar and Analysis* were assigned for each of these grades. Grammar did appear under the heading "Language" for the fifth grade, but there it was to be taught orally, without a textbook, and teachers were directed to use the blackboard in those lessons. In the lower grades, claiming 60 percent of total instructional time, the same broad heading was for reading, composition, industrial drawing, and rote singing. The policy of deferring formal textbook grammar until completion of the first five grades of school was continued in the revised course of instruction approved in 1898. The grammar content for Grades 6 through 8 was defined by sections of a new textbook, Meiklejohn's *Short Grammar and Composition*, first authorized in 1891.

In Prince Edward Island after the 1840s, attempts to reform grammar teaching by both reducing teachers' dependence on textbooks and by postponing formal instruction to the older classes preoccupied the Province's school visitors for more than half a century. According to their annual reports, the school visitors or inspectors found the use and misuse of grammar textbooks to be a perennial issue. The frequent references to the dislocation caused by changes in the authorized grammar texts suggest that grammar teaching was heavily dependent on whatever text was available. In 1877, Mr. Stewart reported that books in use on the Island included Lennie's, MacCabe's, David's, and Currie's grammars. In 1879, Peter Curran said that "The teaching of grammar has been retarded by the frequent changes of textbooks in former years, from the evil effects of which the schools have not yet recovered." It appeared that teachers and pupils were confused by different versions of grammar. (That complaint was still being voiced in the 1894 report.) The problem seemed to be, as Visitor McNeill reported in 1845, "Our teachers in too many instances have entertained the idea that nothing could be done in [grammar] without a book in the hands of each child."

Complaints about reliance on memorization of material from the grammar text and about failures to achieve application and transfer continued through the rest of the century. In 1894, for example, Alexander Campbell observed, "English grammar is very well taught as to definitions, rules and analysis; but as to its practical utility it remains a mystery to the majority of pupils" (1894).

By the 1880s, attempts to reserve the formal study of textbook grammar for older pupils were being reflected in the provincial course of study. The 1882 course of study introduced grammar in the Fourth Class with oral lessons on the parts of speech, followed by a study of analysis from the first part of the grammar textbook, Currie's *Rudimentary Grammar*. Fifth Class pupils were expected to study the entire text and then go on to analysis, syntax, and prosody in the next two classes.

Teachers appear to have heeded the 1882 policy, because in 1894, Visitor John Balderston reported that "Elementary grammar is disappearing as beginners are taught orally" (1894). Presumably the word *elementary* referred to grade level, not to level of grammar.

A comment by Visitor Campbell in 1895 suggested that the spirit, if not the exact letter of the program of studies, was being followed. He noted that Prince Edward Island teachers introduced grammar orally in Grade 3, while study of the textbook began in Grade 4. In the 1900 Report there was a suggestion that grammar teaching at all levels was becoming less dominated by the textbook in the quotation from a newspaper report that, "The study of English is changing. Currie and Linney are no longer Sovereigns in the Kingdom of English." (*Linney* was probably a misspelling of Lennie.)

A number of early twentieth-century references to the issue, however, suggest a continuing need to promote alternatives to textbook grammar. The School Visitors' report for 1902 made reference to the Teachers' Association meeting of that year, at which a Mr. Stewart had made a plea for abolishing grammar textbooks in the lower grades, doing away with rote grammar entirely. The 1905 Report said that children were still being given the grammar text when they were too young. In the following year, the recommendation was made that children should observe the facts of language for themselves, and that grammar books were more of a hindrance to pupils in the junior grades. In 1910, a Commission on Education report said of grammar in the public schools, "At the last stage only should a textbook be placed in the pupil's hands" (p. 14)—a sentiment almost identical to the one expressed in the 1883 *An English Grammar for Schools* text quoted earlier.

By the first decade of the twentieth century, the other Canadian provinces were following similar policies of assigning formal or textbook grammar to the higher classes. In the 1870s, it was apparently the practice in Quebec to begin formal grammar instruction in the third year, based on the "limit table," or syllabus, prepared by the Protestant Board of School Commissioners for a four-year program leading to high school entrance. Two twenty-minute lessons per week were to be taught on the structure of sentences in the third year. A note said that a textbook for this work was in preparation. For the final year, the whole of the Ontario text, Davies' *Grammar for Junior Classes*, was to be studied.

In the 1898 course of study, grammar began in the third year with memoriter work, sentence drills, and parts of speech, and textbook study began in the fourth year. That was still the pattern in the 1906 course of study. However, in 1907, the Protestant Committee of the Council of Public Instruction directed that the textbook grammar was to begin in the seventh year of schooling with the first ninety-nine pages of West's *Grammar for Beginners*. This text was to be completed in the following year, while the ninth-year classes were to study West's *Elements of English Grammar*.

Manitoba's first program of studies, issued in 1882, began textbook grammar in the seventh of twelve five-month standards of work. This class was to begin the study of Mason's *Outlines of English Grammar*, while pupils completing the eighth standard were to have a thorough knowledge of the whole book. Mason's *English Grammar* was assigned to the ninth and tenth standards. In 1899, an item in the *Educational Journal of Western Canada* noted that in Manitoba "grammar is not begun until Grade 7 on account of the logical and psychological character of the subject." (p. 137) In the other two Prairie Provinces, formed out of the old Northwest Territories in 1905, the policy of the territorial Department of Education was continued with formal grammar beginning in Standard V (which corresponded to Grade 8, the final year of elementary schooling). The syllabus specification for Standard V grammar was simply, "An intelligent comprehension of the prescribed text," the *New Elementary Grammar* by David Goggin (who had been superintendent of education in the Northwest Territories). This was a widely used grammar text in the early years of the twentieth century, authorized in British Columbia, Manitoba, and Prince Edward Island, in addition to the two new Prairie Provinces.

Australia and New Zealand

In Australia and New Zealand, syllabus prescriptions for primary schools were usually not stated in terms of particular grammar textbooks. South Australia's syllabi were an exception to this practice, both before and after the New Education reforms. In the 1901–1902 syllabus, for example, the Fifth Class was "to learn as much grammar as is explained in Davidson and Alcock's first English grammar, and also the analysis of complex sentences." The 1910 syllabus prescribed pages from Arnold's *Lessons in Language* series.

The distinction between formal and functional grammar cannot, therefore, be made on the basis of use of grammar textbooks in courses of study approved by departments of education in these two countries, neither before nor after the great reforming syllabus revisions of the early 1900s. The general policy was to designate grammar, sometimes in some combination with composition, as a named part of the English studies program in Class Three and above. Again, South Australia was an exception, since grammar as such was specified for the Second Class as late as the program revision of 1910. In spite of the recommendation of the 1904 conference committee, the Queensland course of studies as revised in 1905 retained grammar in Class Three. So did the revisions in Victoria in 1905, in New South Wales in the same year, and in Tasmania in 1910.

The wording of the syllabus prefaces and notes suggested that the Australian reforming directors of education, Frank Tate, Peter Board, and William Neale, did not want any formal grammar taught in the primary schools. Referring to the program in Victoria's more senior primary classes, Tate was forthright about the need for a more practical approach to the subject.

> Parsing and analysis have been given, in the past, more than their due share of attention, and the grammar lessons have often meant little more than written exercises in these branches. ... It will be noted that only such grammatical rules and forms as are likely to be of practical use to the children are included, and the memorizing of rarely-used inflexional [sic] forms, and the dealing with rare syntactical rules and grammatical puzzles will not be required. (Course of Study and method of inspection and examination, 1905)

Director Peter Board expressed similar sentiments about grammar in New South Wales' revised syllabus, which set out guidelines for teachers in the preparation of their teaching programs. Formal grammar was to enter the syllabus "only in a very limited extent" before the beginning of the Higher Primary Course in Classes Six and Seven, when pupils had reached the age of thirteen to fifteen. The meaning of *to a very limited extent* may be inferred by contrast with the prescriptions for the more formal study of grammar for the two Higher Primary Classes, Class VI and VII. These were: "Parsing in full, analysis of sentences to show the relationships of clauses, subject and predicate, and the force of qualifying and modifying phrases." (p. 14) Presumably, pupils in Classes Three through Five were not to engage in these activities. In the two higher classes, one hour per week of formal grammar was permitted. As far as grammar textbooks were concerned, only pupils in the Upper Division of the primary course (Third and Fourth Readers) were permitted to study the subject from textbooks and then only if they were far advanced in it. Another condition was that the understanding and not the memory was to be exercised. The syllabus claimed that, "Grammatical accuracy does not demand a knowledge of formal grammar—it depends on imitation and on correction of errors as they occur."

In the Tasmanian syllabus revision of 1910, grammar was listed beginning in the Third Class for children who would have reached the age of ten. The emphasis in the Third and Fourth Class program, which allocated two lessons per week to grammar, was on a functional approach. In the next two classes, the Fifth and Sixth (pupils aged about twelve and thirteen), the study of grammar became more formal, and the lesson allocations for grammar were increased to three per week. The emphasis turned from synthesis to analysis, and full parsing was required by the end of the Sixth Class.

In its attitude to formal grammar, South Australia seemed to be at some variance with its state counterparts. The syllabus of 1873 had included a very rigorous grammar course, starting in Class One. However, John Anderson Hartley, the influential first inspector-general, "was never an enthusiast for English grammar" (Theile, 1975, p. 37). As early as 1885, the syllabus listed grammar and composition under the heading "English," and in the 1890s, the term *language* replaced *grammar* in the inspectors' register (Chant, 1985).

However, by the late 1890s, school inspectors were commenting about an official revival of formal grammar in the primary school syllabus. For example, Inspector Clark noted in 1899 that, "Formal grammar is in 1900 to have more attention given to it." A 1901 comment by the same inspector suggests that the rigor and perhaps method of the grammar examinations used by inspectors had something to do with its teaching in that more attention had been given to the examination of formal grammar. Also in 1901, another inspector, Mr. Smyth, hinted that there had been a return to a more rigorous form of written examination in grammar. "The written grammar, introduced after an interval of ten years, was very disappointing" (Report of the Board of Inspectors, 1901, p. 18).

It seems likely, therefore, that as the new liberal ideas about education were reaching the continent, South Australia, which had been recognized as a progressive state in education before 1900, was experiencing a conservative reaction to an earlier reduction in grammar's role in the primary curriculum. The political pressure from this reaction might explain why the syllabus of 1901–1902, in spite of its prefatory criticism of formal grammar teaching, contained a surprisingly heavy and traditional grammar component, beginning in Class Two—a practice, as pointed out above, that was retained in the 1910 syllabus revision.

In spite of the proclaimed intentions of the Australian syllabi, the actual prescriptions for the different classes of pupils did not speak so clearly and emphatically about the removal of formal grammar from the primary classroom. Much of the wording of the specifications for grammar had failed to pass beyond the formal study of language structures to a genuine functional approach. In Victoria's case, for example, grammar work was predominantly defined in the old vocabulary of propositional knowledge, such as "to have an intelligent knowledge of," "to distinguish," "to know," and "to analyze." Less prominent was the vocabulary of functional grammar: "to be able to use," "to arrange in the most effective manner," and "to construct." Only New South Wales succeeded in expressing the content of the grammar syllabus in a language that matched its intentions, giving more emphasis to synthesis than to analysis and to function than to definition. The old formal grammar terms, parsing and analysis, were retained.

Perhaps the dilemma for program developers was to present ideas about the pedagogy of grammar to teachers, using the vocabulary of the subject, without inadvertently authorizing the teaching of that vocabulary to school children. The reform syllabus that was adopted across the Tasman Sea in New Zealand in 1904 seemed to be more successful using the language of functional grammar in its explanation of its grammar content. Hogben's hostility to formal grammar was made very clear in the revision. He cautioned that although grammatical terms had been used in defining the work of composition for the standards, they were used only for the guidance of teachers, and it was "not intended that any grammar shall be introduced into the course of primary instruction except for the practical end above mentioned." Technical grammatical terms should be used very sparingly indeed. The syllabus for composition spent almost as much time on denials as on prescriptions.

What is required is not any exact definition of the terms *subject* and *predicate*. Complete analysis is not to be expected, nor are the children to be required to pick out adjective phrases and clauses, except in answer to such questions as those indicated above ... They need not even know the terms 'adjective phrase', 'adjective clause', etc., although the use of these terms may be found convenient. The distinction between the various tenses of the indicative, including the perfect forms, is to be taught by their use in sentences, but no parsing is to be insisted on, except such as is implied in analysis—e.g., the distinction between subject and object should be known but the terms *nominative* and *accusative* (or *objective*) need not be used. (p. 277)

Although the old terms *analysis* and *recognition* were used, much more emphasis was given to *synthesis*, building up sentences from other grammatical units. Recognition of parts of speech was to be by function. Variation in the form of sentences was to be taught and practiced. By the use of detailed examples, the concepts involved in teaching functionally were made clearer than in the Australian syllabi. That is not to say that the revised syllabus necessarily communicated more effectively to teachers; but there was a much greater congruence between the intentions as stated in the introduction and commentary and the wording of the prescriptions. To misinterpret the New Zealand syllabus as an authorization of formal grammar teaching would have been a more culpable offence than similar misinterpretation across the Tasman Sea.

Hogben's treatment of grammar represented the most radical reform of all the colonial jurisdictions. Formal teaching of the subject was to have no place whatever in the primary standards, and he offered only grudging acknowledgment that such teaching of grammar might have a role in secondary schooling. His syllabus was most explicit about the boundary between functional and formal grammar. For the new Standard VII, which would grow into state-sponsored secondary education, the syllabus noted that, "... the pupils might be expected to have a more explicit knowledge of the formal grammar implied in the composition of lower standards." (p. 277) The intention was to make formal grammar study a matter for the secondary school.

One of the achievements of New Education reforms was that the study of English grammar as an abstract, formal, and autonomous body of propositions about language structure, whose educational value lay in its training of the mind, was officially recognized as unsuitable for younger children, whether they were Canadians, Australians or New Zealanders. As the administrative distinction between primary and secondary education, the latter becoming recognized as a state responsibility by the end of the nineteenth century, became clearer, formal grammar defined by a textbook was in the process of being designated as a subject of study suitable only for the secondary level. Formal textbooks such as Nesfield's *Manual of English Grammar and Composition*, Seath's *High School English Grammar*, or Mason's *English Grammar* became revered or feared artifacts of secondary education. Although formal grammar was not entirely exorcised from the primary school as experienced by thousands of children, the arguments that it should be and the official policies to back the arguments up were in place by 1910.

Except that these last few statements are not really true. Formal grammar *was* banished from early Grades 1 through 6 in most, but not all, cases, but it was retained in Grades 7 and 8 (still elementary primary grades), to crystallize as a junior high school issue by the 1930s.

CHAPTER 14
The Effect of Examinations on Grammar Teaching

NAME THE PARTS OF SPEECH IN THIS SENTENCE: THE LADY SAID, IN SPEAKING OF THE WORD THAT, THAT THAT THAT, THAT THAT GENTLEMAN PARSED, WAS NOT THAT THAT, THAT SHE REQUESTED HIM TO ANALYZE.

A typical country day.

Beginning of school examinations

Together with official courses of study and prescribed textbooks, external examinations developed as a mechanism of central control of schools in the colonial educational systems. The central authorities could exercise great influence on what would be taught, even in remote schools, by what subjects were examined and by what kinds of questions were included on the papers. Set and marked by bodies external to the school, examinations served the purposes of determining promotion from one class to another within a level of education, such as the primary level; or from one level of schooling to the next, such as from primary to secondary or from secondary to university. They were also used to select pupils for scholarship purposes. In addition, examinations acted as credentialing devices, sorting school leavers for employment purposes.

Their significance for teachers was two-fold: first of all, teachers' professional ability was often judged by the examination performance of their pupils, and, secondly, they themselves had to pass examinations in order to gain admission to and graduation from teacher-training programs, as with pupil teachers or students in normal schools. Their career development through the levels of teacher licenses was also controlled by external examination.

While these uses of examinations are still found in modern education, it was the extent to which they pervaded public education in the second half of the nineteenth century and in the first part of the twentieth that made them uniquely significant in that period. In those years, preparing for examinations and writing examinations were inescapable annual ordeals for pupils and teachers in all jurisdictions.

Referring to the colony of Newfoundland, which created external examinations in 1893, Andrews (1985) called the seven-level system that soon developed, "A monster which made curriculum development at levels under its influence virtually impossible." Over sixty years earlier, a Canadian, H. J. Coleman, had complained that the formal and formidable high school entrance examination was "the greatest evil in our Ontario education," and a source of misery to parents, teachers, and pupils alike. Coleman went on to extend his criticism to the Canadian examination system that, he said, "Made an unwholesome appeal to the competitive instincts and overemphasized intellectual education at the expense of the emotions and the will" (Tompkins, 1986, p. 238).

EXAMINATIONS AT THE END OF PRIMARY

The New Education syllabus reforms in all three countries had to contend with an external examination at the end of primary schooling. Set and marked by departments of education, this examination consisted of separate papers in the main subjects taught n primary school. Called the Entrance Examination, it was in place in Ontario by 1873. By 1900, the other provinces had followed suit. New Zealand had formalized its examination, called the Certificate of Proficiency Examination, by 1902, and by 1912, the Australian states had their Qualifying Certificate Examination in place. The examination was based on the objectives of the primary course of studies. Candidates, aged approximately twelve to thirteen, would have completed the Canadian Standard IV (Standard V in the NWT) or Grade 8, Standard VI in New Zealand, and Class VI in Australia. This was the examination that maintained a tight grip on the primary school course of studies through the first three or four decades of the twentieth century, until it was replaced by school-based assessment in the 1930s and 1940s.

The examination had great educational and social significance. Its original function in Australia and New Zealand had been to provide school-leaving credentials as a sorting device for employment purposes. In New Zealand, for example, applicants for clerkships in both the Post Office and the Railways Department required a Certificate of Standard VI Attainment—the precursor of the Proficiency Certificate —after 1891 (McKenzie, D., 1982). In addition, as the state began to play a larger role in secondary education, the end-of-primary examination became a means of controlling passage from a universal system of primary schooling to a restrictive and selective secondary education.

This can be seen in the boosting of the prestige of New Zealand's Proficiency Certificate when, in 1902, Hogben introduced a system of free places for two years of post-primary education. The Certificate became a prerequisite for admission to these free places. Since there were more applicants for the free places than the post-primary system could accommodate, Proficiency Certificates became objects of fierce competition and community pride. New Zealand teachers became adept at preparing their Standard VI pupils for the Proficiency examinations.

However, success in examinations came at the expense of the principles of the New Education, not only in Standard VI but throughout the primary school, as the work for each standard became oriented to eventual success in the examination. In other words, the popular demand for examination preparation had a conservative effect on the curriculum, one of the worst being the encouragement of cramming.

These school-leaving or entrance examinations had evolved from more informal and local assessments. In the early years of the new colonial school systems, local inspectors were responsible for examining pupils for both promotion and graduation purposes. A description of an early examination conducted as part of a school inspection comes from an 1887 report from Quebec. Having arrived at the school of Miss Euphemia Clarke of Geneva in the County of Argenteuil at 11:30 a.m., the inspector announced the afternoon inspection to the children, asking them to invite their parents to attend. He then was to call on parents who lived near the school and offer them a personal invitation. At 1:00 p.m. the inspection began. Scholars who could take dictation were separated from the younger ones, and the inspector dictated "some simple, comprehensive questions in history, grammar, and geography" and wrote some arithmetic problems on the board. While the pupils were answering these questions, the inspector collected attendance figures from the teacher and inspected the copy books. He then tested oral reading individually, using what he called simultaneous reading. "An exact imitation of an exemplar set by the teacher … After recess, the children were called up with slate and copy book in lines as they sat, [waiting] to 'stand up,' 'stand out,' 'face,' and 'come up' with as much military precision as possible." Each was then marked for dictation, written answers, copy books and sums, the slates and copy books being passed from visitor to visitor. Prizes for proficiency and for attendance were awarded, bonus proficiency points being awarded to younger pupils and bonus attendance points to those who had to travel further to school. The first prize was for attendance and the second for proficiency. The names of the winners were forwarded to the local newspapers (Percival, 1946).

In New Zealand, it became practice in the 1880s for inspectors to examine children orally in the first two standards and to use written or printed questions in the higher standards, including Standard VI, where the examination determined graduation and the award of a school-leaving certificate. Inspector Smith of Westland stated in 1881 that his written tests in Standard III and up caused many children to "fail to do themselves and their teachers justice." Presumably, they were unused to written examinations. Petrie, the inspector for Otago, described his procedures in 1883; he gave Standard III pupils printed questions in grammar to be answered at their desks on either paper or slates. This would permit the busy inspector to carry out the other aspects of an inspection visit while some of the children in the school were writing the examination.

Smith of Westland noted in 1889 that he used passages from the Reading books in his grammar examinations in Standards V and VI, the practice in other inspectorates, but that because of poor results in Westland, he was going to limit his selections to the first half of each book in future. In 1885, Taylor of Otago thought that a low percentage of passes in Standard VI grammar that year had been caused by his use of a passage of poetry in the parsing question. With regard to passing grammar examinations, Hill of Hawke's Bay reported in 1883 that he set 60 percent for a pass in grammar in Standard IV and up.

However, by this time, in the interests of uniform standards, departments of education were beginning to exert control over the examination function of local inspectors. In New Zealand this took the form of published test cards distributed to inspectors and teachers to guide promotion and school-leaving examinations. Their convenience rather than compulsion made these tests the option of choice. In South Australia, on the other hand, control was exercised by regulation. In 1882, Chief-Inspector Hartley sent a letter to all his local inspectors directing them on the preparation and conduct of their school examinations. The following were to be the procedures for examinations in English grammar:

> Class Two. On slate. The inspector may make his own sentences to examine from unless teachers prefer to have one taken from the Reader. Children to write in columns all the nouns, adjectives, verbs and pronouns (at least 12 words) and to give the reason (as in Abbott) of two words selected by the inspector. Time allowed one minute for each word that should be picked out by children. Two errors allowed. Words leading to more than one mistake to count as one error only. Sentences containing abstract nouns to be avoided.

> Class Three. Inspector to select twelve words from a sentence of his own composing or from a passage in R. Reader if the teacher prefers it, six of them to be above words for the second class standard. The parts of speech and the reason (as in Abbott) of each word to be given by the children. Three errors in the whole allowed, four errors to fail. Time allowed twenty minutes. Same word leading to two mistakes to count only as one.

> Class Four. Parsing and at the discretion of the inspector re inflections, etc.

> Class Five. Parsing and analysis of simple and complex sentences. Inflections at the discretion of the inspector. (Extracts from the confidential letterbook of the south Australian Inspector of Schools, 1880–1914)

Grammar could be a separate paper or it could be linked with some other part of English study, such as composition, orthoepy, dictation, or spelling.

Sometimes, especially later, grammar questions could appear in a paper called Language or English.

A major effect, one that is entirely predictable, is that cramming and memorization were encouraged. An 1894 comment by an examiner included the comment that although the average of marks on the junior grade examination had been fairly high, the favorable impression produced had to be modified by, "the consideration that a considerable proportion of the marks was gained by mere memory work; the questions which involved thought were not, on the whole, so well done." In 1902, the examiner complained that in the Primary Level grammar paper there had been, "Meaningless reproduction of what had evidently been committed to memory without being understood." In 1915, a comment on the results of the same paper noted that in the answers, "Terms were used and matter given which could hardly have been understood at this (Grade 6) level." Sixteen years later, the Grade 7 and 8 examiner noted that, "Hundreds gave a good definition of gerund and then proceeded to name all the six words in the passage with -ing ending as geruduns" (1931).

In a few cases, memorization too obviously affected answers on the composition questions. In 1934, a comment on the Grade 9 composition paper noted. "In a few cases essays were written that had been learned by heart," the subject being "A Winter Landscape." The same examiner also reported, rather triumphantly, that "A group of very pretentious essays on a ship-wreck, all with the same wording, were discounted accordingly."

EXAMINATION QUESTIONS ON ENGLISH GRAMMAR PAPERS

The fact of external examinations in English grammar was a statement about the subject's importance; the nature of the questions that candidates were required to answer shaped the content of the grammar course. Questions that examiners used made different demands on grammatical knowledge and skill. Five kinds of questions can be identified:

- a. recall of propositional information
- b. analysis and parsing
- c. correction
- d. language manipulation; and
- e. language production

A. Recall of propositional information

Many questions, especially those on nineteenth-century papers, required recall, with or without comprehension or propositional information. They could ask for the definition of grammatical terms, the statement of rules, the explanation of grammatical processes, the listing of paradigms, the explication of theories, and the account of grammatical changes in the language. To answer these questions required no use or application of the information; they tested some degree of mastery of grammar as information about language structure and its classifications, and in some cases questions asked for textbook-specific information.

An 1850 grammar examination from the Upper Canada Normal School shows the dominance of propositional questions in the middle of the century. Of the twenty-nine questions on the paper, twenty-six could have been answered on the basis of recall of either textbook or lecture information, while only three required analysis and some manipulation of samples of text (Martyn, 1932).

The following is a list of examples of propositional questions culled widely from the Colonial records.

1. Give a full account of the verb. (New South Wales Examination for Candidates in Training at the Model Normal Schools, 1859)

2. When is 'who' applied to inferior animals? (List of 101 questions for local examining boards prepared by the Superintendent of Education for Lower Canada, 1861)

3. When does Shakespeare use the subjunctive mood after 'if'? Give examples. (1889 Class I Teachers' Licence Examination, New Brunswick, p. 51)

4. How many kinds of conjunctions are given in Lennie's *Grammar*? Give examples of each kind. (New South Wales Pupil Teachers' Second Class Examination, 1891)

5. Distinguish (with examples): (a) transitive and intransitive verbs; (b) simple and gerundial infinitives. (Tasmania Junior Public Examination, 1892)

6. Define Adjective, Gender, Imperative Mood, Syntax. (Newfoundland Junior Grade Examination, 1894)

7. Write all you know about the indefinite pronouns as they are treated in Meiklejohn's *Grammar*. (1896 Quebec Model School Grade 111/ Academy Grade 1 English Grammar, p. 236)

8. Why are adjectives compared? (1904, South Australia Qualifying Examination)

9. Classify pronouns and give examples of each class in sentences. (Manitoba Grade 9 Grammar, 1925)

10. What does Bradley mean by phonetic change? (Nova Scotia Grade 12 English, 1958)

B. Analysis and parsing

These questions were the most enduring on English grammar examinations, lasting, in a reduced form, in some jurisdictions until the 1960s. In a sense they were application questions, since they required the allocation of previously unseen words and structures to grammatical categories. However, these questions were designed to test mastery of the categories—they dealt with the propositional content of grammar, not its application to language performance. Proponents of analysis and parsing would, however, have claimed that the activities laid bare both the grammatical structure of the samples involved and their thought structure; therefore, those questions were testing skills related to reading comprehension. Nevertheless, comprehension itself was not assessed, except, in a most generous interpretation, that successful analysis might depend on prior comprehension.

The level of difficulty in parsing and analysis questions could easily be adjusted by means of the samples provided for dissection. Sentences could be relatively simple or exceedingly complex; prose or poetry passages could be straightforward or convoluted. The following is a listing of parsing and analysis questions from a broad range of grammar papers.

1. Give the general analysis of:
   As he plucked his cursed steel away,
   Mark how the blood of Caesar followed it,
   As rushing out of doors to be resolved,
   If Brutus so unkindly knocked or no. (Class I Teachers' Licence Examination, New Brunswick 1884)

2. Analyze the following passage (from Milton's Paradise Lost):
   Too well I see, and rue the dire event,
   That with sad overthrow, and foul defeat
   Hath lost us heaven, and all this might host
   In horrible destruction laid thus low,
   As far as gods and heavenly essences

Can perish. (Class II Teachers' Licence Examination, Prince Edward Island 1886)

3. Parse each word of the following sentence:
But me no buts. (Class I Teachers' Licence Examination, New Brunswick 1884)

4. Parse the words ending in -ing in the following passage:
"He told me with a bumpkin grin,
A weakly intellect denoting,
He'd rather not invest it in
A company of my promoting." (Class E and Junior Civil Service English Grammar and Composition, New Zealand 1888)

5. You are to teach a lesson to a primary class on subordinate clauses. Your students furnish you with the following examples:
His being king displeased the nobles, for who would reverence such a king as he?
Hadst thou been there, my brother had not died.
Select, classify and give the relation of the subordinate clauses in these sentences. (Ontario School of Pedagogy Methods in English Paper (for Specialists) 1895)

6. Write out a long sentence of your own making, then analyse it, and tell what part of speech each word in it is. (Quebec Protestant Committee 1895)

7. Point out the adjectives in:
Under a spreading chestnut tree
The village smith stands.
The smith, a mighty man is he,
With large and sinewy hands. (Grade 1 Model School English Grammar, Quebec 1906)

8. Give a detailed analysis of the following sentence, and parse the italicized words:
Almost the first act of William after establishing his power in England, was to distribute the unredeemed lands of the English among the nobles who had aided him in the conquest. (Grade 9 Grammar, Manitoba 1925)

9. Analyze the following passage and parse the eight words in italics:
   When winter nights are piercing chill,
   When through the hawthorn blows the gale,
   With solemn feet I tread the hill
   That overlooks the lonely vale. (Qualifying Certificate Examination, South Australia 1932)

10. Analyze the following passage:
    When I came to my castle, I fled into it like one pursued; whether I went over by the ladder or went in at the hole which I called a door, I cannot remember; for never frightened have fled to cover with more terror of mind than I to this retreat. (Grade 9 Examination, Newfoundland 1934)

C. Correction

As both practice and assessment, exercises in false syntax (also called false grammar, or false English), date back to the first half of the nineteenth century. Grammarians had enthusiastically mined English literature for examples of infelicitous sentences found wanting by their normative rules. As an instructional activity, exercises in false grammar had become controversial by the end of the century, as educators began to worry that if children indeed learned language by imitation, as the new theories were claiming, the presentation of bad examples might lead them astray.

In spite of this worry, questions calling for the correction of grammatical errors remained popular in grammar examinations. This activity was a more authentic application of grammar knowledge to language use, except that an examination candidate might be able to correct a sentence on the basis of a more intuitive sense of linguistic propriety rather than by an appeal to the explicit and conscious body of knowledge that constituted grammar. To prevent this bypass, examiners simply asked candidates to justify or give reasons for their corrections, thereby retaining an emphasis on propositional knowledge. The following are examples of such questions:

1. Criticize the following expressions; account for any alternations you would suggest:
   The mail is arrived.
   A large quantity of people was present.
   Etc. (Examination Papers of Candidates in Training at the Model National Schools, New South Wales 1859)

2. Correct or justify:
   During the three or four first years of its existence.
   The hay smells sweetly.
   Etc. (Class E Teacher and Civil Service Examination in English
   Grammar and Composition, New Zealand 1881)

3. Discuss the grammar of these passages:
   Better than him I am before knows me.
   What he is indeed more suits you to conceive than I to speak of.
   (Senior Public Examination in English, Tasmania 1891)

4. Point out the faults in the following, and rewrite each sentence so as
   to avoid the faults:
   Every competitor will only be allowed to get one medal.
   Those kind of things are no use.
   Etc. (English B. Examination for Junior National Scholarships
   and Free Places in Secondary Schools, New Zealand 1905)

5. Correct where necessary, and give reasons for correction:
   The boy drunk the water.
   Being a wet day I wore my raincoat.
   Etc. (Grade 10 Grammar, Manitoba 1925)

6. Rewrite the following sentences in improved form with the least
   possible alteration (no comment is required):
   The judge imposed a heavy fine on the prisoner, who, being
   unable to pay, the police arrested him.
   Etc. (English Language and Literature for Training College
   Entrance, New Zealand 1930)

D. Language manipulation

Another form of grammar question involved changing a given piece of text in
some way. At the word level that could consist of changing words from one
part of speech to another. At the sentence level it could involve operations
such as changing the verb from active to passive voice or from present to
past tense, reducing clauses and phrases to adjectives or adverbs, completing
partial sentences by adding subjects or predicates, or joining simple sentences
to form compound or complex sentences. Questions calling for this type of
manipulation required a level of grammatical knowledge that was much more
functional and more related to the kind of language choices that have to be

made in composition. However, even here some knowledge of grammatical information was required, because the questions often used the technical language of grammar in the instructions. Some examples follow.

1. Write down the past tense and past participle of 'sing,' etc. (Junior Public Examination in English Grammar, Tasmania 1892)

2. Vary the expression in each of the following sentences by changing the voice:
    The boy struck the ball.
    Paris Green destroys potato bugs.
    Etc. (Entrance Examination, Manitoba 1920)

3. Change the following compound sentences into complex:

    Wolfe died from a wound received on the Plains of Abraham, but his body was buried in England. etc. (Grade 9 English Examination, Nova Scotia 1925)

4. The verb in the sentences below is in the present tense and active voice. Rewrite the sentence, putting the verb in the past tense and passive voice:
    George is doing the work very carefully. (Grade 8 Grammar, Alberta 1931)

5. Combine the following into two sentences:
    This scheme was blown up. I had some thoughts of shipping back to England again. I fell into company with an Irish student. He was returning from Louvain. Our conversation turned upon topics of literature. There was no Greek taught in the University of Louvain. Not two men in the whole university understood Greek. This I learned from him. I was amazed. I resolved to travel to Louvain instantly. I resolved to live there by teaching Greek. (Public Service Entrance Examination, New Zealand 1940)

E. Language production

Whereas questions calling for classification required candidates to place given samples of language into unique grammatical categories, a variation was to present a category and ask the candidate to give an example. Questions like these were slightly more open-ended but still demanded knowledge of technical terms, which must have made their answers more difficult to mark.

1. Construct a complex sentence of not less than twenty-five words. This sentence must not be compound. (Grade 2 Academy Examination 1898)

2. Give examples showing how the predicate may be modified by (a) a word, (b) a phrase, (c) a subordinate sentence. (Exhibitions and Bursary Examinations, Grammar 1905)

3. Write a sentence to illustrate each of the following: infinitive adjective phrase; participle in the absolute construction. (Matriculation, Prince Edward Island 1920)

4. Illustrate each of the following in sentences: (a) nominative absolute, (b) adverbial adjunct ... etc. (Grade 11 Composition, Manitoba 1925)

5. Construct sentences showing the infinitive form used as a noun and as an adjective. (Training College Entrance Examination, English Language and Literature, New Zealand 1931)

END-OF-PRIMARY EXAMINATIONS IN NEW ZEALAND

It is difficult to assess the precise impact of the Proficiency Examinations produced by the New Zealand Department of Education on teaching between 1900 and 1936, when the external examination at the conclusion of primary education was finally abolished. Complete sets of the English papers included in the annual examinations have not been retained in New Zealand archival collections. Goddard (1967) was able to find copies of seven English papers in the Proficiency Examinations set between 1928 and 1935. While he did not identify the actual papers, they were probably the formal language papers, which, together with papers in comprehension, dictation, and spelling, comprised the English part of the examination. Goddard provided an analysis of grammar questions on these formal language papers using two categories. The first he called formal grammar, which included analysis and parsing activities, questions on case, tense, mood, voice, number, structure of sentences (complex, compound, etc.), and grammatical explication of sentence faults. The second category he called "fringe" grammar, into which fell questions that involved punctuation, correction and improvement of sentences without explanation in grammatical terms, phonology, and word structure. The results of this analysis showed considerable variation from year to year.

In his unpublished Diploma of Education thesis, Goddard (1967, p. 23) assessed the percentages of grammar questions, fringe grammar questions, and non-grammar questions in selected Proficiency examinations from 1928 to 1935.

Year	Percent Grammar Questions	Percent Fringe Grammar Questions	Percent Non-Grammar Questions
1928	32	16	52
1932	0	80	10
1933	40	60	0
1934	100	0	0
1935	50	50	0

Table 2 P. R. Goddard, Proficiency Exam Results

None of the four papers that I was able to examine showed the extreme emphasis on formal grammar that Goddard found for his two 1934 examples. One was from 1932 and the other three were from 1935. All were entitled *English Part I Formal Language*; all were allotted fifty marks and were of thirty-minute duration. There were to be no formal grammar questions, while on each of Papers Six, Eight, and Twelve for 1935, two out of the ten questions would be classified as formal grammar. In each case one question called for the identification of the parts of speech in a sentence, and the other required sentence and clausal analysis. In all four cases the remaining questions would have been what Goddard called "fringe grammar" questions, requiring punctuation, correction without reasons, and various kinds of transformations of given words, phrases, or sentences.

From this analysis of a very small sample of English papers from the later years of the Proficiency Examination, it seems that pupils taking the examination were liable to encounter questions about formal grammar, although they did not appear every year, and in most years they did not constitute a majority of the questions. The fact that most of these analyzed papers were set after the 1929 syllabus revision, which once again had asserted the futility of formal grammar teaching, raises the possibility that the proportion of formal grammar questions might have fallen from the level that prevailed after the 1919 regulations were introduced. This, however, is conjecture.

The survival of formal grammar questions after the Red Book's strong condemnation of that approach to language teaching is another example of the mismatch between the department's curriculum aims and its evaluation practices. There is no doubt that, faced with discrepancies between syllabus and examinations, teachers would put more faith in preparing their pupils for the examination than for the syllabus. This was likely the reason why the Red Book's criticism of formal grammar was still relevant so long after Hogben's syllabus had tried to get rid of it.

It is worth noting that the *New Zealand Education Gazette* carried a notice in 1926 explaining changes in the proficiency examinations. These changes, the notice said, were to achieve greater objectivity in marking and to eliminate the personal factor.

END-OF-PRIMARY EXAMINATIONS IN AUSTRALIA

In 1903, the *South Australia Education Gazette* listed the provisional prospectus for the primary public examinations to be held in August of 1904. There were to be three papers in English: grammar, composition, and dictation. In the grammar paper, candidates could expect to find questions on "elementary grammatical distinctions, including inflexions; parsing and analysis of sentences; the detection of grammatical errors; and the meaning of words in common use."

The 1904 examination paper itself was published in the *South Australia Educational Gazette* in the following year. It was a two-hour paper worth eighty marks, and Inspector Burgan was the departmental official responsible for it. All ten questions required knowledge of formal grammar. One question required recall of propositional information in the form of definitions of the given terms: proper noun, neuter gender, passive voice, weak verb, gerund, and imperative mood. Another propositional recall question asked for an explanation of why adjectives are compared.

Three questions involved parsing and analysis, two of them using the sentence, "In this foolish way they would have pursued their *journey*, but *passing* together through the next village they *met* a little boy *who* looked up and said, 'Why do they travel in this silly way?'" (1905, p. 53) There was one question in the category of sentence correction, with reasons to be given. Three questions required candidates to give their own examples to illustrate particular grammatical concepts, such as writing three sentences to show the use of the word "that" as a conjunction, as a relative pronoun, and as a demonstrative pronoun. Finally, two questions involved manipulation of given examples according to technical instructions. For example, "Give the comparative and superlative degrees of 'bad', 'much', 'little'," etc.

Although the questions were a psychometrically varied set, the variation was all in the different ways of testing the candidates' knowledge of formal grammar; no question could have been adequately answered without knowledge of the technical language of formal grammar (1905, p. 122).

END-OF-PRIMARY EXAMINATIONS IN CANADA

Manitoba

In 1920 the Manitoba Entrance Examination paper in grammar, mandatory for all schools, was heavily weighted towards formal grammar. There were questions on parsing and analysis; the kind of verb that can be changed from the active to the passive voice; changes to be made in the voice of verbs in sentences; and possessives; one called for sentences to be corrected and reasons given. The 1930 paper, two years before the department abolished the entrance examination, still emphasized classification, analysis, and parsing. Tabular forms for analysis and parsing were very popular on this 1930 paper; one form for a parsing question using the headings Classification, Inflections, and Syntax.

Prince Edward Island

Pupils seeking entrance to high school in Prince Edward Island in 1921 were required to write six papers in their Public School Certificate Examinations covering the elementary course of studies. English was one paper dealing with the "Fourth reader throughout, spelling, grammar (textbook throughout)." The grammar text in use was still Goggin's *New Elementary Grammar*. On the English paper of that year, three questions were concerned with formal grammar, with the italicized words to be parsed: "Give the clausal analysis of the following: '*This people*, which thus *became British* by a campaign and a treaty, was destined to form the solid core around *which* should grow the vast Confederation of Canada.'" The third formal grammar question required correction of sentences with reasons for changes. Other questions involved dictation, recall of information from the reader, memorized poetry, and a business letter (PEI Examination papers, 1921, pp. 8–9).

Atlantic Provinces

In Nova Scotia in 1925 and 1926, formal grammar was represented by analysis and parsing questions on the Grade 8 County Academy Entrance Examination paper, The English Language. In 1926, candidates had to analyze the following: "(a) *Tell me* not in mournful *numbers*, life is *but* an empty *dream*. (b) The fact *that* the man had been in prison *could* not be *denied*." A question requiring sentence correction with reasons was also included, and another formal grammar question required candidates to pick out adverbs, prepositions, and adjectives from sentences.

A 1927 item in a Halifax newspaper complained that "Teaching English in Nova Scotia has been too much of a parrot fashion learning of a textbook on English Grammar by the students in order to answer questions on an examination paper" (*A Nova Scotian Looking On*, 1927). Similar complaints about the formal nature of questions on grammar had been made earlier in New Brunswick, as well as clear across the country in British Columbia.

In the colony of Newfoundland, examinations were a particular scourge. In 1893, the government created the Council of Higher Education to prescribe syllabi and textbooks and to organize examinations for Newfoundland secondary schools in an attempt to bring some uniformity to the diverse denominational schools of the colony (Andrews, 1985, p. 21). The Council had been the brainchild of Brother Slattery, a teacher with the Irish Christian Brothers, a religious order that operated schools in the colony. He had won the $100 prize offered by the Colonial Government for the best essay addressing the problems of education in Newfoundland, and the government enacted legislation to implement his proposals. The Council contracted with the Joint Examining Board of Cambridge and London Universities for the setting and marking of the examinations. This contract was later switched to the College of Preceptors, an affiliate of London University. In 1932, responsibility for the examinations was transferred to the Common Examining Board of the Maritime Provinces and Newfoundland.

At first there were two levels of examination: junior grade for pupils who had reached the age of twelve and senior grade. By the early twentieth century, the number of levels rose to as many as seven, covering Grades 6 through 12.

The effects of these external examinations on schooling in Newfoundland were described by a 1933 report by British inspector Richardson, commissioned to advise on education in the colony. "Every child," he said, "is regarded at any rate through the greater part of his school life as a potential examination candidate," and is put through "the same machine irrespective of his individual qualities and capacities," the curriculum machine being "predominantly of a formal and artificial nature" (Andrews, 1985, p. 164). The inspector also noted that public opinion tends to judge schools and teachers by examination results.

Since it was the practice to publish the results of these public examinations in the newspapers, candidates being listed in order of marks obtained, there was a particular poignancy to Richardson's final comment. He also noted a special inappropriateness about the examination-driven curriculum in Newfoundland. Whereas in Britain the examination syllabi were used in selective secondary schools, attended by only 10 percent of children over the age of eleven years—presumably the most able selection—in the colony, the formal abstract program was used for *all* older children attending school. In 1900 this comment was made on the Primary Level grammar paper, which was written by children at the Grade 6 level:

> The paper set appears to have been beyond the capabilities of the candidates. This is to be regretted because otherwise they would undoubtedly have acquitted themselves better than they have done. (1900, p. 58)

Prairie Provinces

In Alberta and Saskatchewan, the entrance examinations at the end of Standard V were a significant marker in a pupil's schooling. John Charyk gave an account of the Entrance Examination in the prairies in the early years of the century:

> The Entrance Year was certainly the most important year as far as rural teachers and students were concerned. It meant writing the all-important Final Examinations set by the Department of Education. Rural teachers soon became aware of the fact that their competence was judged on the ability of their students to pass these examinations. For many students it was the end of their formal education as the examination meant a great deal to them too. [...] Examination results were published in the daily newspapers in mid-August and reprinted in the local community weeklies. (Charyk, 1973, pp. 252, 287)

Alberta's elementary syllabus was reformed in 1922 (see Chapter 16), and major changes were made to the grammar program. Its role was redefined and its introduction as a formal subject delayed until Grade 7 on the grounds that young minds lacked the reasoning power required to understand the explanations and had to resort instead to memorization.

The new syllabus acknowledged that the teaching of grammar in the public schools had formerly had little effect on speaking and writing and that the role of the syllabus was to make knowledge of grammar conscious and explicit, to provide a set of terms that children should learn in order to talk about language, to prepare pupils for the advanced study of foreign languages, to facilitate comprehension, and, even more surprisingly, to discipline the mind. An inductive method was recommended. In the actual prescriptions for Grade 7 and 8, the grammar content followed the old grammar of the word, with parts of speech being allocated to Grade 7 and sentence analysis to Grade 8.

In spite of this reform in the direction of functional grammar, questions on the grammar paper in the Grade 8 Public School Leaving Examination remained formal in their demands on candidates. The 1922 paper, called "Grammar and Composition," was a two and one-half hour examination that had fifty marks for grammar and seventy-five for composition. The grammar section started with a short passage, rather dated even for that year. Its content revealed what seems to modern readers a quaint, patriotic attachment to the British Empire.

> We pray that when the end of this long and glorious reign comes,
> the subjects of Her Majesty in South Africa shall have learned
> to appreciate those British institutions which in this age and in
> every land signify liberty and equal rights.

Candidates were required to indicate the subordinate clauses and explain the grammatical relations of each. They were also required to give particular forms of words and to classify parts of speech. A passage of poetry was given for further analysis, and two underlined words were to be parsed.

> Around her lovers, newly <u>met</u>
> 'Mid deathless love's acclaims,
> <u>Spoke</u> evermore among themselves
> Their heart-remembered names.

Perhaps the new syllabus had not had time to influence the 1922 examination, but nine years later the grammar questions on the same paper were just as formidable.

1. Parse each word in this sentence: So, without undue delay or inconvenience, everyone should arrive safely.

2. Give a detailed analysis of this sentence: The depth of that swift and silent stream no one has yet estimated accurately. (Alberta Department of Education, Departmental Examinations, 1931. Grade VIII. Grammar and Composition)

Mr. Tim Byrne, former deputy minister of education for the province of Alberta, described how one Alberta teacher in a one-room rural school prepared her Grade 8 pupils for the grammar paper. He recalled his eighth-grade year in a rural school west of Edmonton in about 1918. His teacher, a woman from Nova Scotia, had decided that he was to be entered for the Grade 8 provincial examinations. He proceeded to study grammar from the textbook, largely as an independent study, since only four pupils in the school were preparing for the examination. Byrne was the only one of the four who passed the grammar paper. He did not recall learning any grammar before the Grade 8 year; it was the Reader that dominated the curriculum before Grade 8 (Byrne, 1984).

As was the case in many jurisdictions, the Manitoba Department of Education often published examination papers in subsequent editions of their teachers' magazine. This was a means of showing teachers the standard to which they were expected to teach, and it was unashamedly a means by which teachers could coach and rehearse their Standard V or Grade 8 pupils for their forthcoming ordeal. In 1899, the *Western School Journal* published grammar papers, used in a few schools, "With the hope that they will prove valuable term tests in many of the schools of the province." The Grade 8 examination paper for 1908 would have been the source of considerable rehearsal, as it consisted of a particularly strong emphasis on classification, analysis, and parsing of parts of speech. Other questions called for production of examples of grammatical concepts, definitions, and paradigms. A manipulation question involved combining sentences according to a keyed code.

In 1925, the *Western School Journal* published a Grade 8 examination paper in grammar, "So that all teachers will be able to help their classes as well as make them familiar with the new type of questions" that would be used in the next department examination. The novelty referred to was mainly in the use of fill-in-the-blank question formats, with pupils answering on the paper itself. The emphasis on formal grammar, however, was not reduced. The 1930 paper kept the new format, except that tabular forms instead of small blanks were used for the answers. Perhaps it was all to make the task of marking easier!

This use of past examinations is described in the following anecdotes. At about the time of the First World War, Mrs. Nordstrum from Wildwood, Alberta, built a collection of departmental examinations, and every May and June she would prepare her students for the Entrance or Grade 8 Departmental Examinations by giving them practice in working typical questions (Charyk, 1973).

Miss Helen Fowler, who began her rural teaching career in Nova Scotia fresh from the Truro Teachers' College in the early 1930s, described how she would spread out her ten-year collection of departmental examinations in her lodgings and try to detect patterns in the sequences of questions from year to year. She then short-listed likely questions for the coming June and had her examination pupils in the one-room school rehearse their answers to them. From her own school days in the 1920s, she recalled that Grade 8 pupils practiced writing examinations in April and May. They were allowed to study at home or in school during these months, but they were exhorted to stay out of local cafes (Fowler, H., 1983).

Teacher Certification

Initially, as state systems were struggling to establish themselves, teacher certification was left to the local decision of school boards and superintendents. The rustic nature of early certification procedures is seen in an account of the interview experienced by an applicant for a teaching position in King's County, Nova Scotia, under the system of County Boards of Commissioners, set up in 1826. The commissioner to whom the candidate had first applied confessed his own lack of qualifications to conduct an examination and referred the man to a better qualified member of the Board.

> This gentleman was found in the act of shaving. Pausing occasionally during the operation, he put to the candidate a few general questions. When his toilet was completed, however, he requested the young teacher to go with him to his general store. Here the candidate was required to solve a question in vulgar fractions, to read a few lines from Milton's *Paradise Lost*, and parse a portion of the passage read. All this having been done to the examiner's satisfaction, the certificate was made out and signed, first by him and then by the commissioner earliest called upon. (Eaton, 1910, pp. 342–343)

A colorful account of an early grammar examination from Upper Canada (Ontario) for a teaching licence has survived. R. W. Bigg, prospective teacher in the Midland District, presented himself for his certificate examination at the home of William Hutton, school superintendent for the county. Bigg found the superintendent ploughing a field, and the examination was conducted as they both walked behind the plough.

> [After a test of spelling] Hutton's grand attack was in Grammar, and he asked me to state what part of speech were each of the nine 'that's' which were in the following sentence: 'The lade said in speaking of the word 'that' that that that that that gentleman parsed was not that that that she requested him to analyze.' Having gone through this satisfactorily, I was complimented by the superintendent and informed that I was the first teacher he had examined who had parsed all the 'that's' correctly, and … at the house he wrote me out the required Certificate of Qualification (Martyn, 1932, p. 18).

Central control over teacher certification was tightening, as revealed by the rules and regulations published in the 1861 Report of the Superintendent of Education for Lower Canada (Quebec). Local boards of examiners were given detailed instructions on the examination of candidates for teaching licenses. Candidates who were at least eighteen years of age and of good moral character as testified by a clergyman were to complete a dictation exercise using a page randomly chosen from the Third Reader. In the event that an excessive number of errors in orthography occurred or that the handwriting was poor, the examination could be terminated at that point. Otherwise the candidate was to go on to read aloud and explain a portion of the same text. This exercise was followed by an individual oral examination in different subjects, including English grammar. To assess knowledge of this subject, examiners could choose from lists of questions provided by the Superintendent's Office. The list for an elementary teaching certificate consisted of 101 questions about grammar. Examples were "What is grammar?," "What is a verb?," "Conjugate negatively and present and perfect indicative of the verb 'to love'."

By the 1860s, the Australian states had regulations in place governing the classification of pupil teachers, teaching assistants who were employed in an apprenticeship capacity under a regular teacher. Tasmania, for example, following the example of New South Wales, adopted this method of teacher training in 1854 from the pattern of the Irish National Board. Pupil teachers had to have reached the age of at least thirteen. In 1859, the report of the Board of Education listed requirements for five levels of pupil teachers, specifying topics in English grammar to be mastered as part of the criteria for classification at each level. By the 1860s, the Tasmanian Board of Education had written examinations in place to test pupil teachers' mastery of these requirements, and textbooks were prescribed as preparation for the examinations. Performance on the papers in English grammar featured prominently in annual reports.

In New South Wales, the 1855 Report of the Commissioners of National Education included a regulation on teacher certification.

> Attainments of teachers will be tested by a written examination ... Before a certificate is granted it is absolutely necessary that ... he should pass a satisfactory examination in all the subjects usually taught in National Schools, viz: Reading, Writing, Arithmetic, Grammar, and Geography. (p. 5)

The Victoria Board of Education Report for 1862 spelled out the requirements for teacher certification. These included the rather intimidating warning that unless teachers reached a satisfactory level in the examination for certain subjects, including grammar, "No notice will be taken of their replies in any other subject." (p. 29)

CHAPTER 15
The Tyranny of the Textbook

Jean Galbraith's class, Coaldale School, Alberta, 1930.
(courtesy Galt Museum & Archives, UID 20001076107.)

By 1900 most school jurisdictions prescribed the grammar textbooks that could be used in their schools. By this time, most grammar texts so prescribed were written and published in each respective Dominion. Authors were usually superintendents or normal school instructors. Generally, approved textbooks enjoyed a long shelf life, sometimes as long as twenty-five years, because the purchase of new textbooks was a considerable expense to education departments or to parents. Parvin (1965) listed authorized textbooks approved for Ontario with prices in 1896; the public school grammar was priced at 25 cents. (p. 150) Many teachers did not like a change in the textbook because they had become used to the old one and did not want to have to learn how to use a new one. As a result of these factors, grammar books were a particularly highly significant influence on what teachers taught and what pupils learned over a lengthy period time. The smallest provincial jurisdiction in the three countries involved in this study, the province of Prince Edward Island, had an interesting experience with its school grammar textbooks in the first several decades of the twentieth century.

PRINCE EDWARD ISLAND 1900–1940

In 1903, Mr. Anderson, the chief superintendent of schools for Prince Edward Island, announced the decision of the Board of Education to adopt Goggin's grammar as the only textbook for that subject in all schools after June 1904. It was clear that Mr. Anderson was optimistic that the new text would satisfy the critics of the old list of grammars, which included Currie's *Rudimentary and Advanced Grammar* and Swinton's *Language Lessons*. Approved teacher references, Abbott's *How to Parse* and Angus's *Handbook of the English Tongue*, as well as Mieklejohn's *Grammar,* used in the normal school, were de-listed.

The need for a new textbook was linked to reports from the inspectors that grammar was badly taught in the schools in PEI. Teaching grammar was too frequently "by the book," mechanical, without any application to speaking and writing. In 1902, a Mr. Stewart gave a lecture at the September meeting of the PEI Teachers Association on the subject of teaching grammar. He made a plea for doing away with the textbook, rote learning, and other ridiculous methods. He urged that schoolrooms be the domain of plain English, rather than so-called proper speech.

However, with the adoption of the new Goggin text in 1904, these problems did not disappear. The litany of complaints from inspectors continued: "Too many weary months and years at parsing and analysis"; "too much time spent on endless technical terms of formal grammar; young children memorizing definitions from a textbook of formal grammar." Inspector Shaw said in 1924, "Formal grammar as a separate subject was still being taught to pupils too early in the course." (p. 65)

Some suggestions were made by inspectors as to the various factors that might have caused this instructional failure, including teachers' low salaries, the advent of the First World War, and out-migration to the West.

The chief superintendent noted that the new Goggin text had been examined by "many" of the teachers and tried out by some, and the agreement was that the new text was a "practical book and greatly in advance of any one heretofore in use." He then remarked with great confidence, "[T]hat from this time forward I trust to observe and to hear through the inspectors that in this important subject there is conspicuous improvement." In the following year, 1905, Mr. Anderson was still confident in the new text and claimed that teachers showed a greater interest in the subject.

However, the Goggin text was a grammar, and only cursory treatment was afforded to composition; there was no other text authorized for composition. The complaints soon started to appear in the annual reports of inspectors. In the same year, Inspector Matthews included the grammar text in his list of books that were "more of a hindrance than otherwise to pupils in the junior grade." In 1913, Inspector Devereaux recommended that a textbook largely devoted to composition be prescribed and that the study of formal grammar be omitted except for pupils in the advance grades. Opposition continued to rise, until by 1920 the book was being verbally condemned by inspectors, including the president of the PEI Teachers' Association, Inspector Doyle. In the same year, Inspector Court reported fair results in language work "considering the difficulty of the textbook we have." Inspector Doyle made a direct attack in 1922.

> The textbook fails in synthetical [sic] arrangement and is wanting in exercises for the profitable application of instruction given. It is unattractive and cannot be made use of by teachers not possessing a superior knowledge of the subject. We need a better textbook in grammar.

In 1923, teachers launched their own direct attack on the unpopular grammar text. They approved a motion at the annual meeting of the Teachers' Union condemning it and urging the Board of Education to authorize a more suitable grammar. Inspector Court pointed out at this meeting that there were more suitable textbooks in use in other provinces.

At last, in 1928, twenty-four years after it was first prescribed and after years of criticism, the Board of Education replaced Goggin's grammar text with two widely used in other provinces: Cowperthwaite and Marshall's *Public School Grammar* for pupils up to the end of Grade 8 and their *High School Grammar* for Grades 9 and 10.

The new text for the younger grade levels was probably easier for teachers to use. Examples were more concrete, and the material was set out less densely on the page. However, it was still just a grammar text. The authors showed their commitment to what they called a thorough course in grammar, denouncing the "short-lived notion that Grammar can be set aside for loose and nontechnical 'language lessons' ... High school teachers, as well as businessmen, demanded that students of the 'teen years know at least the rudiments of technical English Grammar." They did not explicitly state that their text was a treatise on formal grammar, but their text was not based on the widely accepted principle that in the junior grades, at least, grammar should be taught as a support for composition. The new text paid even less attention to composition than did the Goggin book that it was replacing.

In the 1940 Table of Studies, Donalda Dickie's textbook *Learning to Speak and Write* was listed as the textbook for language in Grades 2 through 5. This signaled a change from a focus on grammar to direct instruction in composition. However, the Cowperthwaite and Marshall grammar text was still firmly entrenched in Grades 6 through 9. Grade 6 children were to study Parts 1 and 2, Elements of the Sentence and the Parts of Speech. Grade 7s were to study Parts 3 and 4, Classification and Analysis of Sentences and Classification and Inflection. (Curiously, Grade 9 students were to complete the grammar text despite the fact that Part 4, studied in Grade 7, was the final part of the book.) However, the progressive textbook *Junior English Activities, Book 2* was also listed for Grade 8. In Grade 9, the first year of high school, the texts listed were *English Grammar for Secondary Schools* and *Junior English Activities, Book 3*. Grade 10 students were to continue as in Grade 9.

In 1948, a supplement to the course of studies was issued by the Department of Education. This document advised teachers against using the grammar text (presumably the one by Cowperthwaite and Marshall) prior to Grade 6. It was suggested that teachers in Grade 3 through 6 use the new textbook for language, *Language Comes Alive*. A penciled note in the margin of this supplement said these recommendations were part of the "assault on Cowperthwaite and Marshall."

The recommendation for high school grades was that a single teacher's copy of *Junior English Activities* be placed in each classroom, Book 1 for Grade 8, Book 2 for Grade 9, and Book 3 for Grade 10. A loosening of central control over curriculum materials was shown in the final suggestion that teachers could use other materials for language study recommended by supervisors of schools.

In 1963, the Provincial Curriculum Advisory Committee expressed dissatisfaction with the language arts program and proposed to send out a questionnaire to all teachers in PEI asking for their opinions about the program. The first question was "What areas of the curriculum needs most urgent reform?" Those who identified language arts as the most serious problem gave reasons; there was not enough grammar; the textbook, *Language Comes Alive*, "babied children"; Grades 9 and 10 "needed a textbook that had more grammar"; Grades 7 and 8 had too little grammar and composition; there should be more emphasis on clausal analysis and parts of speech and on a sequential presentation of grammar; and language; teachers had to supplement the program with extra grammar.

Many of the teachers who urged more grammar probably went to school themselves during the days when Goggin, Cowperthwaite, and Marshall dominated the language curriculum, forgetting, perhaps, that those years had also been a time of widespread discontent with grammar teaching.

TEACHER SNAPSHOT: AGNES RAMSAY, PEI

This section provides a brief glimpse into the classroom of a skilled teacher of grammar in the period just before the Progressive Education Movement took hold in Canada (discussed in next chapter). This snapshot of traditional school grammar in the hands of a gifted teacher shows the nature of the challenge facing the new reform ideas about to enter the ring. Agnes Ramsay was a teacher in Summerside, Prince Edward Island, where she began her teaching career in 1890, retiring in 1944. She taught all subjects in Grade 9, but English grammar seems to have been her favorite. One of her former students, Marjorie McCallum, writing in 1980, recalled Agnes's teaching in the year 1928. Marjorie wrote a vivid account of a typical grammar lesson in Agnes's classroom, in which she recalled with great detail, undiminished over fifty-two years, her experience as a student in that Grade 9 classroom.

> When I look back on that particular year (Grade 9), I remember most clearly the analysis and parsing sessions. Analysis with Aggie was almost a religion. Day in and day out we analyzed everything in sight, it seemed to me, and often parsed every single word in a particular sentence or paragraph ... After more than fifty years, I can still remember many of the passages which Aggie chose ...
>
> One day she wrote on the blackboard:
> Analyze into clauses and parse the underlined words in the following:
> It is a marvel that I was not drowned: for when I was brought to

a <u>stand</u> at last, <u>my</u> mouth was so <u>dry</u> that I must wet it with sea water before I was <u>able</u> to <u>shout</u>.

It is almost automatic even today to follow the instructions.
Analysis
It is a marvel—Principal clause
That I was not drowned—noun clause in apposition with 'it'
For my mouth was so dry—adverbial clause of reason, modifying 'is'
When I was brought to the stand at last—adverbial clause of time modifying 'must wet'
That I must wet it with the sea water—adverbial clause of result, modifying 'was so dry'
Before I was able to shout—adverbial clause of time modifying 'must wet'.
Parsing
Is—copula or relational verb, part of the verb to be which takes the same case after as before it; principal parts: as, was, been, indicative mood, present tense, third person singular to agree with its subject 'it' (McCallum-Gay, 1980, p. 89).

So thorough and intense were the grammar sessions that pupils remembered them years afterward. One former pupil said, "I loved the analysis and parsing—such training for the mind. I've forgotten the history and the geography, but oh, those grammar sessions!" (p. 90)

No matter which side of the grammar debate one takes, Agnes Ramsay was an outstandingly successful grammar teacher at a time when many teachers in PEI (and elsewhere) were having trouble with the subject. Following years of criticism by teachers, the old authorized text, Goggin's *English Grammar* was de-listed in 1928, replaced by the Cowperthwaite and Marshall text. McCallum-Gay noted that Miss Ramsay used many different reference books, some bought from England, and when the approved texts were insufficient, teacher and students had a wealth of resources in which to solve grammar problems. Aggie was both a grammarian and a teacher. She knew what she was teaching, and she had a passion for it. Moreover she was a teacher with a great presence in the classroom, a stern disciplinarian, much loved and respected by her pupils.

Her purpose in grammar teaching

According to McCallum-Gay, Agnes encouraged students to apply grammar to writing, but not in a big way. She would assign them to write sentences using particular words and parts of speech. However, it seems that Aggie was not troubled by questions about the value of grammar; it was a system of rules and categories that had to be mastered, and that was that. Mastery achieved was its own reward for successfully learning grammar. The sentence analysis component of her course in grammar dated back to 1852 and John Morell. After eighty years, this analysis program was something that schools just did; it was a commonplace of schooling, needing no justification for conservative school teachers.

It is likely Agnes Ramsay's implicit allegiance was to the humanities curriculum, developing the powers of reasoning and sensitivity to beauty and high moral character. She would probably have agreed that her teaching of grammar was, partly at least, designed to imbue her students with a passion for the English language as part of the Canadian cultural heritage in its finest, standard form. David Goggin, author of the retired textbook of grammar, was a prominent educational leader in the early years of the nineteenth century, whose motto was "one empire and one language," and his grammar text represented that world view. Agnes would likely have approved.

There is no evidence that Agnes believed that learning traditional grammar had any benefit for composition. The sentences she assigned for written practice seem to have been more an exercise in learning the grammar concepts than developing composition skills. For her, the slogan about grammar being the handmaiden of composition was reversed to make composition the real handmaiden.

Her teaching methods

It is not to criticize Agnes's Grade 9 grammar program to say that it was made up of formal concepts, often remote from the students' experiences, isolated from real language use, and part of a ritual of schooling that often placed memorization and recitation ahead of comprehension (although not in Agnes's case). It was a perfect fit with the subject-centred curriculum, in contrast with the student-centred that focused first of all on the needs, interests, and capacities of students. Her methods were formal and academic. Since her students were in Grade 9, they would generally have the required ability to deal successfully with abstract ideas and language; and as fee-paying high school students, they would have passed all the school leaving examinations at the end of Grade 8 to be eligible for admission to high school. Hence Agnes's students were a select academic group, motivated to learn, and able to acquit themselves well in any departmental examination in English grammar.

Her teaching was mainly authoritarian, in the sense that what happened in the classroom was under her control: the topics, the examples, the explanations, the practice activities, and the evaluations. Her teaching was deductive, as opposed to inductive (called the "scientific approach" at that time), in that she first presented the sentence or the grammatical structure, which she explained with examples, and then assigned exercises to reinforce the learning.

For example, a teacher could write on the board the puzzle sentence "I like cats like me." Then the teacher could ask the students to suggest what the sentence meant. A discussion of the two versions of "like" could lead to the idea that words can have different roles in sentences; for example, the word "like" could have two different functions in a sentence, first as a noun and second as a preposition. The test for a preposition could then be applied by asking what other prepositions could take the place of the second "like" in the same sentence. In other words, the concept appears and is named towards the end of a teaching episode, not at the beginning.

STUDENT SNAPSHOT–ANNETTE CHRISTOFFERSON, ALBERTA

In 1925, Annette Christofferson, a school girl from High River, Alberta, recorded in her notebook for Composition, Grammar, and Vocabulary her attempts over thirteen days in April and May to complete exercises in clause analysis. She was probably in Grade 8. On April 29, Annette copied into her notebook a passage to be analyzed, under the heading "Grammar."

> As we came on, I observed the general sway. The general pushed forward again. Then I lost sight of him for I saw what gave the battle new interest for me.

As taught by the grammars in use in Alberta at that time, one would expect the following analysis:

> Clause 1. As we came on. Subordinate adverbial clause modifying the verb "observed"
> Clause 2. I observed the general sway. Principal clause
> Clause 3. The general pushed forward again. Principal clause
> Clause 4. Then I lost sight of him. Principal clause
> Clause 5. for I saw. Subordinate adverbial clause modifying the verb "lost"
> Clause 6. what gave the battle new interest for me. Subordinate noun clause, object of verb "saw"

This, however, is Annette's analysis, according to her notebook:

> Clause No. 1. As we came on I observed the general sway. (As we came on I observed the general.)
> Clause No. 2. Push forward again. Principal clause coordinate with Clause No. 1.
> Clause No. 3. I lost sight of him. Princ. Clause coordinate with Clause No. 1 and No. 2.
> Clause No. 4. I saw what gave the battle new interest for me. Principal clause coordinate with clauses No. 1, 2, and 3.

Poor young girl! She was hopelessly lost in this ordeal. However, she persevered with the same exercise the next day with a little more success—one nearly correct clause: "As we came on. Sub. Adv. Cl. Mod. 'observed'." The fact that she was modifying the wrong verb suggests the partial success was not based on any real insight into the mysteries of English clauses. Perhaps her teacher could have drawn some advice from a 1922 article in the *Alberta Teachers' Association Magazine*. This advice came from a qualified source—it was written by David Sullivan, the third author of the last of the old-time grammar textbooks authorized for use in Alberta schools. This was the *Alberta Public School Grammar* (Cowperthwaite, Marshall & Sullivan, authorized for intermediate Grades 7 and 8 for the years 1926 through 1936).

In his article "An Exhausting Subject," Sullivan referred to a recent survey that had shown that many Grade 9 students found grammar to be a distasteful subject. To overcome this negative response, he suggested the following steps in teaching clause analysis in Grade 9. First, the teacher should find an interesting sentence and read it aloud to the class, and then have pupils identify and underline all the verbs. This would reveal the clauses. Then all the subordinate clauses should be bracketed. With the hard part over, the students should then proceed to write out the analysis as follows:

> Sentence: In Scotland they have narrow open ditches which they call sheep-drains.
> Kind of sentence: complex sentence
> Clause 1. In Scotland they have narrow open ditches
> Kind of clause: Principal clause
> Clause 2. Which they call sheep-drains
> Kind of clause: subordinate, adjective clause. (Sullivan, 1922)

One would doubt that these suggestions could have helped Annette. First of all, the sentence about Scottish sheep-drains hardly qualifies as an interesting specimen of writing for adolescents in southern Alberta. And Annette's grasp of parts of speech was likely not strong enough for her to reliably find and underline the verbs. Finally, Sullivan is rather glib about the ease of identifying and bracketing the one subordinate clause in the sentence. In any case, the following day Annette moved on to a new exercise calling for the pupil to write out sentences that contained adjective clauses (all wrong), adverbial clauses (all correct), and noun clauses (one correct) (Notebooks of Annette Christofferson).

In spite of her difficulties with grammar, Annette was able to enter the teacher training program at the Calgary Normal school. Who knows? She may have gone on to teach clause analysis, or she may have embraced the new reform movement that was going to impact her teaching career. Certainly her career as a teacher would have spanned a period of intense debate and change in Alberta schools. The edifice of English grammar that Annette had to endure as a student—formal concepts, remote from the student's experience, isolated from real language use, and a ritual of schooling that placed memorization ahead of comprehension—can be seen as a perfect fit with the ideology of the old subject-centred curriculum, embraced by Sullivan's 1922 pedagogy and about to be challenged by Progressive educators.

CHAPTER 16
Grammar and Progressive Education

Davina Sang in front of her classroom, Spring Coulee School, Alberta.
1918. (Courtesy Galt Museum & Archives, UID 19981061015.)

The New Education Movement had, by the end of the 1920s, achieved significant changes in the role of grammar in the primary or elementary grades. Functional grammar, in its role as a support for composition ("the handmaid of composition") was widely accepted as the form and rationale for grammar teaching up to and including Grade 6. Generally that meant that the purpose of grammar teaching was to help students overcome errors in their speech and writing. Mental discipline was much less likely to be invoked as a reason for teaching grammar to younger children. Formal grammar was reserved for high school study because it promoted logical thinking and provided a necessary prerequisite study for pupils who would go on to study linguistics and other languages. Grammar study should not confine itself to English grammar; rather, it should be a study of "pure grammar."

At least that was the official doctrine, supported by official programs of study

195

and most authorized textbooks. Some inspectors did not like the relegation of grammar, and many teachers did not understand the implementation of functional grammar in their often overcrowded classrooms. Members of the public and prospective employers were uneasy about the consequences of downgrading grammar from its traditional status.

As we have seen, the New Education reforms did not complete the task of putting the right kind of grammar instruction for the right kind of reasons into primary classrooms—indeed, after the 1904 reforms in New Zealand, there were several attempts to restore aspects of formal grammar to the primary program. There was still work to be done, and that work was enthusiastically incorporated into the massive reforms undertaken by the **Progressive Education Movement** in the 1930s. The goals of the Movement were much broader than just the reform of grammar teaching, but grammar was a kind of whipping boy that epitomized all that was wrong with the old authoritarian schooling.

Progressive Education was a loose amalgamation of three major orientations to change in the public schools. **Social Efficiency** emphasized scientific measurement, such as tests and surveys. An example applied to grammar and composition was Martyn's 1932 book *Grammar in Elementary Schools*. Martyn's book was based on large-scale surveys of children's grammatical errors in speech and writing in Ontario as observed by teachers. Using categories of grammatical errors developed in the United States, Martyn was able to list frequencies for different grade levels. For example, in Grade 3 he tabulated 201 errors involving case and order, compared to 298 errors in Grades 5 through 7, and 25 for Grade 8. An example of this error is "Me and my brother went" (Martyn, 1932). The aim of the study was to show what errors were being made at what levels so that schools could teach according to scientific measurement of need.

The second orientation was towards efficient school management, or **Administrative Progressivism**, a topic that is not included in the scope of this paper. The third orientation, most important from the point of view of this book, was **Progressive Pedagogy**. Based on Dewey's writing, this called for replacement of the old focus on subjects with a new focus on the social aspects of learning, expressed as group work, projects, experiential learning, and engaging activities.

The **enterprise**, a new term borrowed from England, was the core concept of progressive teaching. An enterprise was a large-scale project for the whole class or school; for example, "The Story of Wheat." Under guidance from the teacher, children would collect information in a collaborative way and share their findings with the class. Language and other skills would be developed in the course of the enterprise as children gave oral reports or written presentations. The teacher would note children's errors or weaknesses in skills and provide instruction to help them to strengthen their skills. Grammar study would not be a separate subject; a functional approach was intended to help pupils to identify their errors in writing and speaking.

The Progressive Education Movement reached Canada in the early 1930s. As its principles and practices became mandated by provincial departments of education, school grammar found itself under attack, this time with a clear alternative, "activity learning," as the new contender. Grammar's role in the English Language programs was reduced to that of dubious support for oral and written composition.

ACTIVITY LEARNING

The most powerful term in Progressive Education was **activity**, as in "activity learning," "activity curriculum," or "activity system." Education was viewed as a matter of the continuous reconstruction of the pupil's experience. It was a process of living by developing and redeveloping one's needs, purposes, interests, ideas, and actions. For this to be of maximum effectiveness, teachers had to know the interests and needs of their pupils.

Activity methods of teaching emphasized:

- the importance of pupils' needs and interests
- the acquisition of functional knowledge through purposeful work and problem-solving
- appropriate opportunities for expression
- involvement in cooperative experiences

Functional education was the kind of teaching and learning that could be seen by teachers and pupils to have a purpose that they could approve. Problem solving involved the following steps: (a) becoming aware of a dilemma or perplexity, (b) gaining practice in gathering and evaluating data, (c) putting forward and testing hypotheses, (d) reaching appropriate conclusions, and (e) presenting them effectively (Connell, 1987).

Expression was important as an activity. Teachers should help children in their attempts at expression to be more than effective in speaking and writing or using media such as art, music and drama: the aim should include sincerity. It was the teacher's task to teach pupils to express their experience aptly and accurately in whatever was the appropriate and preferred medium.

Of course these complex requirements of activity learning were very demanding for the teacher. Superintendents sometimes complained in their annual reports that enterprises were sometimes shallow, lacked rigour, and allowed the activity work of pupils to "degenerate into pure manual exercises."

In Canada, progressive reforms of the school curriculum and instruction occurred in all provinces in the period between 1931 and 1945: Saskatchewan in 1931, British Columbia in 1932, Nova Scotia in 1933, Alberta in 1936, Ontario in 1937, and Newfoundland (not then a Canadian province) in 1940. Of all the provinces, Alberta undertook the most ambitious reforms with the most detailed planning, the most radical changes to curriculum, the most retraining for teachers, and the most aggressive leadership.

ALBERTA'S PROGRESSIVE EDUCATION REFORMS 1935–1945

In 1935 in Alberta, a new Social Credit government was elected, with a new premier and minister of education in William Aberhart, a high school principal and radio evangelist. Led by Deputy Minister Fred McNally and Supervisor of Schools Hubert C. Newland, Alberta began an ambitious ten-year period of radical school change. McNally and Newland had earned doctoral degrees in education at, respectively, Columbia University and the University of Chicago. They were thoroughly aware of the theoretical foundations of progressive education and committed to its implementation in Alberta schools. Assisted by other department officials and instructors at the three normal schools, many of whom had also received training in England and the United States, Newland transformed schooling in Alberta.

The timing of the reform project could not have been more challenging. Nineteen twenty-nine had ushered in the Great Depression, which hit the mainly agrarian economy of the province very hard. Then there were the droughts of the early 1930s that ruined many farmers and led to an unemployment rate of over 24 percent. School districts found it impossible to collect school taxes; teachers' salaries were slashed; schools were closed; many students, completing elementary schooling and failing to find jobs, stayed on to take secondary courses, straining the system, as these students and unqualified teachers struggled with academic courses without real motivation. There was an oversupply of teachers in spite of the low salaries, which were often unpaid or in arrears. In spite of these enormous difficulties, the reforms took place, and many teachers found themselves teaching in new ways.

Alberta followed British Columbia into progressive education with major curriculum revisions that began in 1935 and took four years to complete for all twelve grade levels in elementary, intermediate, and high school. By then it was apparent that curriculum change was not a one-shot reform; progressive education required continuous modification. By 1938 all programs of study for Grades 1 through 12 had been revised at least once; thousands of experienced teachers had been trained in the new theories and teaching methods through special summer courses; normal schools had revised their programs to train new teachers in line with the new orientation; examinations had been reduced in number and reformed; and classrooms were starting to look different. Teachers found they needed movable desks, sand tables, and reference materials to encourage activity learning on the part of pupils: sharing, researching, cooperating, reporting, and demonstrating, in contrast to the old classrooms with fixed desks for passive listeners and memorizers.

Grammar received little attention during this period of change; it was part of the old subject-based curriculum of authoritarian teaching, book learning, verbalization, single subject textbooks, and memorization. The role of grammar under the new program was as part of language skills embedded in the enterprise unit, taught as needs were revealed by children's oral and written work. Programs of study forbade the formal study of grammar; it was to be taught functionally to overcome errors, such as so-called troublesome verbs, like "Has the constitution been wrote?" Newland's 1936 report said that grammar will be taught "not for its own sake, but as a tool for effective expression." (p. 18)

In the 1937 Annual Report, written one year after the new program of studies for elementary grades (One through Six) had been fully mandated, Newland offered a full account of the enterprise as the fundamental unit of the students' learning experience.

> A well chosen enterprise—
>
> - is centred in the interests of the pupils
> - is within the range of their ability
> - suggests several kinds of work to be done
> - provides different types of social experience
> - is susceptible of completion in a reasonable length of time (p. 16)

Newland often warned teachers that skills were important and should not be overlooked amidst the enterprise's individual and group activities. In the same 1937 report, he listed the outcomes of an enterprise as, "Generalizations and insights, attitudes and appreciation, abilities and traits of character, skills and knowledge."

A starting point for the committees that were set up to draft the new programs was a report by a legislative committee, which had been set up before the election that brought Social Credit into power. This committee, which studied the problem of rural schools, reported on the problems caused by the old system of education and compared them with the progressive conception of education, and claimed that the great handicap of the traditional type of one-teacher schools was the large number of 'recitations' required for many subjects in many grades. The progressive conception of education was to replace verbal recitation with socialized activity; integration of subject matter would be effected through large units of work developed around genuine life interests and experiences. Children would not be classified in closely homogeneous groups on the basis of achievements in skills or factual knowledge, but work together, as people do in life outside the school, on enterprises of common interest in which each would participate according to his ability.

Elementary program of studies

It comes as no surprise to find that grammar had only a small role in the new curriculum for the elementary grades. The term used was *language skills*, referring to accurate and effective expression in oral and written work—*grammar* did not even appear as a heading. In Division II (Grades 4 through 6), language skills included using the correct form of the four kinds of sentences and using complete sentences in speech. Students were to know how to use subjects, predicates, and objects in order to strengthen their feeling for completeness in sentences. Certain usage demons were identified for elimination by drills and games.

The three-volume textbook series authorized for Division II in 1939 was specially written for the enterprise program by Dr. Donalda Dickie, a normal school instructor and member of the curriculum committee that drew up the program. The author had completed doctoral studies at Oxford and the University of Toronto. The new series was called *Junior Language*. The emphasis of these textbooks was on the social use of language. Children were taught how to speak well, how to make conversations pleasant, how to write descriptions, how to vary sentences, and how to give a talk to the class. Some few grammar concepts were included under language skills: using pronouns properly, making new adjectives, using phrases for descriptive purposes and clauses for explanatory purposes. These terms were used and occasionally definitions were given, but the emphasis was on the effective use of these elements and not on the terms themselves, other than as convenient labels with which to talk about language forms.

Intermediate program of studies

As noted earlier, the Depression in the 1930s coupled with the prolonged drought in the rural areas put an enormous strain on Alberta's economy. Many students reaching the end of Grade 8 could not find jobs, so they chose to continue their schooling by enrolling in Grade 9. The percentage of pupils enrolled in classes beyond Grade 8 went from about 6 percent of the overall school enrolment in 1921 to over 17 percent in 1932. Given that most pupils were educated in one- or two-room schools, the large increase in high school enrolment meant that the educational system was stressed in several ways: resources were scarce, teachers' salaries dropped, and although there was a surplus of teachers, most were not qualified to teach high school classes.

Because of these factors, the extra students entering Grade 9 were often students who did not have the necessary skills to succeed in formal academic studies. Many rural teachers were not able to teach them, either because they were unqualified to teach at that level or because they could not spare the time to work with high school students, given their arduous responsibilities to students in the elementary grades. The situation was most serious in the small rural schools, where the Grade 9 class would likely have been a handful of young adolescents sitting at the back of the room, many not really motivated for academic study and unable to receive much help from a teacher preoccupied with younger children, who was likely challenged by the material to be taught.

One part of the solution to the Grade 9 dilemma was to change the purpose of that year of study. Instead of Grade 9 being the first year of high school, it was designated as the third intermediate year, following Grades 7 and 8. In his 1936 Report as Supervisor of Schools, Hubert Newland explained the change with respect to the whole three years of intermediate school.

> The work of the intermediate school is not primarily a preparation for the high school programme [sic]. It is complete in itself, and will appeal to many hundreds of boys and girls who may never go to high school. (p. 14)

The second target for curriculum reform in 1936 was the intermediate program, Grades 7 through 9. The Grade 9 program was the first to be drawn up because Grade 9 had become the third year of intermediate school—this change was important; the new Grade 9 was no longer to be exclusively academic, focused on students going on to secondary study. While retaining the academic function, it also had to provide an appropriate program for students who would complete their schooling at the end of Grade 9. The program developers had to respond to the growth of enrolment, the need for a different kind of preparation for high school study, as well as the need for more suitable courses for students planning to leave school upon completing Grade 9.

The new program for all three years of intermediate school was drawn up and mandated for September 1937. The revised program of intermediate school studies included a course in English language under two headings, *Literature and Reading*, and *Language*. Under the latter heading appeared "Oral and written work, grammar, spelling, and word study." English was a "tool," not a subject; it was to be integrated with other subjects, such as social studies. The course in language should consist of activities, not formal instruction. It should be unified; grammar could not be isolated from composition and should be taught as a technique of correct and effective expression. The material used in English classes should be socially useful, and emphasis should be placed on practical speech situations that were relevant to students' needs in later life.

> No attempt should be made to undertake a formal study of grammar in the intermediate school. The grammar study should be 'functional' in character; that is, it should be subordinated to and motivated by the work in expression. Some 'phases' of grammar are important for functional treatment. These are: recognition of a sentence and the distinctions among sentences, phrases and subordinate clauses; recognition, without recourse to definitions, of the eight parts of speech; correct use of inflected forms of personal pronouns and of certain irregular verbs. (p. 26)

The Program of Studies went on to briefly list a number of common language errors that intermediate teachers should pay attention to. Interestingly, the amount of time allocated to English was reduced, on the grounds that "a large amount of the purely formal class instruction was undoubtedly wasted effort." English in the new program would be interwoven with other subjects;

there would be less time for the formal teaching of literature and for formal exercises in language.

In the following year, a new textbook series for language was approved, replacing the last of the old-style grammars (Cowperthwaite, Marshall, and Sullivan's) used in Grades 7 and 8 since 1926. The new Grade 9 textbook, Diltz and Cochrane's *Sense and Structure in English Composition,* was the authorized text until 1940, and it was the approved textbook for the revised language component of the Grade 9 English program introduced in 1936. English as a subject was divided into two sections: literature and reading; and language, consisting of composition, spelling, and grammar. There was no other textbook for grammar. In this book, "Functional Grammar" consisted of eight lessons out of a total of seventy-six lessons. (Other major sections included dictionary use, prepared speeches, punctuation, unity and clarity of the sentence, spelling, letter writing, and impromptu speeches.) The justification for the grammar lessons was that the rules to be learned would help to eliminate problems in common expression; this was a late example of grammar serving as the handmaid of composition.

The first grammar lesson in the textbook consisted of common errors related to agreement of subject and verb; the next five lessons considered parts of speech and errors of usage associated with them ("troublesome" pronouns, prepositions, verbs, adjectives, and adverbs). The lesson on adverbs and adjectives included an explanation of certain "crudities" associated with colloquial modifiers such as, "I kind of thought" or "I sort of understood," and the misuse of *less* and *fewer.* The final lesson in the functional grammar section was a lengthy achievement test that required students "to point out all the mistakes you can find in the following sentences. Break up these jumbled ideas and try to express them in short sentences that are correct grammatically and clear in meaning" (Diltz, 1933).

There were no references to sentence analysis, although the focus was entirely on the grammatical rules for sentence structure. Unity and clarity were the goals. It was not an easy book. The explanations were often terse; for example, "'Less' refers to quantity or degree, and 'fewer' refers to number." This laconic instruction was followed by two sentences that illustrated the rule: "Distinguish between the meanings of the following sentences: Our sales are less than last month. Our sales are fewer than last month." (p. 102)

Personally, I am not confident about the right answer. A possible approach to the answer might be to consider *less* to refer to value of the goods and *fewer* to the number of items. I think most Grade 9 students would have needed more and easier examples. Perhaps teachers, too, would have benefited from a fuller set of explanations. Inspector Good from Wainwright reported in 1936 that the new composition textbook was proving to be a challenge for teachers.

> The formal composition for the grade [9] as outlined in Diltz and Cochrane is proving very heavy for the majority of rural schools and probably few schools will be able to cover this text completely this year. The subject matter is admittedly splendid but requires much careful supervision and discussion if effective results are secured.

Newland himself, reporting in the same year on the new intermediate program, warned about the new composition textbook:

> The new text [Diltz and Cochrane] is found to provide definite objectives for both teachers and pupils, but it is agreed that a rigid following of its outlines results in less practice in written expression that was obtained from the old course.

Why was this textbook chosen for the new program of studies? In the absence of a recorded rationale, one can look to the revised Grade 9 program to understand what the curriculum committees were trying to achieve. The Diltz and Cochrane textbook was probably designed to provide Grade 9 students with some autonomy in their study of composition, including grammar. The text presented a concept whose embrace would eliminate some solecism. A brief explanation accompanied by a small number of examples then led to an exercise in the application of the concept, which a teacher might be able to mark and provide, ideally, some extra assistance. But perhaps that particular textbook was not a good choice. Simply stated, it was too hard for the rural students who were poorly prepared and inadequately motivated for rather dry and laconic study.

Its authorized use shows how curriculum and teaching directives are dependent upon more factors than materials and methods; it is an early example of curriculum development responding to demands of the social milieu. High school education was emerging from the economic difficulties of the time as being for the masses, instead of being traditionally reserved for a very selective minority of students. In a sense the whole thrust of progressive education was, partly at least, driven by this social and demographic shift.

The composition text was replaced in 1938 by a much more progressive textbook series, *Junior English Activities,* a three-volume series tailor-made for the new language program. Authorized for Grades 7, 8, and 9 until 1953, its authors were Americans, led by Wilbur Hatfield. (These American textbooks had been revised as a Canadian edition published in Canada.) Hatfield had chaired a National Council of Teachers of English commission in 1935 that published an influential report called *An Experience Curriculum in English*. Essentially, this report was an endorsement of progressive education applied to language's role in the intermediate level curriculum. The key word *experience* in the title signaled an emphasis on real-life communication as encountered by young adolescents. Communication experiences included using the telephone, running a club meeting, writing friendly letters, and engaging in conversation. Each of the theme units was concluded with a section called "Review, Test and Practice," which is where the skills of language were explained and practiced. Errors in speaking and writing were presented, followed by corrective exercises. Grammatical terminology was sparingly used in the explanations. For example, the explanation for the different uses of *lie* and *lay* did not use the terms *transitive* and *intransitive verbs*. "The word 'lay' is a Dr. Jekyll-and-Mr.-Hyde sort of word," the text asserted.

The Program of Studies advised teachers that the treatment of grammar in the prescribed textbooks for English was adequate for the needs of most students, but that in rare cases they could supplement their instruction with references to an older series of texts. Teachers were also encouraged not to try to teach the whole textbook but to make judicious selections in order to meet the needs of their students.

This may explain a rather curious inclusion on the 1941 list of recommended language reference books: C. H. Ward's *Grammar for Composition* (1933). In his introduction to the text, Ward made no secret of his hostility to progressive teaching of composition. "By 1920," he claimed, "the 'fluency-first doctrine' was in the United States regarded as a 'national scandal'." He was referring to the principle that children should develop fluency first in their writing, followed by gradual control over correctness and accuracy of expression. He called it the "flamboyant theory of ultimate ends," which believed that children learning to write were driven by a wish to be clear and interesting. According to Ward, demographic changes in the United States undermined the theory, so that high school students could no longer be assumed to value accuracy, to come from refined homes, or to have a grounding in Latin and Greek. In other words, students needed formal grammar.

This message would hardly be reassuring to intermediate teachers of language who were attempting to implement the 1940 program. On the other hand, recalcitrant teachers may have found this reference to be a licence to continue teaching formal grammar; and it may have reinforced the Canadian suspicion that by the time education theories arrived in Canada, they had been discredited in the country of origin.

High school program of studies

In 1939, the Department issued a Bulletin setting out the reformed program of studies for high school Grades 10 through 12. This program included prescribed courses in English, and it was in force until 1946. Prominence was given to a statement warning students that if their written work were to be deficient in penmanship, spelling, and form, they would be disbarred from admission to the Alberta normal schools. Writing skills, as outcomes of secondary education, were to be taken seriously.

The Bulletin set out some basic principles underlying English courses; composition was to be a shared responsibility among all teachers. The principles underlying clear and correct expression were to be taught in the English class, but drill in these principles was to be a part of the teaching of all classes. (p. 3) What became a well-known and, to some teachers, notorious slogan appeared: "Every teacher is a teacher of English." All teachers shared responsibility for correctness. The English teacher had responsibility to expound the fundamental principles of grammar composition and style, but all teachers would check practical applications. As one sign of progress, the annual report for 1945 noted that it is "No longer fashionable at teachers' conventions to laugh sardonically when the dictum ... is produced and examined for validity." (p. 33)

Teachers were to provide motivation for writing and speaking by building on students' immediate social needs and by meeting their personal needs. Oral expression should receive at least as much attention as written work. Teachers should provide for the needs of remedial students who needed special work and for superior students needing more challenge.

The Bulletin set out a general objective for language courses: to develop the ability of the pupil to express himself clearly, correctly, and, if possible, effectively in oral and written English. Twenty to forty percent of the time devoted to English courses should be devoted to teaching clear and correct expression. The bulletin included a statement about the nature and significance of grammar in the high school program of studies, in line with the progressive view.

> Grammar represents the attempt merely to define the underlying
> principles of language and to supply terms which facilitate the

exposition of these principles. Some knowledge of grammar is, therefore, essential to the correct use of the English language. However, teachers of grammar should bear in mind that they are dealing with a living language, which cannot be fettered by rigid rules of grammar. Grammar can eventually 'wear down' the most logical grammatical rule. It seems advisable then to restrict teaching to those simple elementary phases of grammar that actually function in improving and clarifying the sentence. (p. 5)

The doctrine of correctness still provided a justification for grammar teaching, but there was an interesting recognition that correctness is not rigidly fixed by the rules of grammar, so teachers must acknowledge the dynamic nature of the living language and the importance of current usage.

A checklist was provided for Language: correct form of pronouns; agreement between pronouns and antecedent; distinction between adjective and adverb; correct forms of verbs, especially past participles; agreement between verb and subject; use of subjunctive, as in "If I were to go"; and common errors in sentence structure. The same list was specified for all three high school grades.

The Bulletin provided further direction for teachers of grammar.

The improvement in sentence structure resulting from practice in the analysis of long, involved sentences has probably not been commensurate with the time and effort spent on such exercises. Emphasis in these new courses has shifted from analysis to sentence building, the assumption being that it is more important, from the standpoint of improving his expression, for the pupil to be able to use a subordinate clause in a sentence of his own than to be able to recognize a subordinate in a given sentence. (p. 6)

This statement about sentence analysis, long a staple in language classes, points to a more effective way to develop control over sentence structure. Sentence combining, the inductive and constructive activity of building sentences from component clauses and phrases, was a shift more likely to increase motivational and effective learning than deductive analysis. It is interesting to note that forty years after the publication of this 1939 Bulletin, sentence combining was enjoying a huge popularity across North America, including Canada.

Grammar Textbooks for High School

In the reformed program of studies for 1938, the use of a formal grammar textbook came to an end. The new authorized text for Grade 10 was *Expressing Yourself Book 2*. The series was first published in the United States, but a Canadian version was used in Alberta. In the following year, 1939, the series of language textbooks was authorized for all three high school grades. This authorization lasted until 1954.

Listed as teachers' reference books in 1939 were Ward's *Grammar for Composition*; the *Ontario High School Grammar* (Stevenson & Kerfoot), intended as one year of high school study; and Tressler's *English in Action Practice book* (1939). Also listed was H. W. Fowler's *A Dictionary of Modern English Usage*—this very British reference would have been heavy going for many pupils and teachers.

The new language textbook series presented a wide range of language topics: storytelling; speeches; letter writing, including telegrams; explaining; arguing; forceful expression; and creative writing. Among several appendices was included a "Review of the Fundamentals of Grammar," forty-five pages in length—the first time grammar was put in an appendix. The program of studies suggested that this grammar review could be used as a handbook for students to look up particular topics that were causing them trouble in writing or speaking; "Take one as needed," the textbook suggested. This was an example of a functional approach. Another example of the principle of function was the provision of "diagnostic tests" at the beginning of grammar topics in order to help students see where their strengths and weaknesses lay. After a topic had been studied, students could take what was called a "victory test" to assess achievement. However, the grammar appendix relied heavily on a large array of technical grammar terms, which would have limited its effective use as an independent handbook for pupils, despite the authors' claims that the textbooks were written for an audience of students.

Also included was another appendix on Words Misused. The aim of this section of the textbook was to achieve formal standard usage. Examples included "*Aggravation* means to make worse, not a synonym for annoy, vex or provoke"; "*Ain't* is crude; do not use it."

REFORM OF EXAMINATIONS

As we have seen in the past, examinations were often the stumbling block for curriculum change, teachers being persuaded about what to teach more by the examinations than by the program of studies. However, in this case, the Department of Education did attempt to harmonize the examination with the program. The Department reduced the number of public or departmental examinations to two grades, 9 and 12, and created an Examination Board to be responsible for the design of examinations and their marking. These external examination changes marked a major move away from what Newland in his 1941 report called, "The faulty techniques of testing and examining [that] are in a large measure responsible for the aridity of school courses and the barrenness of their results." (p. 12)

The language examination would be a test of language usage and of the practical application of the more important principles of sentence and paragraph structure. The significance of these regulations in 1941 can be seen in a comparison of its testing parameters with the content of the 1931 grammar and composition examination set for Grade 8 students in their last test before leaving school or going on to high school.

The 1931 examination allocated fifty points to grammar and fifty points to composition. The grammar section contained questions on parsing and detailed sentence analysis. Some manipulation of language following technical instructions was required. One question asked, "What is the force of the auxiliary verbs in each of two sentences?" (Departmental Examinations, 1931).

The new 1936 Program of Studies for Grade 9 promised that the language examination:

> ... will be a test, not of what the pupil can write about the theory
> of correct and effective expression, but of how well he can put the
> theoretical principles into practice. Correct usage and properly
> constructed sentences are the things that will count. (p. 18)

Such a mismatch between the functional grammar specified in the program of studies and the public examination questions on formal grammar explains why the 1922 reforms went unheeded.

Mr. T. C, Byrne, former deputy minister of education, said that the retention in the 1930s of the old examinations with formal grammar questions "did most to undermine efforts to reform grammar teaching." He went on to say that development of the new tests in support of progressive teaching, using unseen passages as in the Grade 9 examinations, had a major impact on high school English in the 1940s and 1950s. Teachers could no longer prepare their students for specific questions, and it was impossible to cram for them. "This," said Mr. Byrne, "drove some teachers wild" (Byrne, 1984).

The 1945 program of studies for high school English courses included an account of the nature of departmental examinations for the following June. There would be two English exams, one Literature and the other Language. Modern techniques of testing were to be applied. There would be fewer "long" questions and a considerable number of "short" questions, including multiple-choice questions. Two reference books on testing were recommended for teachers to study. The Regulations noted that the principle of the new testing procedures was that "examinations are instruments for measuring achievement, not merely hurdles to be jumped, or tests to be 'passed'." (p. 30)

In that same year, the Department announced another new policy on examinations in Grade 12, intended to encourage all teachers to follow the slogan from the 1939 Bulletin and think of themselves as English teachers. Examination papers in subjects other than English Language would be evaluated by a special group of subexaminers for the quality for the written expression. A score for Language would be incorporated into the overall mark. This was a practice that had been introduced into the Grade 9 examinations some years earlier.

SUCCESS OF ALBERTA'S REFORMS

How successful were Alberta's grammar reforms? It is not possible to answer this question very satisfactorily because it is too narrow to allow enough evidence. Once grammar had been put in its proper place as a possible aide to expression, but only as a much reduced part of the curriculum, little was said or written that could help answer the question. Grammar's fate was closely tied to the prospects of progressive education as a whole: if progressive curriculum, teaching methods, textbooks, and examinations prospered, so did the agenda of finding a proper role for English grammar. Thus the assessment question deals with the larger issue.

But there is no objective evidence to answer the even broader question. No one carried out a scientific study of teachers' success with the new programs of studies or methods of teaching, nor formal measurements of teachers' ability to implement the reforms, nor comparative studies of improvement in students' learning or motivation. What evidence we have of the impact of the activity approach in the classrooms of Alberta comes mainly from the Annual Reports of the Department. Reports by the deputy minister, the supervisor of schools, and by school inspectors who reported to Mr. Newland usually carried informal assessments of the new work in the classrooms. Newland was a prolific report writer, and his reports were usually insightful. Of course all those officials had a vested interest in success. Newland and McNally, who were passionate advocates of progressive education, wanted to see the reforms helping to improve the classroom lives of students and their teachers. No doubt the inspectors felt some pressure to give their bosses what they wanted to hear.

Assessments of historians of education

Professional historians of education generally saw the reforms as top-down changes that did not deeply penetrate school practice. Kach (1987) thought that the enterprise approach was not comprehensive enough to provide a full and sequenced program. It was important to distinguish between what occurred at the official level and what occurred in classrooms. Officials were prone to claim widespread implementation when in really it was limited. Those critics who claimed that progressive ideas were taking over in Alberta tended to overstate the impact on teachers.

T. C. Byrne observed that it was the Department of Education and the Alberta Teachers' Association that brought reform to Alberta schools by a process of top-down leadership. Newland was a dominant figure and a demanding leader. Mr. Byrne thought that progressive ideas did not percolate very far down, except where there was strong local leadership. There was always some opposition from teachers to activity learning (Byrne, 1984).

Tompkins (1986) contrasted the enthusiasm of educational leaders for the enterprise and activity learning in the late 1930s with the skepticism of "more than a few" Alberta teachers who resisted the new approach. Many felt pressured into some new, vague procedures at the instigation of a group of theorists. Sheane summed up the real challenge of the enterprise system:

> [It] called for well-trained, adaptable teachers who knew something of child nature and of the laws of teaching. The organization required to arrange study material into teaching units was not possible with inexperienced teachers, nor could they be expected to get the most out of such procedures. Because

of the quality of the teachers, as well as for other reasons, many educators in Alberta claimed that the enterprise had not failed because it had never been tried in the true sense of the word. (p. 196)

Peter Sandiford (1938) observed that although progressive education ideas had originated in the United States and Britain, activity programs were coming under severe criticism south of the border. Critics claimed that children's achievements were sloppy and insecure. Alberta's annual reports made no mention of this pendulum swing, but it must have been on the minds of the Alberta leaders.

Assessment by Alberta education officials

In 1936, Mr. Newland asked his inspectors to evaluate the first-year use of the enterprise method in the elementary schools. Mr. Fuller, chief inspector of schools, summarized these assessments for his 1936 report. This summary noted that the new method of teaching was more demanding of teachers: "It required more ability, resourcefulness, initiative and scholarship" than the old system. (p. 52) He noted further that those teachers who were recent graduates of the normal schools, or who had taken courses in the summer school to prepare them, had the edge over their colleagues who had been unable to study "activity" teaching. The consensus was that teachers had grasped the objectives of the enterprise approach, although some had allowed the pupils' activities to "degenerate into pure manual exercises."

Students were thought to be developing greater power to make abstractions and generalizations, to relate cause and effect, and to do independent thinking. It was felt that there had been a definite improvement in language training. The culmination of enterprises, for the most part, had served their educational purpose; in addition, parents were able to understand the new teaching and learning from these culminations. There was general agreement that the activity program had resulted in increased motivation and interest among pupils. These all sound like a report of a resounding early success.

It seemed to be evident that enterprises were more successful in Division II (Grades 4 through 6) than in Division I, where the children's skills were less developed. Grammar was not mentioned in the summary, but language work, both oral and written, had improved because of the link with other subjects. Some individual inspectors were very impressed. Inspector Crispo, for example, said that virtually all elementary teachers in his district were using enterprises, some even for the whole year's work. The new Grade 9 program was included in the assessment; generally inspectors seemed to be rather more cautious in their assessment of its success. The Literature and Language course drew positive comments in the 1936 report: a reduced tendency for teachers to use a dissecting method and indications that pupils were getting more enjoyment from the subject. (pp. 55–58)

Mr. Newland reported that the new programs in elementary and intermediate schools were "working out with a large measure of general satisfaction." Referring to the enterprise approach, he went on to say that the new program had "quickened the pulse of classroom activity in thousands of Alberta classrooms." (p. 14) And Mr. Fuller reported that the new Grade 9 procedures for examinations had influenced teaching for the good, saying that there was less teaching for examinations and more stress on the application of school studies to life, although he also criticized the teaching of English composition in Grade 9 as too often divorced from the life experiences of the pupils. (p. 42) The chief inspector also noted that inspectors' reports indicated "A very real improvement in the general tone of the classroom and the attitudes of the pupils toward the new activities." He estimated that 85 percent of the teachers were using the enterprise procedure in some form. "Teachers are gradually learning what they may expect from their pupils, and pupils are taking more and more responsibility." (p. 62)

Parents were obviously interested in the new programs and no longer believed that their children should be taught in the same way they had been. Where teachers were seen as business-like and well organized in their teaching, parents and communities were supportive.

Sometimes they were puzzled how their children could be learning when they were playing. A common complaint from parents was that there must be something "phony" about the new course, because their children seemed to be enjoying school. They were sometimes even neglecting their chores at home in order to spend more time on their enterprises. Some school boards were supplying more appropriate classroom furniture in the form of sand tables, work tables, and reading tables.

There were some difficulties: first, a tendency towards half-hearted attempts to adopt the new approach occurred when teachers copied enterprise materials from their colleagues; second, a lack of reference materials; and third, very low enrolments in some divisions, where there were too few pupils to form working groups. In the 1937 report, grammar did not often receive a mention, although Fuller did note that in Grades 7 and 8, "[M]any teachers are still stressing formal rather than functional grammar. Too much attention is being paid to analysis and parsing and too little to correcting expression." (p. 66)

In the same report, high school inspectors Mr. Balfour and Mr. Sullivan made some observations about the quality of instruction in the high schools, referring to the new program at that level. They spoke about weaknesses that were gradually being remedied.

(1) emphasis upon memorization of notes in the content subjects (Language and Social Studies, for example)

(2) assigning textbook material to be learned, without adequate introduction and unrelated to students' experience

(3) limiting the field of study to a single text, or to condensed forms of the texts (p. 38)

It was estimated that 50 percent of all teaching time in schools was spent on the older methods. Uncertainty about what children were learning and difficulties in acquiring reference materials were cited as causes of recidivism (1938, p. 61).

One year later, the enterprise technique was almost universal in the rural schools as well as urban, and perhaps 60 percent of the teachers were successful in using it to good advantage in the integration and revitalization in the curricular activities of the schools. However, there were problems of implementation: some older teachers had not yet grasped the principles of enterprise and the importance of students' activities. They were using prepared materials from the publishing houses, falsely purporting to be designed for the enterprise method, which led to poor preparation for teaching. (p. 61)

An example of these published materials was the series *My Language, Books II through VI*, published in 1940. These contained exercises that were "methodical training in written language." The topics included grammar, as well as exercises in punctuation, telephone etiquette, and conversations. For overworked teachers in one- or two-room schools, one could see how those materials could be used to provide seatwork for students. However, they were not quite in the spirit of activity learning.

In 1939, the Chief Inspector for Schools offered a province-wide breakdown of teachers' success (or otherwise) with the enterprise method: a large group, comprising many new teachers and those who had taken upgrading courses, were using the technique wholeheartedly and successfully; a second group, rather larger than the first, were using a modified version of the technique but without correlation in the teaching of skills; and the third, a relatively small group, were still teaching by the old method. (p. 62)

In 1939, several prominent educators from the United States were invited to assess the elementary program of studies with respect to skills, drills, and integration. This group unanimously affirmed the validity of the activity program, the enterprise procedure, and the principle of successive meaningful experiences. In 1940, the following year, Newland included in his annual report his assessment of the level of implementation in the elementary schools. "Inspectors and superintendents report that the principles and objectives of the revised program are now accepted by a large majority of the teachers." (p. 15)

In the same year, Chief Inspector Fuller pointed to other evidence that the enterprise technique was being widely adopted. As reported in 1936, Fuller said that classroom furniture in the form of low tables and chair, drawing easels, work tables, and cabinets was increasingly making its way into the classroom to facilitate the new forms of teaching and learning. (p. 63)

In his 1941 report, Newland gave the new education paradigm a clear retrospective explanation. Referring to the changes that the past six years of reform effort had wrought in Alberta's schools, he quoted from a 1937 book[10] published in the United States to show the depth and significance of the changes that had occurred.

> When someone in the year 2000 writes the history of American education for the twentieth century, the decade between the close of the World War and the financial and economic collapse which heralded the great depression will stand out as of peculiar importance. It was in these years that the great battle of educational ideas took place. The death struggle between two opposing types of curriculum practice was fought and decided. On the one side was the very large group of educators who championed the subject curriculum; on the other side was a small group of educators who advocated the experience curriculum. A decision was rendered in 1929. As a result, from the kindergarten to the liberal-arts college, the subject curriculum with its basic

---

10   L. Thomas Hopkins et al., *Integration: Its Meaning and Application*. New York: D. Appleton-Century Co., Inc. 1937.

educational ideas began to decline, and the experience curriculum with its fundamental principles began to increase. The rapid acceleration which began in 1931, has in this year, 1937, almost reached a tidal wave (1941, p. 24).

Newland claimed that Alberta was as far advanced in its implementation of progressive education as any province in Canada. (p. 15) However, his report for 1942 was somber and pessimistic. The war in Europe was drawing young teachers from the classroom into the armed forces and other wartime employment. That was having a serious impact on the quality and availability of teachers. Newland admitted that progressive teaching required high-caliber teachers who both understood the principles underlying activity teaching and learning and the more democratic interactions that modern classrooms required. Young people coming into teaching with only emergency training or older people without re-training were reverting to the older methods of teaching: formal, authoritarian, textbook-based, and subject-based, negating much of the progress made in the previous eight years. However, he took some solace in the positive effects of the New Education on children who had experienced it throughout the five years of their school experience since 1936. Speaking of the reports from the inspectors, Newland offered this assessment:

> … in the majority of the schools there is a slow but clearly discernable advance from the old to the new education. The spirit of the latter is becoming more prevalent in pupils' attitudes, dispositions and responses in social situations. The social attitude of the pupils is more desirable. Cooperation is increasingly the rule of classroom life. Discipline is less rigid and dictatorial and more spontaneous and reasonable. Pupils seem to be getting more out of their school experience than was usual under the old regime. They read more, and they express themselves more freely. (p. 29)

Referring to the intermediate grades, Newland admitted that because the enterprise and activity methods were not mandated at that level, there was a tendency to neglect oral English and to teach formal rather than functional grammar. (p. 31)

The year 1945 saw the retirement of Fred McNally from the position of deputy minister of education. That was also the year when Hubert Newland resigned as supervisor of schools. The two men were the mainsprings of progressive reform in their province. When they left office, official support for progressive teaching went into a decline, and progressive policy no longer enjoyed the full sanction of the Department of Education (Kach, 1987).

In 1946, a subcommittee chaired by David Sullivan drew up a statement on high school grammar; his pronouncement reads like a rehabilitation of English grammar teaching. Mr. Sullivan had a long career in the Department and had been listed as one of the three authors of the old approved grammar text, *An English Grammar for Public Schools, Alberta Edition* (Cowperthwaite, Marshall & Sullivan, 1926). His statement appeared in a revised 1946 Bulletin under the heading, "Grammar Requirements."

> In order to emphasize the importance of functional grammar and to give further directions to teachers, an outline of the grammar requirements for each high school grade was included in Bulletin I. The outline of grammar for each grade is sketched under the heading 'Functional Grammar'; it will be the duty of the teacher to make the applications in writing and speaking. It is felt that the successful application of this knowledge to the language habits of the students is one of the most important parts of the entire language program. The outline indicates only the minimum attainment for every student. Any teacher should feel free to carry his class further in grammar than is suggested in the outline. (p. 52)

This statement has the appearance of a Trojan horse, giving licence to those teachers who believed in lots of grammar to teach it.

The program of study included another statement about grammar teaching.

> Grammar is the guide to correct and forceful expression … the emphasis is on 'functional' grammar. Through a definite, systematic and progressive study of grammar for two years from the functional (that is, usable), point of view, students achieve style in writing and speaking as well as accuracy of expression. (p. 35)

Mediocre grades from the historians and failure to establish a universal and permanent system of education based on progressive principles do not mean that the Progressive era in Alberta was unsuccessful. Connell (1987), writing about the Progressivists in general, pointed out their innovative contributions to public education: "They broke the traditional mode [of teaching] more drastically than had ever been done before. They allowed new methods suitable for the new societies of the twentieth century. They were the first to use pupil activity as the central component of teaching and learning."

Connell went on to give the Progressive Movement credit: "Exploring the connection between action and intellectual development, they made wide use of teaching through problem solving, and encouraged creative kinds of expressive activities. They did, in fact, bring a new dimension into teaching." (p. 213)

As far as grammar was concerned, the clock could not be turned back. Certainly there was some reaction against the so-called "neglect of grammar." But after a decade of grappling with the subject of grammar teaching, there was no attempt to bring back the "grammars." New textbooks authorized for English Language included some grammar in appendices and topics, but the concept of language arts (reading, writing, speaking, and listening) that should be taught in an integrated manner and presented that way in textbooks did not encourage a widespread desertion to grammar.

As a result of the progressive reforms, children's encounters with subject grammar were closer to the ideal of grammar instruction: the right material for the right students in the right way. Adjustments of this three-part balance would continue to be made in future decades, but in the general direction provided by experiences between 1935 and 1945.

CHAPTER 17

Reform in New Zealand and Australia 1943-1959

Pupils at Lake Eloida school, Ontario. 1895. Located approximately 25 km NW of Brockville, Ontario. (Courtesy Galt Museum & Archives, UID 19730115000.)

A committee set up in 1942 to consider the curriculum implications of the proposed introduction of accrediting for university entrance presented the Thomas Report in 1943 and published it the following year. Its recommendations on curriculum were broadly influential and were incorporated into later syllabus revisions for primary schools.

In its discussion of English teaching, the Committee extended the 1929 primary syllabus revision's stand against formal grammar teaching to post-primary. "We have passed through the stage where formal grammar was regarded as the principal part of the syllabus in English, and where detailed parsing and analysis, correction of sentences, and rules and exceptions learned by rote in isolation from composition occupied almost all the school time devoted to the subject." (p. 18)

The Committee went on to say that "[G]rammar is useful for the general student only in direct, applied relation to the use of English, written or spoken. No substantial transfer of grammatical knowledge to written and spoken English is proven." After those statements, the Committee offered teachers a choice, consistent with its view that the State should not impose a "cut-and-dried philosophy on the schools" or control the curriculum in any detail. The Committee did not wish to restrict teachers to one view, believing that they would be more successful using methods in which they had confidence, although it did strongly condemn the isolated teaching of grammar, separate from composition. "Some very successful teachers of English have found by experience that good English is better fostered by extending very widely the time devoted to reading, writing and oral discussion of the subject matter read than by systematic training in formal grammar. Other teachers retain their faith in a varying minimum of formal grammar as an effective working-tool." (p. 20)

The climate of opinion in the 1940s, especially among secondary teachers of English, was not yet ready to accept a completely liberal position on grammar teaching. The Committee, therefore, was obliged to make concessions to both conservative and liberal thinking on the issue. Some teachers in the 1920s even felt that formal grammar teaching was completely barren—the material used for grammatical analysis was often taken from Shakespeare, in spite of its elliptical and colloquial structure.

Many Englishes

The influential Thomas Report made a major break with one tradition of English teaching. After stating two primary aims of English teaching (to develop the power of expression in speech and writing, and to develop the ability to understand the spoken and written thoughts of others), the Report turned to a consideration of "good English." Posing the further question "Good for what?" the Committee turned its back on the notion of a single form of English against which all speech and writing could be unambiguously judged.

"There is an English which is good for conversation, there is an English which is good for serious discussion, there is another English which is good for imaginative writing, and for oratory, and for description, and so on." Apart from a reference to "English for everyday life" as the main concern of the schools, the Committee did not attempt to further describe the characteristics of these different "Englishes," but it related each to function, the position from which teaching should start. The likelihood is that the variation allowed in this discussion extended to matters of rhetoric—the effective arrangement of thought in writing—rather than grammatical form.

On first glance, the Committee seemed to be granting parity of esteem to these varieties of English. However, its real conviction on the issue may have been revealed by a metaphor it used to explain its view of oral and written composition. "Expression," the Committee said, "may be carried to the point of high art in conversation and oratory, in imaginative literature and in scientific and philosophic exposition. Likewise comprehension can be carried to literary appreciation." The teacher's role was "to take each pupil as far as possible along both roads," to give control of the mother tongue that was as full and flexible, as sensitive and efficient as possible. The notion of a road to be travelled along suggests that destinations in oratory and philosophic exposition involved qualitatively better forms of language than other functions.

In terms of general aims, the Report dealt with personal development and preparation for an active role in society and did not see those as contradictory. According to the *New Zealand Education Gazette,* it wanted a shift from a curriculum consisting of formularized knowledge as determined by demand for attainments to a liberal core and set of options. It asserted that a liberal education could be achieved through practical and technical subjects, that there was a need to acknowledge individual differences and creativity, and that the program should emphasize preparation for later life (1946, pp. 9–20).

Writing was the first component of the primary English curriculum to be modified by the Department's appointed revision committee for English. A draft had been circulated as a supplement to National Education, the final approved version taking into account comments and reactions from teachers. The new syllabus analyzed the teaching of writing in two aspects: helping children to achieve technical correctness through control over spelling, punctuation, and grammatical usage and helping them to develop the ability to express clear, effective writing for the purpose and audience involved.

Language variability

Variability in language was acknowledged in the new syllabus, although not as directly as in the Thomas Report. First of all, the syllabus pointed out that

"Grammar is merely the description of the forms of language established by the usage of the educated; if this changes, the rules of grammar must be changed to conform with it." In cases where usage was changing, the teacher was urged to be tolerant and flexible and to consult reliable references, such as Fowler and Jesperson, in resolving issues of pupil usage. The variability allowed reflected the slow change in standard usage. However, at any one time the prevailing standard, as defined by the usage of the educated members of the community, is capable of arbitrating any differences of opinion that might emerge in the classroom. The concept of correctness of form to which writing for all purposes and audiences must adhere had not been abandoned. The term "correct idiomatic English" still appeared in the syllabus.

The discussion in the syllabus about "free expression" revealed an epistemological position on the nature of language learning. Acknowledging that the "theory of free expression" had emerged as a reaction against the "stilted correctness" of traditional composition, the syllabus writer warned against the opposite danger of acquiescing in "inferior, commonplace writing, familiar to children in their books, magazines, films and radio series." In other words, it was not sufficient to regard writing as a skill that emerged from its practice, as an inside-out process of experiential learning. Guidance on the part of the teacher was essential.

Two other sources of language variability were discussed in the curriculum, one related to rhetoric, the other to levels of ability in children. With respect to the first, an emphasis on the role of purpose and audience in shaping writing implied that writing was more than a neutral vehicle for the expression of thought; rather, its rhetorical arrangement was influenced by the nature of the writing task.

With respect to the second, the syllabus emphasized the effect that varying abilities had upon what written achievements could be expected of children. While the "simple English of purposeful communication is the staple kind that all pupils above the age of nine or ten, whatever their ability, should be taught to write," brighter children could go further, and backward children should focus more on the "most obvious and practical uses of language."

The syllabus did not belabour the grammar question. It stated that "abstract definitions of grammar were not required and that terms used should be clear and simple. By the time the child has completed Standard IV, he should use the more common orthodox terms." It asserted the belief in the importance of "the simple grammar of function as an aid to correct speech and writing."

In the prescriptions, two headings were used: "written expression" prescribed the constructive aspect and "formal English" the technical part. In Standard II, the concepts of naming words and doing words were introduced, as were notions of number and tense. In Standard III, functions of adjectives and adverbs were to be introduced. By the end of Form II, the functions of most of the parts of speech were to have been taught, as well as the naming of clauses (adjectival and adverbial—time, reason, manner, place, condition) although without formal analysis. Pupils were also to understand phrases and the use of prepositions and participles in their introduction.

In spite of the de-emphasis on grammar, there was enough terminology used to allow teachers who wanted to spend considerable time on a more formal approach. The term "simple grammar of function" seems to be a key term in the intention of the prescriptions.

Reference was made to textbooks that were in preparation. The new syllabus was only to be compulsory when the new texts were available. It has been noted that the syllabus emerged at a time when there were recurrent complaints about the standards of English in schools, and this gave the syllabus a sober, practical bias, dampening free expression by criticism of it.

ENGLISH IN THE PRIMARY SCHOOL

A supplement to National Education was released in August 1959 and was circulated as part of the consultative process. Called "The Report of the Standing Committee for the Teaching of English in the Primary School," the existing syllabus was described as having separate parts for reading, writing, speaking, and listening. There was also a separation between the practice and exercise of language skills and real situations. A statement of principles included:

> Teacher's role is to set up contexts for effective and correct use
> Activities must acknowledge children's developmental levels
> Prescriptions must be avoided
> Use of a single integrated framework recommended
> Technical skills must be placed at the service of effective use

The Committee recommended that official textbooks for English be dispensed with, and there was a definite move away from the notion of a single standard for language. "The general criterion for the use of language is its fitness for the occasion, and its effectiveness in carrying out the user's intention." Standards were therefore expected to be variable, taking into account the ability of the child. Major function categories were: private satisfaction, private communication, addressing an audience and writing for publication, and class business and daily work. In the case of the last, the standard to be aimed at was that of the educated adult community—i.e., "clear and coherent expression; and correct usage, including grammar, spelling and punctuation."

On grammar, the report noted that the Thomas Report of 1944 had said, "We have passed through the stage where formal grammar was regarded as the principal part of the syllabus in English, and where detailed parsing and analysis, correction of sentences, and rules and exceptions learned by rote in isolation from composition occupied almost all the school time devoted to the subject." The report asserted that it was well established by then that there was little connection between knowledge of the rules of grammar and language performance. Functional grammar should be developed out of the children's work. Under skills to be taught, the grammar listing for Standards III and IV were present and past tense, singular and plural number, the use of comparatives and superlatives. The correcting of actual errors common to the class should all be discussed as the teacher saw the need. From Forms I and II, children should be helped to develop the sense of function in relation to the parts of speech. Terms should be used freely, but recognition and classification of parts of speech was not recommended. A functional approach was recommended towards phrases and clauses, defined as "many-worded adjectives and adverbs."

A Study of New Zealand syllabus development

Language in the Primary School: English

The New Zealand Department of Education presented *Language in the Primary School: English* (1961), which was reprinted in 1969 and 1973. It refers to two earlier revisions, 1928 and 1946.

The report offers no changes in aims or in content and focuses on conditions for learning, suggesting direct teaching whenever the teacher thinks it necessary. This implies that the norm for primary school English teaching is child-centred individual and/or group activities. While not prescriptive, it does insist on comprehension by the children and their being able to see the point of what is done. Writing was to be judged on the basis of intention: to inform, describe, persuade, express an imaginative concept, and establish relations with others. Grammar (term not used), would have a role in the preparation phase of writing when "the idea that groups of words (phrases or clauses) can be classified and named according to the way they are used—that is according to their function—should be developed." Terms, such as *noun, pronoun, adjective, adverb, conjunction, verb, subject of the verb, object of the verb, phrase* and *clause,* should be used freely by the teacher at those times and whenever language was being discussed and be taught by frequent use and occasional explanation.

The document also provided the syllabus for post-primary school. It noted that grammar was useful for the general student only in direct, applied relation to the use of English. No substantial transfer of grammatical knowledge to English use had been proven. It noted, however, that some teachers retained their faith in a varying minimum of formal grammar as an effective working tool. It outlined the elements of grammar for use in practice: recognition of various parts of speech by their function (not definitions, types of nouns, etc.); common usages of the apostrophe; practical exercises in number and in the efficient use of pronouns; correct use of comparative and superlative; concord of subject and verb; analysis as an aid to comprehension—an exercise in the subordination of ideas, logical rather than grammatical. As one of the basic requirements of the course, "the recognition of parts of speech by their function" was included. Cedric Croft, who started his teaching career in 1961, said that the revision was a watershed in the teaching of English and that newly graduated teachers were able to assume leadership roles in schools because of their training in the new approach.

The NESC Curriculum Development Project, 1969–1983

The previous English syllabus for Forms 3 through 5 dated from 1945 and resulted from the Thomas Report. In 1969, a committee was struck to examine the 1945 syllabus and prepare guidelines for its revision. In 1970 the NESC began its work. Warwick Elley made a presentation to the 1969 Committee on Research in the Teaching of English in which he devoted considerable time to the question of the role of formal grammar or linguistics. Research since 1906 had been unanimous, even with older students. He suggested that skill in writing was more the result of forming habits than learning abstractions. He quoted a number of linguists who maintained that one should not expect a relationship between the study of language and its effective use. He said that "the general picture is that grammar is slipping," although he noted that some evidence suggests that a focus on synthesis rather than analysis may be fruitful. Overseas syllabi showed grammar being played down.

In describing the process of curriculum development through the 1970s, the NESC noted the significance of the Dartmouth Conference in 1966. In 1972, a statement of aims outlined three assumptions about language: it is a form of human behaviour; it is central to personal growth; and it starts with oracy. The student's own language was the starting point. Group work and cooperative planning were important. In 1979, the School Certificate Examination Board began to investigate the possibility of assessing English in accordance with the principles of the new syllabus. In 1981, the New Zealand Association for the Teaching of English was established. In 1982, the Minister of Education announced that he approved a new syllabus for English, Forms 3 through 5, to replace the 1945 version. The question of internal assessment as part of the certificate of education was under consideration.

Forms 3–5 Statement of Aims, 1983

The New Zealand Department of Education's *Forms 3–5 Statement of Aims* (1983) referred to 1945 as the last official statement on secondary English. These aims were based on the recommendations of the Thomas Committee as part of the core curriculum. The new statement was of principles, based on New Zealand experience (as opposed to overseas opinion), for the guidance of schools in drawing up their materials and methods to meet the needs of their own pupils. A list of truisms in the statement included that language is developed principally by use, and language is partly governed by convention and habit.

Language aims were to increase ability to understand language and use it effectively; to extend imaginative and emotional response through language; to extend awareness of ideas and values through language.

In relation to Aim 1, awareness that language is influenced by convention and habit so that students can develop sensitivity and competence; recognize and be sensitive to the effects of social, cultural, and technological changes on language; appreciate that language is modified by situation and language mode; adapt their language to audience and purpose; develop respect for national, regional, and cultural differences in the use of language; awareness that judgments about appropriateness of language are often affected by established attitudes and personal preferences. The document does not make any commitment to the role of propositional information in the development of these attitudes and awarenesses; none is endorsed nor denied.

Forms 6 and 7 English Syllabus, Discussion Paper 3: Linguistic Diversity, Language and Learning (undated)

This paper states that a current characteristic of educational systems is a move to linguistic diversity and recognition of the rights of people to an education in languages with which they feel comfortable, in a move from exclusive concern with English. All students have the right and need to use their first language in school programs; growth in English is dependent on strength in any first language; pupils have to be ready to live in multilingual communities.

The argument, presented in a short document accompanied by a questionnaire, is that language is central to learning, not a neutral vehicle. Therefore language effectiveness is crucially important. Since effectiveness in English is built on strength in any first language, schools must foster first language learning as an avenue to effective use of English. However, since there is growing acceptance of multiculturalism and multilingualism, this strategy also can achieve goals that are important in themselves. The result is that schools are now considering language as a much more diverse phenomenon and much more broadly than English.

If these ideas, presented tentatively for reaction, were to be implemented as official policy, they would have the effect of broadening the pluralistic concept of English even further, to include language as a whole.

The Massey University Study Group (1984), in a critique of the 1984 *A Review of the Core Curriculum for Schools* (Department of Education, 1984), noted that whereas the Working Party's draft report for the review had used the broader term *language* in its policy recommendations on Language/English, the Review itself in its final draft had returned to the term *English*, thereby restricting the notion of language to that of the English language. (p.16) The defeat of the National Government in the 1984 election led to the Review being reopened by the new Labour Government; it was never officially implemented or accepted.

Stuart Middleton ("New Zealanders are good at English but is English good enough for New Zealanders?", 1987) recommends that the time has come for English teachers in New Zealand to see themselves as language teachers. His argument is that language has an active relationship to thought and that the first language is the language through which children mediate their world. Given the country's inevitable move towards two official languages, English and Maori, and given the increase in immigration from the Pacific Islands, it is time to acknowledge the full implications of the theories of language development that are espoused today in the name of the personal growth model of English, that first language is a necessary basis for learning.

CHAPTER 18
Final Word

Written by Stephanie Sedgwick

In reading the research, notes, and manuscripts that my father, Dr. Laurence Walker, gathered over thirty years, one begins to notice several things. The most obvious, of course, is that the teaching of grammar has been a contentious issue, one that involves not only the teachers but also parents and other educators at many levels. This contention dates right back to the advent of a state curriculum and therefore the notion of certain standards of education; one could then take this discussion into the realm of curriculum development, but that is a scope best handled by another book.

Some observations can be made that are common to all of the countries studied: the concern for the so-called degradation of the English language, a social recognition based on the type of English spoken, the confusion between what is mandated in the curriculum and what is actually being taught. Although each country and even each province/state has developed its own methods of dealing with how grammar is taught, the similarities in their experiences—frustrations, reforms, reactions, regressions, and progressions—are very close.

The most interesting observation to be made is that in two hundred years of history of grammar teaching, the debate continues, in much the same fashion as it originated. Although no longer in the centre of education development, as Dr. Walker was for many years, it seems that the comments and observations made today by current teachers and students virtually echo those made by educators and pupils in this book.

Even those on the periphery of education, people with no direct involvement in the development or execution of education, have some opinion on English language, and their opinions tend to have something to do with grammar's function in language.

The intent of this book is not to provide a definitive answer for how grammar should be taught, nor even to say with great certainty that it should be taught today (although my father's position on this subject can probably be intuited between the lines). As my father mentions in the introduction to this book, this is an attempt to provide access to a civil discussion of grammar's role in the curriculum and its educational significance.

However, this book does provide a framework for how the context of the politics around grammar teaching affects the teachers and students themselves, as well as the different approaches and techniques that have been used, whether successful or not. It may also allow current teachers and students to gain some objectivity in the debate or to get involved in the debate themselves. It might even spur them on to explore different methods of teaching language (English or others) or even grammar in their classrooms, or to take inspiration from teachers of the past.

Works Cited

"Address by the Director." *Educational Gazette*, 1927: 3-5.

Andrews, Ralph L. *Integration and other Developments in Newfoundland Education 1915-1949*. St. John's: Harry Cuff Publications Limited, 1985.

Annual Report, 1850. Department of Education of Nova Scotia. Halifax. Public Archives of Nova Scotia.

Annual Report, 1865. Department of Education of Nova Scotia. Halifax. Public Archives of Nova Scotia.

Annual Report, 1866. Department of Education of Nova Scotia. Halifax. Public Archives of Nova Scotia.

Annual Report, 1869. Department of Education of New Brunswick, 1869.

Annual Report, 1873. Department of Education of Nova Scotia. Halifax. Public Archives of Nova Scotia.

Annual Report, 1875. Department of Education of Nova Scotia. Halifax. Public Archives of Nova Scotia.

Annual Report, 1878. Department of Education of Nova Scotia. Halifax. Public Archives of Nova Scotia.

Annual Report, 1880. Department of Education of Nova Scotia. Halifax. Public Archives of Nova Scotia.

Annual Report, 1881. Department of Education of Nova Scotia. Halifax. Public Archives of Nova Scotia.

Annual Report, 1883. Department of Education of Nova Scotia. Halifax. Public Archives of Nova Scotia.

Annual Report, 1884. Department of Education of Nova Scotia. Halifax. Public Archives of Nova Scotia.

Annual Report, 1889. Department of Education of Nova Scotia. Halifax. Public Archives of Nova Scotia.

Annual Report, 1891, Department of Education of Nova Scotia. Halifax. Public Archives of Nova Scotia.

Annual Report, 1891, Department of Education of Wanganui, New Zealand. NZCER.

Annual Report, 1891. New Zealand Ministry of Education.

Annual Report, 1896. Department of Education of British Columbia.

Annual Report, 1936. Department of Education of Alberta.

Annual Report, 1937. Department of Education of Alberta.

Annual Report, 1938. Department of Education of Alberta.

Annual Report, 1939. Department of Education of Alberta.

Annual Report, 1941. Department of Education of Alberta.

Annual Report, 1942. Department of Education of Alberta.

"Annual Meeting." *Canadian Council for the Teaching of English*. Winnipeg, 1987.

Anonymous. *Nova Scotia Journal of Education*, 1871: 72.

Archibald, deWolfe, Rosamund, R.M. *The King's English Drill*. Toronto: Ryerson Press, 1921.

Atkinson, Clara. "Language Lessons." *Education Review*, Jan 1888: 154-155.

Baker, Harold S., and Charles H. Campell. *Words and Ideas*. Toronto: W.J. Gage, 1953.

Bassett, Patrick F. "English Grammar—Can We Afford Not to Teach It?" *NASSP Bulletin*, 1980: 58.

Bornstein, Diane. *Readings on the Theory of Grammar*. Cambridge, MA.: Winthrop Publishers Inc., 1976.

Braddock, R., R. Lloyd-Jones, and L. Schoer. *Research in written composition*. Urbana, IL: National Council of Teachers of English, 1963, 37-38.

Brown, Goold. *The Grammar of English Grammars*. 4th Edition. London: Sampson, Low, Son & Co., 1858 (orig. 1832).

Buckler, Ernest. *Ox Bells and Fireflies: A Memoir*. Toronto: McClelland and Stewart, 1968.

Bulletin II. Program of studies for high school grades, Alberta Department of Education, 1939.

Byrne, T.C., interview by Laurence Walker. (September 1984).

Cameron, Agnes Deans. "The old Broughton Street school." *Educational Journal of Western Canada* 4 (1902): 137.

Carroll, Lewis. "Through the Looking Glass." *Project Gutenberg*. June 25, 2008 (orig. 1873). http://www.gutenberg.org/files/12/12-h/12-h.htm (accessed August 11, 2011).

Chant, Colin. "Changes in Curriculum (Primary)." Compiled by South Australia Department of Education. unpublished paper, 1985.

Charyk, John. "The Little White Schoolhouse (1925-26)." In *Educating Canadians: A documentary history of public education*, by E.W. Nichols, edited by Douglas A. Lawr and Robert D. Gidney, 114-118. Toronto: Van Nostrand Reinhold, 1973.

Christofferson, Annette. "Notebooks of Annette Christofferson." Calgary, Alberta: Glenbow Museum Archives.

"Class E and Junior Civil Service English Grammar and Composition, New Zealand." 1888.

"Class E Teacher and Civil Service Examination in English Grammar and Composition, New Zealand." 1881.

"Class I Teachers' Licence Examination, New Brunswick." 1884: 87.

"Class II Teachers' Licence Examination, Prince Edward Island." *Education Report*. 1886. Appendix F, 102.

Cobbett, William. *A Grammar of the English Language, in a series of letters*. London, 1833 (orig. 1817).

"Cohen Commission on Education." New Zealand, 1912.

Cohen, Murray. *Sensible words: Linguistic practice in England, 1640-1785.* Baltimore: The Johns Hopkins University Press, 1977.

Connell, W.F. "History of Teaching Methods." In *The International Encyclopedia of Teaching and Teacher Education*, by Ed. Michael J. Dunkin, 208-9. New York: Pergamen Press, 1987.

"Controversy of Teaching Grammar." *Your Dictionary.* http://www.yourdictionary.com/grammar-rules/Controversy-of-Teaching-Grammar.html (accessed June 25, 2010).

Cross, A.E. "English in the schools." *Educational Record of Quebec*, December 1915: 357-366.

Curme, George. *A Grammar of the English Language.* 2 vols. New York: D.C. Heath and Company, 1931.

Daniels, Harvey A. *Famous Last Words: The American Language Crisis Reconsidered.* Carbondale & Edwardsville: Southern Illinois Press, 1983.

Davies, H.W. *An English Grammar for the Use of Junior Classes.* Toronto: Copp Clark, 1882 (orig. 1868).

Denny, L.R.R. "The teaching of English in technical schools." *New Zealand Education Gazette*, Dec 1, 1926: 206-9.

Departmental Examinations, 1931. Alberta Department of Education.

Dickens, Charles. *Nicholas Nickleby.* Charleston: BiblioLife, 2008 (orig. 1838).

Dickie, Donalda. *Junior Language, Books A, B and C.* Toronto: W.J. Gage and Co. Ltd., 1945.

Diltz, B.C. and Cochrane, Honora M. *Sense in Structure in English Composition.* Toronto: Clarke Irwin & Co. Ltd., 1933.

Dilworth, Thomas. *New Guide to the English Tongue: in five parts.* New York, 1827 (orig. 1761).

Dunlop, E.J. "The Teaching of English." *New Zealand Education Gazette*, August 1, 1929: 144-6.

Eaton, A.W.H. *The History of King's County, Nova Scotia.* Salem, MA.: The Salem Press, 1910.

eds: Simpson, John, and Edward Weiner. *Oxford English Dictionary.* Oxford: Oxford University Press, 1989.

Education Report, Prince Edward Island, Appendix F, 1886.

Educational Review. "Composition - Grade III: One Teacher's Method and the Result." December 1891.

Edwards, C.B. "What should be taught in the Canadian public schools?" *Annual Report and Proceedings* (Ontario Education Association), 1894.

Elley, Warwick B., I. H. Barham, H. Lamb, and M. Wyllie. "The role of grammar in a secondary school curriculum." *Research in the teaching of English*, Spring 1976: 5-21.

Ellwood, A. *Lists from the Elementary School Teacher.* Victoria: Education Department, 1943.

"English B. Examination for Junior National Scholarships and Free Places in Secondary Schools." New Zealand, 1905.

English from 5 to 16. London: Her Majesty's Inspectors of Schools, 1984.

English from 5 to 16, Second Edition, Incorporating Responses. London: Her Majesty's Inspectors of Schools, 1986.

"English Language and Literature for Training College Entrance." New Zealand, 1930.

"Entrance Examination, Manitoba." 1920.

Ewing, John L. *Origins of the New Zealand primary school curriculum 1840-1878.* Wellington: New Zealand Council for Educational Research, 1960.

"Examination Papers of Candidates in Training at the Model National Schools, New South Wales." *Report of the Department of Education.* 1859: 23.

"Exhibitions and Bursary Examinations, Grammar." *South Australia Educational Gazette.* 1905: 53.

Eyres, Ian. *Primary English.* London: Sage Publications, 2000.

Florey, Kitty Burns. *Sister Bernadette's Barking Dog: The Quirky History and Lost Art of Diagramming Sentences.* Brooklyn: Melville House Publishing, 2006.

Forrester, Alexander. *The Teacher's Text-Book.* Halifax: A. & W. MacKinlay, 1867.

Foucault, Michel. *The Order of Things: An archaelogy of the human sciences.* London: Tavistock Publications, 1970.

Fowler, Helen, interview by Laurence Walker. (1983).

Fowler, Henry. *A Dictionary of Modern English Usage, Second Edition.* New York: Oxford University Press, 1965 (orig. 1926).

Geertz, Clifford. "Ideology as a cultural system." In *Ideology and Discontent,* by D.E. Apler (Ed.), 46-76. New York: The Free Press, 1964.

Geike, The Reverend A.C. "Canadian English." *Journal of Education for Lower Canada,* Jan 1857: 128-131.

Gilman, E. Ward, ed. *Webster's Dictionary of English Usage.* Springfield, MA.: Merriam-Webster, 1989.

Goddard, P.R. *A History of the Place of English Grammar in Secondary Schools from 1920 to 1967.* Diploma of Education thesis (unpublished), Auckland: University of Auckland.

Goggin, David J. *New Elementary Grammar.* Toronto: W.H. Gage & Co., 1899.

"Grade 1 Model School English Grammar." Quebec, 1906: 240.

"Grade 10 Grammar." Manitoba, 1925.

"Grade 11 Composition." Manitoba, 1925.

"Grade 8 Grammar." Alberta, 1931.

"Grade 9 English Examination." Nova Scotia, 1925.

"Grade 9 Examination." *Report of the examinations conducted by the Council of Higher Education.* Newfoundland, 1934: 52.

"Grade 9 Grammar." Manitoba, 1925.

Groome, Thomas. *Christian Religions Education: Sharing Our Story and Vision.* San Francisco: Harper and Row, 1980.

"Guardian." March 15, 1988: 23.

Gzowski, Peter. *Morningside.* CBC Radio One, 100.1 FM, 1986.

Halifax Herald. "A Nova Scotian Looking On." February 17, 1927: 100.

Halliday, M.A.K. *A Functional Grammar.* London: Edward Arnold, 1985.

Hanna. "Memorandum by the minister dealing with some phases of educational progress and reviewing existing conditions in the light of national requirements." Compiled by Sundry Educational Reports 1878-1936. June 30, 1916.

Harris, William T. *Psychological Foundations of Education.* New York: D. Appleton and Co., 1898.

Hartley, J.A., A. Williams, and M. Maughan. *Extracts from the confidential letterbook of the south Australian Inspector of Schools, 1880-1914.* Adelaide: South Australia Department of Education.

Hartwell, Patrick. "Grammar, grammars, and the teaching of grammar." *College English*, February 1985: 105-127.

Hatfield, Wilbur W., E. E. Lewis, L. A. Thomas, and L. A. Woody. *Junior English Activities, Books 1, 2 & 3.* New York: American Book Company, 1937.

Heck, W.H. *Mental discipline and educational values.* London: John Lane, The Bodley Head, 1912.

Hodgins, Jack. *The Broken Ground.* Toronto: Emblem Editions, 1999 (orig. 1998).

Howat, A.P.R. *A history of English language teaching.* Oxford: Oxford University Press, 1984.

Jeffries, J. "Aims and methods in the teaching of English grammar." *Annual Report and Proceedings.* Ontario Education Association, 1894: 218-219.

"Journal of the Legislative Council of PEI." 1845.

"Junior Public Examination in English Grammar." Tasmania, 1892.

Kach, Nick. *Essays on Canadian Education.* Calgary: Detselig Enterprises, 1987.

Kemp, J.A. *John Wallis's Grammar of the English Language.* Facsimile and translation from 6th ed, 1765. London: Longman, 1972 (orig. 1653).

Kennedy, and Marshall. *Lessons in English.* Halifax: A. & W. MacKinlay, 1899.

Kliebard, Herbert M. *The struggle for the American curriculum 1893-1958.* Boston: Routledge & Kegan Paul, 1986.

Kolln, Martha. "Closing the books on alchemy." *College Composition and Communication* 32, no. 2 (1981): 140.

Leahey, Thomas H. *A History of Psychology: Main currents in psychological thought.* Englewood Cliffs, NJ: Prentice Hall, 1980.

Lennie, William. *Principles of English Grammar: Comprising the Substance of All the most Approved English Grammar Briefly Defined and Neatly Arranged with Copious Examples in Parsing and Syntax.* Toronto: Brewer & McPhail, 1851.

Leonard, S.A. *The Doctrine of Correctness in English Usage, 1700–1800.* New York: Russell & Russell, Inc., 1962.

Lyman, Rollo Laverne. *English Grammar in American Schools, Bulletin No. 12.* Department of the Interior Bureau of Education, Washington, D.C.: Government Printing Office, 1922.

MacCabe, J.A. *An English Grammar for the Use of Schools.* Halifax: A. & W. MacKinlay, 1873.

Martyn, H.G. *Grammar in Elementary Schools.* Toronto: Ryerson Press, 1932.

Mason, C.P. *Outlines of English Grammar.* London: Bell & Daldy, York St., Covent Garden, 1882.

"Matriculation." Prince Edward Island, 1920.

McCallum-Gay, Marjorie. "Learning Grammar Fifty Years Ago: A lasting experience." *The Atlantic Advocate*, April 1980: 88-90.

McKenzie, David. *The Growth of Credentialing in New Zealand, 1878-1900.* Dunedin: New Zealand College of Education, 1982, 54-94.

McKenzie, M.I. "School Memories." *Alberta Historical Review,* Winter 1959: 14-17.

McKillop, A.B. *A Disciplined Intelligence: Critical inquiry and Canadian thought in the Victorian era.* Toronto: McGill-Queens University Press, 1979.

McLeod, Marion. "Getting things down on paper." *New Zealand Listener,* October 10-16, 1987.

McMorran, George. *Some Schools and Schoolmasters of Early Wellington.* Wellington: S. & W. MacKay, 1900.

Meiklejohn, J.M.D. *A Short Grammar of the English Tongue.* Toronto: W.J. Gage & Co., 1891.

Michael, Ian. *The Teaching of English.* Cambridge: Cambridge University Press, 1987.

Middleton, Stuart. *New Zealanders are good at English but is English good enough for New Zealanders?* Hamilton: Conference of the New Zealand Association for the Teaching of English, 1987.

Middleton, Thomas H. "Don't Grammar Count?" In *Literacy as a Human Problem,* by James C. (ed.) Raymond. Tuscaloosa, AL: University of Alabama Press, 1982.

Morell, John Daniel. *The Analysis of Sentences Explained and Systematized: With an exposition of the fundamental laws of syntax.* 2nd edition. London: Robert Theobald, 1852.

Morgan, George Allen. *Speech and Society: The Christian linguistic social philosophy of Eugen Rosenstock-Huessy.* Gainesville: University of Florida Press, 1987.

Morris, William and Mary. *Harper Dictionary of Contemporary Usage.* New York: Harper & Row, 1975.

Morse, William I., ed. *Acadiensia Nova 1598-1779.* 2 vols. London: Bernard Quaritch, 1935.

Moutoux, Gene. "Sentence Diagramming." *German Latin English*. 2004. http://www.german-latin-english.com (accessed June 1, 2010).

Munro, Alexander. "The English Language." *Instructor*, July 1880: 1-2.

Murray, Elizabeth K.M. *Caught in the web of words: James Murray and the Oxford English dictionary*. New Haven and London: Yale University Press, 1977.

Murray, Lindley. *English Grammar Adapted to the Different Classes of Learners*. London: Thomas Allman, 1843 (orig. 1795).

Neuleib, Janice. "The relation of formal grammar to composition." *College Composition and Communication*, no. 23 (1977): 248.

New South Wales Education Gazette. "Grammar examination." 1891-2.

"New Zealand Standards Regulations 1878." *ANZHES Journal* 6, no. 2 (Spring 1977): 56-63.

Newbolt Report on the Teaching of English in England. Board of Education, London: HMSO, 1921.

Newkirk, Thomas, ed. *Only Connect: Uniting Writing & Reading*. Upper Montclair, NJ: Boynton/Cook, 1986.

Nova Scotia Department of Education. "Journal of Education." 1871.

Nova Scotia Department of Education. "Journal of Education." 1898.

Nova Scotia Department of Education. "Journal of Education." April 1910: 107-111.

Nunberg, Geoffrey. "The Decline of Grammar." *The Atlantic Monthly*. December 1983. http://www.theatlantic.com/past/docs/issues/97mar/halpern/nunberg.htm (accessed June 30, 2010).

O'Casey, Sean. *I Knock at the Door*. London: MacMillan, 1960.

"Ontario School of Pedagogy Methods in English Paper (for Specialists)." 1895.

"Papers relating to the new syllabus on instruction." *Educ/A787*. Queensland State Archives, 1904.

Parvin, Viola Elizabeth. *Authorization of textbooks for the schools of Ontario 1846-1950*. Toronto: University of Toronto Press, 1965.

Petrosky, A.R., and C. Cooper. "Evaluating the results of classroom literary study." *English Journal*, 1978: 98.

Phillipps, K.C. *Language and Class in Victorian England*. Oxford: Basil Blackwell, 1984, 3.

Phillips, Derek. *Making More Adequate Provision: State Education in Tasmania, 1839-1985*. Hobart, Tasmania: Department of Education, 1985.

Polanyi, M. *Personal knowledge: Towards a post-critical philosophy*. Chicago: University of Chicago Press, 1958.

Prentice, Allison. *The School Promoters: Education and social class in mid-nineteenth-century upper Canada*. Toronto: McClelland and Stewart, 1977, 68.

Priestley, Joseph. *The Rudiments of Grammar: Adapted to the use of schools with observations on style*. London: R. Griffiths, 1761.

Program of Studies for the Intermediate School, 1936. Alberta Department of Education.

"Public Service Entrance Examination, New Zealand." 1940.

QCA. "Perspectives on the teaching of grammar in the national curriculum." *The Grammar Papers*, 1998.

Quebec Protestant Committee. "Grade 1 Model School Examination." *Educational Record*. 1895: 203.

—. "Grade 2 Academy Examination." *Educational Record*. 1898: 193.

Report of the Committee of Inquiry into the Teaching of English Language. (Kingman Report.) Department of Education and Science, London: Her Majesty's Stationery Office, 1988.

"Report of the Superintendent of Education for 1877-78." In *Across the Years: a century of education in the province of Quebec, 1846-1946*, by W.P. Percival. Montreal: Gazette Printing Co. Ltd., 1946.

Report of the Commissioners of National Education, 1855. New South Wales.

Rorty, Richard. *Philosophy and the Mirror of Nature.* Princeton: Princeton University Press, 1979.

Ryle, Gilbert. *The Concept of Mind.* New York: Barnes and Noble, 1949.

Sandiford, Peter. "Curriculum Revision in Canada." *Journal of Education (Nova Scotia)*, 1938: 211-215.

Scheffler, Israel. *Conditions of knowledge: An introduction to epistemology and education.* Chicago: Scott Foresman, 1965.

"School Visitors' Reports." *Appendix to the Journal of the Legislative Council,* 1849.

"School Visitors' Reports." *Appendix to the Journal of the Legislative Council,* 1874: 89.

Selleck, R.J.W. *Frank Tate: A biography.* Melbourne: Melbourne University Press, 1982.

"Senior Public Examination in English." Tasmania, 1891.

"Shall and Will." *ATA Magazine,* October, 1930: 11.

Shaw, Beatrice Hay. "Rosamund de Wolfe Archibald Crusades for Better English." *Maclean's Magazine,* August 1, 1924.

Smith, Olivia. *The politics of language, 1791-1819.* Oxford: Oxford Clarendon Press, 1984.

South Australia Education Gazette. March 1905: 53.

"South Australian Qualifying Certificate Examination." 1932.

Steinmann, Martin Jr. "Rhetorical Research." *College English* 27, no. 4 (1966): 278-285.

Stevenson, O. J., and H. W. Kerfoot. *Ontario High School Grammar.* Toronto: The Canada Publishing Co., 1925.

Sullivan, David. "An Exhausting Subject." *ATA Magazine,* 1922: 11-12, 31-32.

Swinton, William. *Campbell's New Language Lessons: An elementary grammar and composition.* Toronto: Canada Publishing Co., 1878.

Sydney and the Bush: A Pircotial history of education in New South Wales. Sydney: New South Wales Department of Education, 1980: 139.

"Syllabus of Instruction." *The New Zealand Education Gazette*, 1904.

Syllabus of Instruction for Public Schools. Wellington: Department of Education, 1929.

Tait, The Rev. Thomas. "A Plea for Pure English." *Educational Gazette of South Australia*, June 1920: 132-3.

The Course of Instruction for the Primary Schools. Hobart, Tasmania: Department of Education, 1915.

The New Zealand Education Gazette. "The writing of English, revised syllabus for Primary Schools." February 1, 1946: 9-20.

The Public Instruction Gazette, April 1908.

The Teaching of English in England. Board of Education, London: HMSO, 1921.

Theile, Colin. *Grains of Mustard Seed: A narrative outline of state education in South Australia, 1875-1975.* Adelaide: Education Department, 1975.

Tompkins, George S. *A Common Countenance: Stability and change in the Canadian curriculum.* Scarborough: Prentice-Hall, 1986.

"Training College Entrance Examination, English Language and Literature." New Zealand, 1931.

Tressler, J.C., and Claude E. Lewis. *Mastering Effective English.* Toronto: Copp Clark, 1937.

Wade, Harold H., John E. Blossom, and Mary P. Eaton. *Expressing Yourself: a Textbook in Language. Canadian Edition for Canadian schools.* Edited by Lorene E. Maguire. Montreal: Houghton Mifflin Co & Renouf Publishing Company, 1939.

Walker, Laurence. "More a torment than a benefit: English grammar in Nova Scotia schools in the 19th century." *Curriculum Inquiry*, Winter 1986: 439-462.

Walker, Laurence. "English Teachers' Beliefs about Teaching Writing." *The English Quarterly* 15, no. 1982-1983 (1982): 55-62.

Webbe, Joseph. *Lessons and exercises out of Cicero, Edited R.C. Alston Menston, 1972.* Scolar press facsimile n.322, 1627.

Western School Journal. "Canadian Musical Speech." September 1914: 179.

Willoughby, Jeremiah. "Progress of education in Nova Scotia during fifty years." (Nova Scotia Printing) 15 (1982-3 (orig. 1884)): 55-62.

Wilson, J.D. (Eds). *Canadian Education: A history.* Scarborough: Prentice-Hall of Canada, Ltd., 1970.

Woods, William F. "Nineteenth-century psychology and the teaching of writing." *College Composition and Communication,* Feb 1, 1985: 23.

Other Sources of Data

1. The Annual Reports of provincial departments of education. Valuable sources of information, especially for the period up to 1915; after which they become much more general in content. They contain statements of purpose for different branches of instruction, statements of curriculum, and textbooks prescribed for each level: even, occasionally, copies of public examinations for pupils and teachers. In addition, comments by local inspectors of schools included in the reports are maintained in one or more of the following repositories for each province: Provincial Archives, Education Department Archives, Legislative Libraries.

2. Textbook collections. In the nineteenth century in particular, a textbook defined the course of study quite closely. There was usually an introduction in which the author offered a rationale for the study of grammar and brief suggestions about method for teachers to follow.
    Collections vary in completeness. University libraries appear to be the hosts of most collections. For example, at the University of Alberta, there is the Sandercock Collection, maintained by the Department of Educational Foundations. At the University of Regina, the Faculty of Education Library is building a collection of Saskatchewan school texts.

3. Newspaper clippings. Public attitudes to language and language instruction are sometimes revealed by feature articles and letters to the editor. Provincial archives often maintain indexed clipping files.

4. Periodicals. Professional journals of education, like the *Western School Journal* that was published in Winnipeg from 1905-1938, *The Nova Scotia Journal of Education*, and the *Education Review* contain relevant articles. Other non-educational provincial journals like *Farm and Ranch Review* and *Agricultural Alberta* contain articles about schooling that sometimes include useful informal data about the school curriculum.

5. Curriculum guides. After about 1915 these appear to have been issued separately from the annual report for the provinces. By the 1970s and 1980s, very comprehensive and explicit guides are available for language arts and English. Department of Education archives are the usual repositories for these guides.

6. Miscellaneous sources. Some provincial archives have sets of school notebooks deposited there by individuals. Some of these show what grammar exercises pupils actually completed. Family papers on deposit are worth searching, as are Educational Scrapbooks for 1908–1909, sets of school reports, and sets of examinations.

7. Extant tape-recorded interviews. The Provincial Archives in Regina has a set of audio tape recordings of interviews with retired teachers.

8. Retired teachers and educators. The recollections of teachers whose careers began in the 1920s can be helpful in providing human details about the grammar program of those periods.

9. Personal collections. A number of people collect educational artifacts, such as textbooks and notebooks.

10. Published anecdotal accounts of grammar lessons. In my study of grammar teaching in Nova Scotia, I found several vignettes about nineteenth century classroom practices in a variety of published sources, such as autobiographies, memoirs, collections of letters, and local community histories.

Appendix A: A Discussion of H. G. Martyn

The emergence of the doctrine of usage coincided in the United States with a significant curriculum movement. Social efficiency, one of the new concepts of the early 1900s, saw education as preparation for life. The curriculum should be based on those skills, attitudes, habits, and forms of knowledge that people needed to live productive lives; those needs could be identified scientifically by observation in the workplace. The curriculum could then be designed to overcome so-called "shortcomings"—those skills or abilities that could not be expected to develop naturally: for example, errors in language usage. The elimination of such errors could form part of the instructional program in English. For education to be efficient, it had to attend to "essentials," and in terms of English usage in speaking and writing, this meant direct teaching of what scientific inquiry revealed as needing to be taught.

In 1915, W. W. Charters inaugurated the science of usage surveys when he studied the errors in speaking and writing committed by pupils in the schools of Kansas City. The aim of Charters' work was to identify "shortcomings" in children's language performance, which could then be used to build a scientific curriculum in English designed to meet actual, proven needs in an efficient manner.

The influence of the usage movement in Ontario led to a survey study of grammatical errors in the speech and writing of Ontario elementary school children. H. G. Martyn reported his study, conducted in 1928 and 1929, as a doctoral dissertation in 1932. (His work is quoted often within this book.) Three hundred and eighty teachers reported on children's grammatical errors as revealed by their speech in the classroom and on the playground. Reports of over 24,000 errors were collected. A sample of 19,000 grammatical errors in the written work of elementary school children was obtained through the cooperation of a further 850 teachers. These errors were analyzed using a slightly modified version of W. W. Charters' classification of language errors.

Martyn presented his results as numbers of errors on particular grammatical elements committed by children in three age groups: Grades 3–4, Grades

5–6, and Grade 8. For example, he found 399 instances of the use of 'me' as the first element in a compound subject such as "Me and Ada saw him." When Martyn rank-ordered those grammatical elements that produced the highest proportion of errors, he found a close relationship between errors in speech and errors in writing. Appearing on both lists of the eleven most serious errors were:

"Me" used instead of "I" in a compound subject

"I" or "me" standing first in a series

"There is" or "there was" used with a plural subject

Plural noun subject with a singular verb

"I (you, he, etc.) seen

"I (you, he, etc.) done

"Can" used instead of "may" (Martyn, p.104)

Martyn noted that errors in verbs constituted the largest category in both oral and written items, with past tenses and participles being incorrectly used most frequently. In the written sample, this category accounted for 57.49 percent of the total errors. Next came misuse of pronoun forms (e.g. "It is me"), accounting for 17.8 percent of the written errors reported. Third came errors in modifiers (e.g. "He drove too slow"), which contributed 8.56 percent of the writing total. Syntactic redundance (e.g. "This here dog ...") accounted for 7.46 percent of the written errors; while double negatives ("I never had no lunch") produced 4.23 percent (p. 98).

Part of Martyn's intention in the study was to evaluate the commonly accepted claim that the teaching of grammar was intended to enable students to speak and write English more correctly. Martyn analyzed textbooks and curriculum documents used in Ontario and found that this was the rationale for grammar teaching that had prevailed through the history of public schooling in that province. It was reiterated in the latest program of studies with the statement:

"The course in grammar should be directed towards giving the pupil such a knowledge of the functions, forms, and relations of words as will assist him in speaking and writing the language with clearness and accuracy." (p. 62)

To check teachers' perceptions of the role of grammar teaching, Martyn distributed a questionnaire to Ontario teachers, in which he asked them to select one of five objectives to work for in the teaching of English grammar. These were:

1. To prepare pupils for the study of languages

2. To enable pupils to speak and write English more correctly

3. To discipline the mind

4. To help pupils interpret literature

5. To lay a foundation for the pupils' work in composition

Of the 652 teachers who replied to the questionnaire, 519 (or 79.6 percent) marked their ballot for the second objective. (p. 64)

To evaluate this belief in the efficacy of grammar teaching as a means to improved speaking and writing, Martyn compared percentages of errors across age groups, a dubious procedure; he did not report numbers of subjects in each age group, nor did he statistically test for the significance of any differences. On the basis of these comparisons, some of which showed increases in the higher grades over lower grades, he concluded that "present efforts are not proving effective in the elimination of errors." (p. 99) "It is very evident," he went to say, "that all our efforts have failed to bring about what has held to be the chief objective of grammar teaching, viz., to enable pupils to speak and write correctly." (p. 105) He claimed that his surveys showed that "right language habits are not developed as the result of grammar teaching." (p. 105) He also claimed that his finding was in agreement with the opinion of eminent authorities, such as George Krapp of the United States, and Henry Wyld and Philip Ballard of England.

Following Ballard, Martyn recommended that the establishment of correctness in expression be a matter of providing a "generous environment of pure English" (p. 109), from which the child could learn by imitation. He advised the use of language games with younger children, recommending Rosamund Archibald's *The King's English Drill* as one source of games. Composition, not grammar, was the subject to which the task of achieving language propriety should be delegated. However, Martyn did not wish to see grammar deleted from the elementary school program: older pupils (those in Grades 7 and 8) should not rely merely upon imitation; they should "seek to use language in a rational way." (p. 110) He provided six reasons for the study of grammar in the elementary school:

1. It provides a standard by which pupils may judge their own language and that of others

2. It paves the way for the further study of English and other languages

3. It provides a "grammatical nomenclature and an organized body of knowledge about language, both of which are useful and even essential in the life of today" (p. 111)

4. It provides a training in logical thinking about language

5. It has a humanizing and civilizing effect (pp. 111, 112)

As regards the course of study defined by textbooks in use in Ontario schools, Martyn thought that it was "fairly satisfactory," except that it neglected the study of phonetics, which, given the primacy of oral language, was indispensable to the study of language structure. (p. 118) The topics he listed as being covered in the textbooks was quite comprehensive: the sentence— kinds, parts, relationships of parts, and analysis, including clause analysis— and the classification of parts of speech and their inflections. This was hardly a reformist proposal.

As far as the method of teaching grammar was concerned, Martyn advised a scientific approach, treating grammar as a science. Referring to it as the "inductive-deductive procedure": pupils were led to the discovery of facts and principles from language samples that were familiar to them; they then applied them to new examples.

What is significant about Martyn's study is his allegiance to the doctrine of usage as it was being used in the United States to promote the ideas of the social efficiency movement in curriculum. It shows that educators could embrace the principles of utilitarianism in their thinking about the curriculum in English, but that it was difficult for them to reject the traditional humanitarian aims of grammar teaching. Martyn was able to accept that correct expression should be established for younger and middle grade children according to the psychology of habit formation and based on a scientific identification of their language "shortcomings"; but the inclusion of the "science of grammar" in the Grade 7 and 8 program was justified on different grounds, articulated in six objectives that were hardly scientific and based on no evidence whatsoever. Given this kind of loyalty to the humanistic curriculum, it is not surprising that grammar teaching did not succumb to the doctrine of usage movement; it might not contribute to improved speech and writing, but it was good for one. Perhaps Martyn was simply mirroring the uncertainties of the Newbolt Report of 1921, which, although he did not refer to its recommendations on grammar, Martyn quoted on the more general issue of the importance of English study in the school curriculum. (pp. 106–7)